# The Working Class in American History

*Editorial Advisors*

David Brody
Alice Kessler-Harris
David Montgomery
Sean Wilentz

*A list of books in the series appears
at the end of this volume.*

*For Democracy, Workers, and God*

# For Democracy, Workers, and God

*Labor Song-Poems and Labor Protest, 1865-95*

Clark D. Halker

University of Illinois Press
*Urbana and Chicago*

*This book is printed on acid-free paper.*

Library of Congress Cataloging-in-Publication Data

Halker, Clark D.
    For democracy, workers, and God : labor song-poems and labor
protest, 1865-95 / Clark D. Halker.
        p.      cm. — (The Working class in American history)
    Includes bibliographical references and index.
    ISBN 0-252-01747-1 (alk. paper)
    1. Working class writings, American—History and criticism.
2. Protest poetry, American—History and criticism.  3. American
poetry—19th century—History and criticism.  4. Working class in
literature.  5. Religion in literature.  6. Working class—United
States—History—19th century.  I. Title.  II. Series.
PS310.W67H35      1991
811'.409355—dc20                                          90-39543
                                                              CIP

*For my grandparents*

*Hilda E. Taylor (1901–1988)*
*Charlie Taylor (1896–1979)*
*Francis M. Halker (1892–1984)*
*Henry M. Halker (1890–1966)*

*From them I learned the meaning of history,*
*compassion, justice, hard work, humility, and simplicity.*

# Contents

# Acknowledgments

I'm happy to say I finished this project without landing in debtor's prison. The cars broke down, the plates expired, the insurance ran out, the teeth got cavities, the guitars never got repaired, and the teaching jobs didn't come through every year. A couple of good friends became ex-friends. However, in a moment of reflection (while I still have a steady income), I might be moved to say that the results were worth the price. Certainly a lot of people offered personal and intellectual aid. I wouldn't have survived without their help. They deserve a good deal of credit, and I apologize for not being able to thank them even more.

While I was a graduate student in the history department at the University of Minnesota, a number of instructors and friends offered valuable suggestions on my research and writing. Jon Gjerde, Melissa Meyer, Joe Stipanovich, Colette Hyman, Bob Salisbury, Russell Menard, John Modell, and Hy Berman gave me ample doses of thoughtful and comradely criticism. More recently John Jentz, Paul Buhle, Lew Erenberg, the members of the Chicago Labor History Group, and a handful of anonymous readers forced me to think about my subject in ways I had previously avoided. David Montgomery's extensive comments and suggestions proved particularly worthwhile as this manuscript neared completion.

A number of institutions and their staffs also came to my rescue. Richard Wentworth proved especially receptive and cooperative as editor and director of the University of Illinois Press. In addition, Cynthia Mitchell edited the manuscript with a precision I greatly admire. At an earlier stage the interlibrary loan staff at the University of Minnesota library managed to locate materials that seemed impossible to find. (They offered proof of divine intervention, or so it seemed to me.) In addition, while I taught at the College of Idaho, the library staff did an excellent job of keeping me seated in front of a microfilm reader. So too did the staffs of the Idaho State Historical Society, the Chicago Public Library–Cultural Center, and the Wisconsin State Historical Society. The Newberry Library's reference division, particularly Emily Clark, did work beyond the call of duty. Emily remains a friend despite my bibliographic questions.

A few places also came through with some financial support when I needed it the most. The University of Minnesota provided a dissertation fellowship when I first began serious research on labor song-poems. Chicago State University gave me a job in the library to hold me over during the summer of 1982 while I did research. The Newberry Library compassionately decided to fund me as a research fellow to revise my book manuscript in the fall of 1986.

Other people aided me in more idiosyncratic ways. Sally Nettleton was a wonderful friend and an excellent editor and critic. Jeff Charles, Wes Dick, Diane Hopkins, Carol Corcoran, and Mona Salmon, my sister, gave heartful support. Mike DiPaolo listened and spoke with a kindness rarely found in men. Ralph Sayre and Frank Specht at the College of Idaho remain the best teachers and colleagues I've ever had. My aunt Marion Taylor gave me a place to stay in Chicago for a summer. That means a lot when you're broke, and I haven't forgotten the favor. As the only academic in a decidedly non-academic family, she has always been an inspiration. My mom and dad acted with exceptional kindness and patience through the ordeal. In fact, they only occasionally questioned the value of my pursuits. I'm thankful for that. After all, writing a book of this sort is a pretty crazy thing to do when it comes right down to it.

A handful of people hardly ever said a word about what I was doing trying to write a book, but they were helpful in their own ways. Don Schraufnagel remains a close friend after having played music with me during a couple of rough years. The members of the D. D. Shamm Band and the Remainders gave me a great creative outlet beyond the confines of the academic argument. After a day of writing one paragraph or teaching in the suburbs, rock and roll really can save your soul.

One person read this manuscript almost as many times as I did, and I know that she too grew to hate it as much as I sometimes did. Nevertheless, Diane Raptosh acted as my best critic and editor. Because she cares about words more than anyone I know, she tenaciously slashed my words, sentences, paragraphs, and pages until they stood for something. She was also my closest personal ally through much of the thick and thin. She taught me the value of a single kiss and a compact sentence. In an age of atomic chance, I'd still rather bet on a good romance.

*For Democracy, Workers, and God*

# Introduction: Rees E. Lewis, Labor Song-Poems, and Scholars

Few people today could recall the name Rees E. Lewis. Even among his Gilded-Age contemporaries Lewis remained nearly anonymous. He and millions of his working-class brothers and sisters rarely gained more than a modicum of recognition. For this reason, we know of Lewis only a few facts gleaned here and there. Nonetheless, such facts enable historians to locate other information and to infer a good deal. Rees Lewis lived in the Pittsburgh region, earned his livelihood in the burgeoning iron and steel industry, and carried a membership card for the union representing his trade. He also had a bit of the bard in him and at least once employed poetic voice to express his feelings for country and class. Seeking an audience for his song-poem, Lewis rendered it singable by adapting it to a folksong melody and then sent it off to the *National Labor Tribune*. On 30 March 1878 that prominent Pittsburgh labor paper included the song-poem in its pages, along with his name and city of residence, as it would the works of other bards of the era.[1]

Thus Lewis gained assurance that his name would appear on more than a census form. More importantly, he would be counted with millions of other Americans living between 1865 and 1895 who believed that the nation's ruling elite had set the nation on a course of ruin and that only workers and their unions could save the Republic:

> Rouse, ye noble sons of Labor,
> And protect your country's honor,

Who with bone, and brain, and fiber,
Make the nation's wealth.

Lusty lads, with souls of fire,
Gallant sons of noble sire,
Lend your voice and raise your banner,
Battle for the right.

Heater, roller, rougher,
Catcher, puddler, helper,
All unite and join the fight,
And might (for right) encounter;
In the name of truth and justice,
Stem the tide of evil practice,
Mammon's sordid might and avarice,
Our land from ruin save.

Ye who aid our locomotion,
Wield the 'cord which binds the nation,'
Honest types of God's creation,
Honor to your names.

Hearts of oak and arms of metal,
Who by dint of skill and muscle,
Fashion bridge and iron vessel,
Ever true and brave.

Heater, roller, rougher,
Catcher, puddler, helper,
All unite and join the fight,
And might (for right) encounter;
Let's be firm, with soul unbending,
'Mid the flash and sparks ascending,
Vulcan's sons are now arising,
Comrades now unite.

The work that follows concerns Rees E. Lewis and his poem, and, more generally, individuals like Lewis and their song-poems. Lewis joined hundreds, if not thousands, whose combined efforts yielded several thousand song-poems between 1865 and 1895. This proliferation marks Lewis's era as the apex of indigenous worker song-poetry in the United States and establishes the labor song-poem itself as a topic worthy of scholarly consideration.

Although the Gilded Age represents song-poetry's heyday, students of folklore and folksong—a logical group to undertake examination—have evinced scant interest in the song and lore of American workers. Laboring under the influence of their intellectual forebear, English ballad scholar James Francis Child, folklorists remained captives of the so-called "Child canon" from the late nineteenth through the mid-twentieth century.[2] True, the key tenets of that canon—an emphasis on ballads as suitable subject matter, oral transmission as a necessary precondition for study, and a preliterate folk population as an appropriate group for fieldwork—engendered criticism and modification early on. American scholars straightaway disregarded the notion of ballad-making as a "closed account."[3] But as D. K. Wilgus put it in 1959, "Despite the main voices raised against subservience to the Child canon, it still cast a long shadow."[4]

Child's shadow most clearly manifested itself in the rural bias of folklorists. Yeomen peasant stock—Child's noble carriers of folk culture—had become less purely "folk" as industry advanced, but proletarian environs still did not inspire fieldwork.[5] The biographer of George Korson, the pioneering collector of labor song and lore in the 1920s and 1930s, remarked in 1980 that "most American folklorists, are, I suspect, Jeffersonians at heart; although they are basically sympathetic to workers, they share Jefferson's lingering bias. There is a distinct ambivalence toward the urban scene and toward the industrial worker."[6]

The author's claims may have been exaggerated, but their general tenor rings true. Today folklorists recognize urban-industrial settings as appropriate study sites. However, the working class has yet to generate significant attention. For two decades Archie Green has been cajoling folklorists, trying to advance the agenda of "labor lore" and "labor song."[7] Nevertheless, his appeals have been only mildly successful.

While working-class lore and song have yet to receive just due, these works have not gone entirely unstudied. Journalist George Korson took up the cause as early as the 1920s. Despite an initially cool reception among academics, he spent three decades documenting folklore of coal miners.[8] His work set an important precedent for other maverick scholars, and in the decades that followed numerous collections appeared: John Greenway's *American Folksongs of Protest* (1953), labor songster Joe Glazer and folklorist Edith Fowke's survey *Songs of Work and Freedom* (1960), Joyce Kornbluh's *Rebel Voices: An I.W.W. Anthology* (1968), and most recently, labor historian Philip Foner's *American Labor Songs of the Nineteenth Century* (1975).[9] In addition, at least two scholars have proceeded beyond collecting such material to asking important questions about it. R. Serge Denisoff has scrutinized the historically varied function of labor and protest songs.[10] From a very different perspective, Archie Green has collected a massive body of labor songs, prodded his colleagues in folklore to do likewise, offered a number of bibliographic and theoretical essays on the subject, and, in *Only a Miner* (1975), explored the interface of folk and popular culture through miners' songs.[11]

Green and his comrades provide a useful starting point for those interested in folklore and the working class.[12] He and like-minded scholars believed that, despite academic conventions, Rees Lewis's and his workmates' compositions merited preservation and examination. It hardly comes as a surprise, therefore, that the scholarship of Korson, Greenway, and Green inspired this work. Issues relevant to folksong scholars—such as transmission, process, textual variation, context, authorship, and "folksong" definition—may surface throughout. Much that follows also bears on topics folklorists address—broadsides, chapbooks, "traditional" tunes, hymns, ballad openings, hawkers, and the impact of mass consumer culture. Yet "folksong" and "folklore" remain of secondary importance to the larger purpose of this book: to expand knowledge of the musical and poetic history of the American working class.

On another level this work addresses more ambitious analytic issues. Song-poets and song-poems offer a lens onto the larger world of Gilded-Age workers and labor protest. This study examines song-poems for insight into that world. Questions of the sort Korson or Green consider occupy small space below. Instead, this work shifts from garnering information about Lewis and his work to posing and addressing broad historical questions about the working class.[13] Although written from the vantage of a historian, this book encompasses Lewis's own larger concerns for his country and class in the battle for the right.

On these concerns Lewis stood arm in arm with a good portion of his peers in Pittsburgh, the iron and steel industry, and the nation generally. Direct encounter with advancing industrial capitalism left many Americans with the impression that something ailed the country, touching everything from the shop floor to the nation's capitol. America seemed hopelessly violated by the nation's elites. What's more, so long as those in power acted out of self-interest, the country would continue its course of ruin. Workers would not receive their just share of the wealth, parasites would leech off wealth created by workers, an aristocracy of wealth would impose its will, and the Republic would become a sham. Even the most basic principles of Christian morality would be disavowed.

Before such scenarios came to fruition, Lewis and his comrades forged a movement for collective improvement of workers, challenging control by the capitalist ruling class as well. Often they fought among themselves over "correct" reform strategies and "correct" alternatives to unbridled capitalism. However, from 1865 until the turn of the century, when changes in capitalism drastically altered the scene, workers mounted an impressive fight, especially when the Knights of Labor emerged to direct the effort. Workers and their allies employed well-known instruments in their campaign—trade unions, federations of trades, city-wide labor bodies, political parties, strikes, boycotts, and labor lobbies. They also battled on a broader front, utilizing tools that may appear anachronistic today—parades, picnics, lectures, reading rooms, singing groups, raffles, concerts, balls, potluck suppers, newspapers, broadsides, banners, auxiliaries, and marching bands. The writing, recitation, singing, and distribution of song-poems had a place in this network as well. Finally, even those essentially defensive "inert" bastions of working-class life—family, church, saloon, and fraternal order—served a purpose in the more consciously "politicized" labor movement.[14]

If Lewis and other individuals have been forgotten, the same cannot be said of the labor movement, which has long occupied historians' attention. Until recently, however, examination tended to be narrow in perspective.[15] Following the example of John R. Commons and the Wisconsin School, labor historians defined labor history almost exclusively as the history of organizations composed of wage-conscious workers seeking redress for capitalism's abuses.[16] As historians well know today, such thinking produced notable flaws in the scholarship of the Wisconsin School. And while this work still has much to recommend to historians, even a partial understanding of Lewis and the movement to which he gave allegiance requires that we consider the past through a lens broader than the Wisconsin School's. A cursory reading of Lewis's song-poem reveals a wider understanding of the "labor question" wherein craft heritage, masculinity, religion, revolutionary principles, common sense, and morality coalesce. For Lewis the struggle might be over wages and conditions, but at base it involved something larger, indeed, more grand. Labor fought nothing less than a battle to ensure the nation's future; a battle for liberty, justice, and equality; a battle for Christian morality; a battle for the rights of all Americans. Citizen-soldiers in a struggle of universal proportions, workers enlisted in nothing less than a battle over the meaning of America itself.[17]

Although historians generally have disregarded song-poems and similar forms of expressive behavior, historians who study the Afro-American experience have been especially sensitive to the value of such sources. Indeed, in *Black Culture, Black Consciousness* Lawrence Levine argued the case for nontraditional sources as critical to understanding oppressed groups.[18] His reconstruction of black consciousness relied heavily on folksongs and folklore and reminded historians that

> the historical use of folklore helps us to recapture the joys as well as the pains, to gain some sense of a people's angle of vision and world-view, to better understand the inner dynamics of the group and the attitudes its members had toward each other as well as toward the outside world, to comprehend the mechanisms members of the group erected to guard their values, maintain their sense of worth, and retain their sanity.[19]

Levine's perspective alerts us to the demerits of the Wisconsin School's constrictive understanding of the past. It suggests not only that a study of labor song-poetry could yield considerable insight into labor history but also that such a study would generate greater analytic potential by employing what has sometimes been referred to as the cultural approach to working-class history.

The cultural approach took shape in the 1960s when New-Left standard bearers turned to writing labor history. The wayward children of the Popular Front, however, were not content with a New-Left variant of their critical forbears. Two other developments in the field prompted wholescale revision of labor history. First, the ascendance of what became known as the new social history revolutionized the writing of history with the introduction of a social scientific methodology and quantitative analysis. Second, and equally important, British historians led by E. P. Thompson rescued Marxist analysis from its Stalinist doldrums.[20] Thompson insisted that understanding the past necessitated class analysis. However, he proposed that class be considered not in terms of workers' relation to the means of production but as a historical process whereby workers' shared experience with capitalism led them to articulate their interests differently from other classes. This process yields what he termed "working-class culture," a culture embodied in the institutions, ideology, customs, and traditions of workers. In turn, this culture shaped the thinking and behavior of workers and informed their collective action.

To American labor historians, Thompson's ideas proved a revelation. What's more, Herbert Gutman's subsequent work along Thompsonesque lines convinced many scholars of its potential for interpreting the American past.[21] In the wake of Thompson and Gutman, the field of labor history would be remade in the late 1960s and early 1970s.

The analysis of song-poems below owes a great deal to the new labor history and to what critics derisively call the "culturalist" approach.[22] Specifically, the concept of culture employed by Thompson informs this work and does much to shape its fundamental direction and character. Emerging from the confrontation of labor and capital, song-poems invoke a rich cultural heritage among the working class but one simultaneously mediated by the more immediate Gilded-Age experience. Conversely, they not only reflect with dramatic clarity a rapidly growing working class increasingly at odds with industrial capitalism but also impress us with the wealthy cultural past that workers carried with them. What's more, song-poems permeated the labor movement and labor struggles and existed as part of a vast cultural apparatus integral to the movement and its success.[23] In short, a cultural approach to song-poems suggests ample analytic rewards for those interested in understanding the working-class past.

Thirty years ago a historian would have been laughed out of the profession for proposing a study of song-poetry. This fact alone serves as testimony to the distance traveled by historians since the 1960s and to the influence of the culturalist approach. Historians employing that approach have found few enemies in the United States. Indeed, in their exorcism of the spectre of Commons, many labor historians fell prey to the same self-satisfaction that inhibited advancement in the field among a previous generation. Much as most practitioners of "culturalism" may have avoided it, a serious exercise in self-criticism seems in order. Indeed, while the following argument relies on studies on "working-class culture," it proceeds as well from an awareness of flaws in the cultural approach and attempts to remedy some of them.

On this side of the Atlantic, criticism of the culturalist approach has been narrow in scope and confined to a few essays.[24] However, some of the charges deserve attention. Critics have correctly charged some culturalists with making broad claims about working-class culture without evidence necessary to support such claims—specifically, with overstating the degree of the oppositional character of working-class culture or cultural traditions. To this has been added a more general charge that culturalists romanticize the working-class past. Searching for alternative traditions, they have sometimes exaggerated the extensiveness of the working-class spirit of mutuality, if not some vague sense of class consciousness itself. Of course, such criticism comes from those who believe that in order to employ the culture concept or the term "working-class consciousness" nearly every worker must possess a clearly defined revolutionary consciousness. Nevertheless, culturalists deserve criticism for not giving account to the ambiguity—the resistance and accommodationist strains—in the culture of traditions they describe.

Romanticism alone cannot account for the degree of singularity sometimes assigned to American workers and working-class culture. As sympathetic critics point out, many historians demonstrated poor judgment in their undiscerning adoption of Thompson's notion of working-class culture.[25] The early new labor history included an implied agenda to discover an American form of the apparently homogenous and autonomous culture Thompson located in England. The impossibility of such a task in the face of a historically diverse and fragmented working class did not deter those intent upon imposing an artificial sense of commonality, if not cultural autonomy, on American laborers. Few probably ever thought an American version of Thompson's work could be written. However, a few spoke of particular groups of workers in such terms without adding the necessary qualifying remarks to put "class" and "working-class culture" in proper context. Too many neglected to question Thompson as a necessary preface.

A more frequent, equally cogent charge has been raised against the culturalists' willingness to jump on the interdisciplinary bandwagon. Thompson suggested the value of applying other disciplines to labor history, but he warned of the pitfalls of uninformed borrowing. Some Americans have thrown out anthropological and sociological buzzwords without appreciating the implications. Daniel Rodgers's thoughtful review of the culturalists demonstrates that careless borrowing from "modernization" sociology produces dangerously simplistic history, portrayed in shallow bipolar extremes and devoid of process. Those engaged in this interdisciplinary shopping spree, he argues, have inadvertently positioned themselves as the intellectual comrades of defenders of the status quo they would otherwise find politically and analytically unacceptable.

On a different note, practitioners of the new social history, culturalists included, have found community studies attractive. The advantages are obvious; in the case study historians possess a manageable unit of analysis. Comforting though that may be, the localism of community studies militates against generalization and synthesis. Studies of a broader scope expose historians to greater criticism, but labor history will remain a series of monographs until historians take risks. While synthesis presses upon labor historians less than some might wish, no one can deny that labor history needs more expansive vistas.

The chapters that follow consider labor in a broad national perspective. Some qualification must be made, however. Although song-poems surfaced throughout the country, they emerged primarily from the ranks of white males, more commonly from the North than the South. Black musical traditions have an important relationship to labor song-poetry, but their bearing must be termed indirect. While song-poems composed by women were not uncommon and find their way into the discussion below, the majority of female song-poets reflect women's concerns, separate from those of men. Understanding female song-poetry ought to be of importance to historians. For that matter, labor song-poetry could tell historians a good deal about gender in Gilded-Age labor. Nonetheless, prior to synthesis, female song-poetry demands examination in its own right, which this study makes no claims to doing. Finally, although southern workers contributed song-poems, song-poetry mirrored capitalism's northern concentration. While southern workers occupied an increasingly significant role for organized labor and labor protest, the working-class presence in the South did not approximate that of the North. Therefore, while proceeding with a recognition of the racial, gender, and regional specificity of the evidence, the chapters below address the need for broader horizons.

Analysis began only after a bibliographic survey of song-poems from the Gilded Age, and additional, though less ambitious, surveys of song-poetry in the eras preceding and proceeding. The Gilded-Age survey included some sixty labor papers or journals, many labor songbooks, personal papers including song-poems, and published collections of song-poems. This undertaking yielded thousands of original song-poems, which were then inventoried with information pertaining to title, author, originality, general theme, publication, place of authorship, union affiliation, specific issues, and tune. Thereafter, hundreds were subjected to textual examination.

Immersion in song-poetry makes one leery of the dualistic world of historians engaged in borrowing from sociology. For that reason, except for certain terms that have a particular and technical bearing on the argument—such as "folksong," "ballad," "oral transmission," "broadside" and others used by folksong scholars—this work avoids terminology from other disciplines.

Avoiding charges of careless borrowing, inadequate evidence, and myopic localism requires sustained effort. Attending the charge of romanticism requires more serious reflection. No doubt a healthy dose of skepticism would temper the most ardent romantic proponents of a usable past. However, the charge proves more substantial when critics have more than temperate scholarship in mind. What they find objectionable is what English historians label "ethical humanism" or, more generally, the culturalists' obvious empathy with the working-class past. To opponents on the Right and Left this romantic proclivity impedes a realistic interpretation of the past. In England, in particular, some "scientific" Marxist historians find the culturalists' romanticism doubly trying because culturalists admit their intellectual debt to the romantics and romanticism.[26]

While this work claims few ties to the likes of Blake or Morris, no attempt has been made to escape romanticism per se. Following scholars as diverse as George Korson and Herbert Gutman, this work proceeds from an assumption that what people such as Rees Lewis said and did deserves historians' attention. The Gilded-Age labor movement generated massive and broad support, even though the thinking behind it appears muddle-headed today. To eschew the legacy of Lewis and his comrades would be to patronize the past and to practice a brand of antirealism and polemic in the guise of social scientific purity. Romanticism and engaged sympathy, therefore, pervade the following chapters, even as the ambiguity of the legacy of labor is laid bare.

To answer the charge that culturalists have been too liberal in their use of Thompson's class and culture concepts is to enter a debate centered in England on the very nature of class and class consciousness.[27] American critics have raised serious questions about the notion of working-class culture. They have sharply-chided culturalists for their failure to account for the materialist, noncultural side of working-class history in favor of an approach given over almost entirely to culture studies. A systematic critique, however, has yet to emerge from the ranks of culturalism's American opponents. The same cannot be said of their English counterparts. Led by Perry Anderson and a vaguely defined group of "structuralist" Marxists, English critics launched a wholesale questioning of the culturalists. They argue that Thompson's "culturalism" constitutes a cultural equivalent of the narrow economism of "vulgar" Marxists. Thompson, they say, proffers a past bereft of class as an objective phenomenon, of "class-in-itself," and of materialist reality. Instead he and kindred spirits substitute class as a subjective phenomenon, "class-for-itself," and a nonmaterial cultural reality in which culture becomes divorced from its necessary material base.[28] For Anderson such thinking constitutes anathema, since he considers Marxism without materialism to be like Marxism without Marx. Anderson has said that Thompson accords us a "cultural voluntarism" in which class conflict becomes cultural conflict and culture becomes the motive force of history.

Thompson's critics pose a significant challenge to the culturalist approach, moving beyond the amorphous criticism of Americans to a higher analytic—not to mention abstract—plane. And despite its acrimonious tenor the debate has greatly enriched the field. In fact, Marxist historians now dominate the field to the extent that the Anderson-Thompson argument has became an inhouse quarrel. What's more, Anderson lately has admitted grounds for rapprochement between the principal parties.

American culturalists have meanwhile steered clear of the exchange, opting for a pragmatic-empiricist approach, adopting the culture concept in some form and then getting down to the topic at hand. Such practicality has merit, especially when one considers the rarified atmosphere in which the continental Marxists render the past. However, after twenty years the analytic potential of the Americans' orientation may have been spent. Indeed, the greatest fault of the new labor history may be an unwillingness to make its assumptions explicit and to examine them critically. Culturalists have left readers to draw their own conclusions about authors' understanding of the nature of class and class culture.

The remainder of this chapter delineates certain particular and general assumptions which inform this work. The next six chapters examine labor song-poetry in both a specific and a broad context. Each chapter examines song-poetry as a particular genre and scrutinizes certain key elements or characteristics of song-poetry.

Chapter 1 briefly reviews song-poetry's topical orientation and its functions, while establishing its integral role in the labor movement. Chapter 2 presents an occupational portrait of song-poets. Chapter 3 identifies the historical and contemporary musical-literary influences on song-poetry and describes its style and form. Chapters 4 through 6 treat song-poem content, searching for the ideological roots of its prominent themes while outlining the impact of the Gilded-Age environment. Finally, the conclusion describes and explains song-poetry's decline at the turn of the century.

A number of critical and recurring themes emerge. Each chapter emphasizes the impact of certain cultural traditions on song-poetry and song-poets. On almost every level song-poetry relied on cultural traditions, evidence that labor protest and the labor movement recalled a rich cultural legacy. This legacy had deep roots in American history—as other historians have argued—frequently dating from the seventeenth century. However, song-poetry also evokes an international flavor, suggesting that the ideology of Gilded-Age labor was not an Americanism. Song-poetry also reminds us that antebellum reform influenced workers and the labor movement. The continuity between antebellum reform and Gilded-Age labor should not be exaggerated, however; song-poets reflect more than just a naive, reactionary, anachronistic spirit in postbellum labor protest. Still, a continuity did exist, imbuing song-poetry, labor protest, and the mainstream of the labor movement with a flavor akin to earlier American reformers. Finally, song-poetry and song-poets are evidence of the shaping hand of burgeoning capitalism and the social environment to which it gave rise. If song-poetry bears the mark of the seventeenth century ballad, the evangelical hymn, the American Revolution, the revolutions of 1789 and 1848, and the Second Great Awakening, it bears the mark of the rising capitalist order and the workplace as well.[29]

Gaining insights from song-poem analysis, however, necessitates considering them in the broader context of workers' battle with capitalists over the meaning of America. In this battle American workers had ample precedent. Since 1776 groups with differing visions of the nation's future had clashed in vicious confrontations. Questions concerning the Articles of Confederation, temperance, nativism, the national bank, Federalists, and slavery stirred people with conflicting views on the exact meaning of America. In the postbellum period, however, class became the focal point of the last major social conflict of the century. Workers rose continuously from 1865 to 1895 to check, if not destroy, the dominant power of the new aristocrats and to gain their share of the nation's increased wealth. What's more, many workers joined together to promote an alternative vision of society and called on every available resource to do so. Within the wider confines of the labor movement, workers and their allies created a movement culture to promulgate the movement's ideals.[30] Setbacks came repeatedly, but until the 1890s progress generally seemed steady and measurable. The combined efforts of these decades, especially the 1880s, constituted "a moment of challenge" as hundreds of thousands, if not millions, joined the cause.[31] That challenge dissipated in the 1890s as economic depression and a ruling-class counteroffensive combined to quash labor protest. Yet even then larger economic processes were transforming the national landscape, restructuring and reconstituting the working class, altering the very environment that made a Gilded-Age labor movement and a movement culture possible.

The following chapters make no attempt to recount the details of the confrontation between labor and capital but emphasize instead the twin themes of culture and class conflict. Labor song-poems—the cultural documents of the working class and of a significant body of non-working-class allies as well—present the outlines of the culture and conflict that pervaded the Gilded Age.

However, song-poems do not represent a homogenous working-class culture. They typically manifest a conscious politicized tone—an outward-looking sensibility, the oppositional, offensive, resistant strand of workers' cultural fabric. Those who contributed song-poems must have realized that they had taken an offensive step. These song-poems find their focus in a massive movement with vague, but nonetheless existing, goals, designed to collectively elevate workers and the nation.

The outward character of the song-poem necessitates a particular understanding of culture, one more specific than the all-encompassing working-class culture scholars frequently employ. The latter presupposes a singularity of purpose and homogeneity of subject unknown to American workers. More importantly, the term masks the defensive character of working-class life, implying that a separate way of life somehow equates with a class-specific, politicized consciousness and purpose. Many working-class institutions, organizations, and practices embodying working-class values, beliefs, and traditions have been part of an alternative culture, but the alternative was often not a conscious choice and only minimally threatened the established order. The saloon, for example, could serve either as a locus for fomenting protest or as a form of social control, part of a culture of consolation. Culturalists have been slow to separate defensive and offensive elements of working-class life.[32]

The chapters below therefore employ a circumscribed notion of working-class culture, namely, "movement culture," to explain the network of activities—from parades, to picnics, to poetry—that surrounded Gilded-Age labor. This movement culture expanded in scope as the movement gained experience and in the 1880s, with the Knights of Labor to give it shape and direction, held momentary promise as an alternative cultural focus for workers, and many other Americans as well. Yet, it was never expansive or self-generating enough to merit the term "working-class culture." Its close ties to the labor movement recall its conscious character. At the same time, movement culture shared ties with less consciously politicized activities also. In fact, these ties were frequently close, as when the saloon served as union hall and site for the recitation of song-poetry. Still, much as movement culture, and the labor movement as a whole, drew strength from that larger cultural milieu, its purposefulness separated it from that environment. Movement culture remained not only "a life apart" but also somewhat distinct from the rest of that life.

The relationship of movement culture to the nation's culture at large remained equally problematic. While it moved toward an alternative cultural system with a more clearly defined class character, it retained an ambiguous relationship with the larger society. Its determination to resist the status quo grew apparent, but it still showed a certain accommodationist character. As citizen workers of the Republic, those who proffered the alternative culture never separated themselves completely from the Republic's trans-class institutional and ideological foundations. Song-poets from both working-class and non-working-class backgrounds believed they were fighting a battle over universally applicable principles, muting a distinctly working-class temperament. Their universal horizons may well explain their success, for while their enemies fought for narrow, self-serving goals, workers fought for real gains but also for something beyond workplace and movement. They fought for true democracy, true wealth, and true religion. That outlook, however, limited the potential autonomy of the movement culture. Acknowledgment of this fact need not lead to the conclusion that "working-class culture," or some variant of the term, offers nothing to historians. It does necessitate clear understanding of the ambiguity of that culture, and for this reason the term "movement culture" seems both apt and accurate.

Since this work focuses on culture, some might assume that it supports a position critics describe as "cultural voluntarism." Certain structuralist historians who lay claim to the most correct version of Marxism and historical materialism find this position repugnant. Certainly this work has everything to do with what most historians would consider the nonmaterial domain. It does not purport to describe or assay class in an objective sense, as "class in itself." Rather, it discusses the subjective side of class, of "class for itself"—purposeful working-class self-activity as it actually existed in this period, as opposed to "class for itself" in the form of the revolutionary consciousness. On a descriptive level culture is divorced from the material base so endearing to culturalism's critics. Indeed, in examining something so nonmaterial as song-poetry, a critical reader might appraise the chapters that follow as the most reified study of culture to date. A few might conclude that the work collapses the process whereby the working class was made into an activity confined to that subjective realm where class is reduced to "class consciousness." Herein the world of the workplace and the means of production figure indirectly at best. Some readers might conclude these have no bearing at all—that culture need not be considered rooted in material life and that workers enjoyed considerable leeway in their purposeful self-activity of culture creation.[33]

Despite its devotion to the cultural realm, this work nevertheless proceeds from an assumption of the material foundations of culture.[34] This does not mean culture should be equated with some reflective phenomenon of the economic base or with a temporary superstructural derivation. Nor does it mean that historians who argue the "primacy" of the economic in such literal terms are correct. The following chapters assume the determinant conditioning impact of the material world on the nonmaterial, but only in the broadest economic context in which capitalism defines the outer parameters for self-activity. The following chapters place the movement culture, and the possibilities of labor's momentary challenge, within a specific economic context in which class formation was an objective structural phenomenon as well as process of "active self-creation."[35]

Economically the years 1840 to 1890 witnessed the triumph of laissez-faire, entrepreneurial industrial capitalism.[36] Plantation agriculture and petty capitalist household farming—once the dominant economic sectors and a key element in the rise of industry—stood triumphant only to be outpaced in a few years by the manufacturing sector. Under the guise of "free labor," capitalism proved its revolutionary potential as it destroyed slavery and marginalized household-oriented agriculture. What's more, manufacturers sought to transfer their economic might into political muscle by consolidating their position in the political arena and molding the federal government into a policy-making ally. More narrowly, manufacturing made significant changes itself. As some industries grew uniformly organized, labor markets became less segmented and haphazard. As methods of production were made more systematic, firms became steadily larger, and machines performed greater roles, some trades became deskilled, the family discovered itself yearly more linked to industrial capitalism, and aggregate production levels quickly outpaced those of earlier decades. Workers from Western Europe found their fortunes tied to American capitalism. Capital generally grew more concentrated; industry finally subjected labor to "formal," if not yet "real," control; and "wage labor" became the rule for most workers.

After unimpeded accumulation and expansion from 1840 to 1870—one of those "long swings" of profitable development for an economy—industrial capitalism encountered obstacles. The next twenty-five years demonstrated the limitations of the social structure of accumulation spawned in an earlier era. Between 1873 and 1896 the aggregate performance of the economy lagged behind previous decades even as general growth continued. The rate of growth in net national product and industrial output dropped sharply. Prolonged business-cycle depressions occurred in each decade, yielding new levels of business failures and unemployment. Prices fell appreciably, pushing business to the margins and forcing it to recognize the limitations of its cost-cutting efforts.

Workers bore the brunt of cost cutting as capital sought to gain more from the labor input into the production equation. On this front, however, capital found itself constrained by the largely "untransformed" character of its work force. Until the 1890s capital accumulation depended on ever-larger numbers of wage workers but not on systematic alteration of existing techniques of production or labor processes. Massive technological innovation remained an exception in most industries and hardly constituted the driveshaft of the industrial revolution. A diversity of production methods still existed in particular industries. Perhaps more important, capitalism depended on workers' knowledge of production. The upswing in capitalist growth from 1840 to 1870, therefore, derived from existing techniques of production and was more a quantitative than qualitative change. The limitations of this situation became apparent to capital near the close of the century. Industry felt itself hamstrung by a work force exercising excessive influence over production and increasingly given to collective resistance to capitalist offensive.

At the beginning and end of the period from 1840 to 1890, workers could not have mounted a major campaign to check capital's power. The speed at which capitalism reworked economy and society negated any such process. However, within the context of the Gilded Age, workers found some brief space for self-activity. For a moment before monopoly capitalism would rework, redivide, and restructure the working class, workers overcame some of the obstacles that had fragmented them in the past. They forged a movement against wholesale domination by industrial capitalism and formulated a formidable critique of the new order. In the process, the divide between capitalists and workers became more politicized, and a movement culture emerged to promulgate workers' vision for the future America. At nearly the same instant, however, economic forces induced a reformulation of the parameters of struggle, and movement culture quickly slipped into the abyss of working-class failure in the 1890s. Material reality had itself changed, and workers found themselves searching for explanations of how the movement and movement culture had failed. By the time workers reorganized on a significant level, however, Rees Lewis and his cohorts were no longer writing song-poetry or taking their place in the battle for labor's rights.

## NOTES

1. Rees E. Lewis, "March of the Rolling Mill Men," *National Labor Tribune*, 30 March 1878.

2. James Francis Child, *The English and Scottish Popular Ballads*, 5 vols. (Boston: Houghton Mifflin, 1882–96). On Child's influence on scholars, see A. L. Lloyd, *Folk Song in England* (New York: International Publishers, 1968); and D. K. Wilgus, *Anglo-American Folksong Scholarship since 1898* (New Brunswick: Rutgers University Press, 1959). Child's considerable impact in America derived in part from the work of a few early scholars who followed their mentor's strictures closely. See, for example, Josiah H. Combs, *Folk-Songs of the Southern United States* (Austin: University of Texas Press, 1967). Combs, who did his fieldwork in the early twentieth century, considered ballad-making a "closed account" and his own work little more than the collecting of cultural relics. In addition, see Lyman Kittridge's introduction to Child's *English and Scottish Popular*

*Ballads*, as quoted in Combs, *Folk-Songs of the Southern United States*, 44; and Cecil Sharp, *English Folk Songs from the Southern Appalachians* (New York: G. P. Putnam's Sons, 1917), and *English Folk Song: Some Conclusions* (London: Simpkin and Co., 1907).

3. For examples of scholarship that challenged some of Child's assumptions, see H. M. Belden, *Ballads and Songs* (Columbia: University of Missouri Press, 1940); Phillips Barry, *The Maine Woods Songster* (Cambridge: Powell Printing Co., 1939), and *The New Green Mountain Songster* (New Haven: Yale University Press, 1939); John Lomax, *American Ballads and Folksongs* (New York: Macmillan, 1934), and *Songs of the Cattle Trail and Cow Camp* (New York: Macmillan, 1919). Between 1910 and 1970, scholars of American folksong compiled numerous occupation-based collections. See, for example, Earl Clifton Beck, *Songs of the Michigan Lumberjacks* (Ann Arbor: University of Michigan Press, 1948); Joanna Colcord, *Songs of American Sailormen* (New York: W. W. Norton, 1938); William Doerflinger, *Shantymen and Shantyboys* (New York: Macmillan, 1951); Austin and Alta Fife, *Cowboys and Western Songs: A Comprehensive Anthology* (New York: Clarkson N. Potter, 1969); Roland Palmer Gray, *Songs and Ballads of the Maine Lumberjacks* (Cambridge: Harvard University Press, 1924); Stan Hugill, *Shanties from the Seven Seas* (New York: E. P. Dutton, 1966); John and Alan Lomax, *Cowboys Songs and Other Frontier Ballads* (New York: Alfred Knopf, 1910); Newman Ivey White, *American Negro Folk-Songs* (Cambridge: Harvard University Press, 1928); and John Weasley Work, *American Negro Songs* (New York: Houghton Mifflin, 1940).

4. Wilgus, *Anglo-American Folksong Scholarship*, xvii.

5. On the rural bias of folklorists, see Lloyd, *Folk Song in England*, 318.

6. Angus Gillespie, *Folklorist of the Coal Fields: George Korson's Life and Work* (University Park: Pennsylvania State University Press, 1980), 5. Similarly, for Great Britain, see the introductory chapter in Robert Colls, *The Collier's Rant: Song and Culture in the Industrial Village* (London: Croom Helm, 1977). On class bias among English collectors, see David Vincent, "The Decline of Oral Tradition in Popular Culture," in *Popular Culture and Custom in Nineteenth-Century England*, ed. Robert Storch (London: Croom Helm, 1982), 20–47.

7. On Archie Green's efforts to convince scholars of the value of "labor lore" and "labor song," see "American Labor Lore: Its Meanings and Uses," *Industrial Relations* 4 (February 1965): 51–69, and "Industrial Lore: A Bibliographic-Semantic Query," *Western Folklore* 37 (July 1978): 213–44. Those sympathetic to Green's cause have sometimes demonstrated less understanding of workers than Green and little of his analytic acumen. See, for example, Roger Abrahams, "Toward a Sociological Theory of Folklore: Performing Services," *Western Folklore* 37 (July 1978): 161–84; Richard Bauman, "Differential Identity and the Social Base of Folklore," *Journal of American Folklore* 84 (January-March 1971): 31–41; Robert Byington, "Strategies for Collecting Occupational Folklore in Con-

temporary Urban/Industrial Contexts," *Western Folklore* 37 (July 1978): 185–98; Robert S. McCarl, Jr., "Occupational Folklore: A Theoretical Hypothesis," *Western Folklore* 37 (July 1978): 145–60; and Bruce E. Nickerson, "Is There a Folk in the Factory?" *Journal of American Folklore* 87 (January-March 1974): 133–39.

8. The most useful source on Korson's life is Gillespie, *Folklorist of the Coal Fields.* Korson's major works, in chronological sequence, include *Songs and Ballads of the Anthracite Miner* (New York: Grafton Press, 1927); *Minstrels of the Mine Patch* (Philadelphia: University of Pennsylvania Press, 1938); and *Coal Dust on the Fiddle* (Philadelphia: University of Pennsylvania Press, 1943). On Korson's reception among some folklorists, see John Spargo, review of *Coal Dust on the Fiddle, Journal of American Folklore* 57 (April 1944): 91–92, and the rebuttal by Ben Botkin in the same issue, 139. Korson's work is not without serious shortcomings, one of which was his exclusion of radical labor songs that he found among miners. Similarly, see Duncan Emrich, "Casey Jones—Union Scab," *California Folklore Quarterly* 1 (July 1942): 292–93. For criticism of this orientation, see Archie Green, *Only a Miner* (Urbana: University of Illinois Press, 1972), 55.

9. John Greenway, *American Folksongs of Protest* (New York: A. S. Barnes, 1953); Edith Fowke and Joe Glazer, *Songs of Work and Freedom* (Chicago: Roosevelt University Press, 1960); Joyce Kornbluh, *Rebel Voices: An I.W.W. Anthology* (Ann Arbor: University of Michigan Press, 1968); and Philip Foner, *American Labor Songs of the Nineteenth Century* (Urbana: University of Illinois Press, 1975).

10. R. Serge Denisoff, *Great Day Coming: Folk Music and the American Left* (Urbana: University of Illinois Press, 1971), and *Sing a Song of Social Significance* (Bowling Green, Ohio: Bowling Green State University Press, 1972).

11. Green's works include, among others, "American Labor Lore"; "A Discography of American Coal Miners' Songs," *Labor History* 2 (December 1961): 101–15; "A Discography of American Labor Union Songs," *New York Folklore Quarterly* 17 (Fall 1961): 186–93; "Industrial Lore"; *Only a Miner;* and "Recorded Labor Songs: An Overview," *Western Folklore* 27 (January 1968): 68–76.

12. See also the work of Duncan Emrich, "Songs of the Western Miners," *California Folklore Quarterly* 1 (July 1942): 213–32; S. Page Stegner, "Protest Songs from the Butte Mines," *Western Folklore* 26 (July 1967): 157–67; and Wayland Hand, "The Folklore, Customs, and Traditions of the Butte Miner," *California Folklore Quarterly* 5 (January 1946): 1–25, and 5 (April 1946): 153–78. In addition, see Wayland Hand, Charles Cutts, Robert Wylder, and Betty Wylder, "Songs of the Butte Miners," *Western Folklore* 9 (January 1950): 1–40. On the relationship between folksong, folklore, and the organized Left in the United States, see Richard Reuss, "American Folklore and Left-Wing Politics, 1927–1957" (Ph.D. diss., Indiana University, 1971), "Folk Music and Social Conscience: The Musical

Odyssey of Charles Seeger, *Western Folklore* 38 (October 1979): 221–38, and "The Roots of American Left-Wing Interest in Folk Music," *Labor History* 12 (Spring 1971): 259–79. See also his discography *Songs of American Labor, Industrialization, and the Urban Work Experience: A Discography* (Ann Arbor: Labor Studies Center, Institute of Labor and Industrial Relations, University of Michigan, 1983). In addition, see David King Dunaway, "Unsung Songs of Protest: The Composers Collective of New York," *New York Folklore* 5 (Summer 1979): 1–20; and Robbie Lieberman, *"My Song Is My Weapon": People's Songs, American Communism, and the Politics of Culture, 1930–50* (Urbana: University of Illinois Press, 1989).

13. A number of scholars have argued the case for the value of folksong and folklore in the study of history. See B. A. Botkin, "Folklore as a Neglected Source of Social History," in *The Cultural Approach to History,* ed. Caroline Ware (New York: Columbia University Press, 1940), 308–15; Charles Seeger, "Folk Music as a Source of Social History," in ibid., 316–23; and John Greenway, "Folk Songs as Socio-Historical Documents," *Western Folklore* 9 (January 1960): 1–9.

14. The term "inert" is borrowed from Bryan Palmer. See "Classifying Culture," *Labour/Le Travailleur* 8/9 (Autumn-Spring 1981–82): 181.

15. On the historiography of labor in the United States to 1970, see Paul G. Faler, "Working Class Historiography," *Radical America* 3 (March 1969): 58–68; Thomas Krueger, "American Labor Historiography, Old and New: A Review Essay," *Journal of Social History* 4 (Spring 1971): 277–85; and Robert Zeiger, "Workers and Scholars: Recent Trends in American Labor Historiography," *Labor History* 13 (Spring 1972): 245–66. On recent scholarship in the United States and Canada, see David Brody, "The Old Labor History and the New: In Search of an American Working Class," *Labor History* 20 (Winter 1979): 111–26; Gregory S. Kealey, "Critiques: Labour and Working-Class History in Canada: Prospects in the 1980s," *Labour/Le Travailleur* 7 (Spring 1981): 67–94; David Montgomery, "To Study the People: The American Working Class," *Labor History* 21 (Fall 1980): 485–512, and "Trends in Working-Class History," *Labour/Le Travailleur* 19 (Spring 1987): 12–22; Robert Ozanne, "Trends in American Labor History," *Labor History* 21 (Fall 1980): 513–21; and Bryan Palmer, "Classifying Culture," 153–83.

16. The most important work of Commons and the Wisconsin School is John R. Commons et al., *History of Labor in the United States,* 4 vols. (New York: Macmillan, 1918–36). See also Selig Perlman's impressive book *A Theory of the Labor Movement* (New York: Macmillan, 1928).

17. The fact that nineteenth-century workers, including those in Europe, frequently saw their struggle in universal, rather than strictly class, terms has only been touched upon. See, for example, Gregory Kealey and Bryan Palmer, *Dreaming of What Might Be: The Knights of Labor in Ontario 1880–1900* (Cambridge: Cambridge University Press, 1982); and William H. Sewell, Jr., *Work and Revolution in France: The Language of Labor from the Old Regime to 1848* (Cambridge: Cambridge University Press, 1980).

18. Lawrence W. Levine, *Black Culture and Black Consciousness: Afro-American Folk Thought from Slavery to Freedom* (Oxford: Oxford University Press, 1977).

19. Ibid., 445.

20. For a survey of the literature of British labor history, particularly Marxist culturalists and structuralists, see Richard Johnson, "Culture and the Historians," in *Working-Class Culture: Studies in History and Theory,* ed. John Clarke, Chas Critcher, and Richard Johnson (London: Hutchinson/Center for Contemporary Cultural Studies, University of Birmingham, 1979), 41–71. See also Chas Critcher, "Sociology, Cultural Studies, and the Post-War Working Class," ibid., 13–40; Edward P. Thompson, *The Making of the English Working Class* (New York: Vintage, 1966). For an overview of Thompson's theory of culture, see Alan Dawley, "E. P. Thompson and the Peculiarities of the Americans," *Radical History* 19 (Winter 1978–79): 33–60.

21. Herbert Gutman, *Work, Culture and Society in Industrializing America* (New York: Vintage, 1977).

22. See, for example, the critical review of historians employing the culturalist approach in David Bercuson, "Through the Looking Glass of Culture: An Essay on the New Labor History and Working-Class Culture in Recent Canadian Historical Writing," *Labour/Le Travailleur* 7 (Spring 1981): 95–112.

23. For a similar attempt at understanding organized labor, cultural activities, and song-poetry, see Vernon Lidtke's work on the "alternative culture" of German socialists, *The Alternative Culture: Socialist Labor in Imperial Germany* (New York: Oxford University Press, 1985).

24. David Bercuson's "Through the Looking Glass" is the only wholesale dismissal of the new labor history and the cultural approach. More balanced is Robert Ozanne's defense of the Wisconsin School, "Trends in American Labor History." Other historians remain generally sympathetic to the culturalists, though a few have offered valuable criticism. See, for example, Brody, "The Old Labor History and the New"; and Daniel Rodgers, "Tradition, Modernity, and the American Industrial Worker: Reflections and Critique," *Journal of Interdisciplinary History* 7 (Spring 1977): 655–81. The best general criticism of the culturalists has come from two of its leading North American practioners: Gregory Kealey and Bryan Palmer. See, for example, Kealey, "Critiques," and Palmer, "Classifying Culture."

25. Of particular value in understanding the difficulties involved in the application of the culture concept to history, see Ian McKay, "Historians, Anthropology, and the Concept of Culture," *Labour/Le Travailleur* 8/9 (Autumn-Spring 1981–82): 185–242.

26. The structuralists charge the culturalists with "romanticism" or "ethical humanism." On this issue, see Johnson, "Culture and the Historians," 68–69, and Kealey, "Labour and Working-Class History."

27. This debate spans nearly two decades and has been intense, acrimonious, difficult, and tedious. Those who wish to follow its course

might begin with Johnson, "Culture and the Historians"; and Kealey, "Labour and Working-Class History." In addition, see Dawley, "The Peculiarities of the Americans"; Palmer, "Classifying Culture," 172–83; and Marcus Rediker, "Getting Out of the Graveyard: Perry Anderson, Edward Thompson, and the Arguments of English Marxism," *Radical History* 26 (1982): 120–31. Thompson offers his own defense and a critique of structuralism, particularly Althusser's, in *The Poverty of Theory and Other Essays* (New York: Monthly Review Press, 1978). For a defense of the structuralists, but one that calls for finding common ground with the culturalists, see Perry Anderson's *Arguments within English Marxism* (London: New Left Books, 1980).

28. The distinction between "class-in-itself" and "class-for-itself" is outlined in Georg Lukacs's historic essay, "Class Consciousness," in *History and Class Consciousness* (Cambridge: M.I.T. Press, 1971), 46–82. Eric Hobsbawm employs these notions, and briefly summarizes their importance, in "Notes on Class Consciousness," in *Workers: Worlds of Labor* (New York: Pantheon Books, 1984), 15–32. On the differing conceptions of class and class consciousness employed by structuralists and culturalists, see Anderson, *Arguments within English Marxism*, 30–43.

29. At this point, some readers may recall Gareth Stedman Jones, *Languages of Class: Studies of English Working Class History, 1832–1982* (Cambridge: Cambridge University Press, 1983), particularly the essay "Rethinking Chartism," 90–178. Jones's analysis of the language of class within Chartism suggests the rewards of such efforts, but it is not convincing and provides an inadequate model for language analysis by historians. For that matter, no historian has yet offered a suitable model for such analysis; like Jones they all rely on well-established methods of historical analysis, whether they refer to it as language analysis or not. For useful commentary on *Languages of Class*, see Joan W. Scott, "On Language, Gender, and Working-Class History," *International Labor and Working-Class History* 31 (Spring 1987): 1–13, and the Response by Bryan Palmer, 14–23, and Christine Stansell, 24–29. For an insightful critique of *Languages of Class* from a more traditional Marxist perspective, see John Foster, "The Declassing of Language," *New Left Review* 150 (March-April 1985): 29–45.

30. I have chosen the term "movement culture" because it conveys a sense of the movement-specific nature of the culture addressed in this work. The term "movement culture" has been used before with some success. See, for example, Lawrence Goodwyn's study of populism, *Democratic Promise: The Populist Moment in America* (New York: Oxford University Press, 1976). See also Kealey and Palmer, *Dreaming of What Might Be*. Vernon Lidtke employs the term "alternative culture" in *The Alternative Culture*. Lidtke's application of this term makes sense in the context of German socialism in the period he studies. However, to speak of an alternative culture among Gilded-Age labor in the United States, with the exception of a few ethnic groups in a few cities, would be to

exaggerate the extensiveness of movement culture and the ability of the labor movement to construct a truly "alternative" culture. Indeed, doing so would imply—as too many historians, including myself, have done—an autonomous working-class culture. See my dissertation, "For Democracy, the Working Class, and God: Labor Song-Poems and Working-Class Consciousness, 1865–1895 (Ph.D. diss., University of Minnesota, 1984). In light of these exaggerated—though sometimes unintentional—claims of an autonomous working-class culture in the new labor history, understatement would seem the best course. For a well-conceived, conservative view of labor's alternative, see Richard J. Oestreicher, *Solidarity and Fragmentation: Working People and Class Consciousness in Detroit, 1875–1900* (Urbana: University of Illinois Press, 1986).

31. Here I have borrowed Lawrence Goodwyn's phrase "moment of challenge." One might correctly argue that the labor movement briefly offered a moment of challenge in the 1880s, just as the populists would do a few years later.

32. On the defensive character of much of British working-class life, see Gareth Stedman Jones, "Working-Class Culture and Working-Class Politics in London, 1870–1900: Notes on the Remaking of a Working Class," in *Languages of Class*, 79–238. See also Penelope Summerfield, "The Effingham Arms and the Empire: Deliberate Selection in the Evolution of Music Halls in London," in *Popular Culture and Class Conflict 1590–1914: Explorations in the History of Labor and Leisure,*, ed. Eileen and Stephen Yeo (Sussex: Harvester Press, 1981), 208–40. On Canadian workers, see Peter DeLottinville, "Joe Beef of Montreal: Working-Class Culture and the Tavern, 1869–1889," *Labour/Le Travailleur* 8/9 (Autumn-Spring 1981–82): 9–40. The best study of the separate cultural life of American workers is Roy Rosenzweig, *Eight Hours for What We Will: Workers and Leisure in an Industrial City, 1870–1920* (Cambridge: Cambridge University Press, 1983).

33. For an useful discussion of the culturalists and structuralists on "agency," see Anderson, *Arguments within English Marxism*, 16–58.

34. For a different view, see Eileen and Stephen Yeo, "Ways of Seeing," in *Popular Culture and Class Conflict*, 128–54.

35. On the cultural activities of the labor movement as "active self-creation," see Kealey and Palmer, *Dreaming of What Might Be*, 223.

36. For an brief overview of capitalist economic development and the rise of the working class, see David Montgomery, "Labor and Republic in Industrial America, 1860–1920," *Le Mouvement Social* 111 (April 1980): 201–15, and Bryan Palmer, "Social Formation and Class Formation in North America, 1800–1900," in *Proletarianization and Family History*, ed. David A. Levine (San Diego: Academic Press, 1984): 229–309.

# 1

# American Workers and Movement Culture in the Gilded Age

THE Civil War brought anything but an easy time for workers. Women, men, and children served on the domestic front in the industrial army, and men became the rank and file of the military effort as well. But as the war dragged on, workers wearied of their sacrifice. From their vantage, workers bore the costs of the war, while the nation's elite not only escaped the carnage but profited from it. Some discontented workers became openly critical of government economic policy and business practices. Many joined those unions that became the foundation for a revived labor movement.

Stepping to the fore, Boston printers defied authorities in 1863. Facing an inflationary spiral and an abhorrent pay scale, they walked out on their employers. An anonymous printer recalled the ideals of his revolutionary forebears and the recent war against slavery in a song-poem written for the occasion:

> Rouse, Workingmen! will ye crouch down,
> Beneath employers' threatening frown?
>   Are ye not men?
> Will ye submissive bow the neck
> To yoke oppressive at their beck
>   Like goaded beasts?
>
> Have ye not rights as well as they?
> Are they to rule and ye obey,
>   Like abject slaves?
> No! Justice, honor, manhood, all
> That man enobles sternly call
>   For union firm.

Yield but the right they now contest
Ye to the winds may fling the rest,
   Nor hope to rise
But lower, deeper, baser sink,
Till robbed of e'en the right to think
   As well as act.

Ye ask but justice, ask but right
These to obtain you must unite,
   And firmly stand,
Unawed by threats, that weakness show,
And from no kindly impulse flow,
   But greed for gain.
The noble souls that think and feel,
For others' wants, in woe and weal,
   Ne'er stoop to wrest
From honest toil its hard-earned gain,
But help to fill instead of drain
   Its scarcity purse.

Your price is fixed, your duty plain,
Your independence now maintained,
   Nor flinch or cringe,
And labor will receive its due,
Though scorned by some, and paid by few,
   Its just reward
For labor is the world's true wealth,
The poor man's capital in health,
   Which who employs
Must pay the usury that is just,
Not what he would, but what he must—
   Its market worth.[1]

Boston printers acted as harbingers of the class conflict common in the next thirty years. Defiant workers throughout the country would take collective action to convince the capitalist elite that they must pay workers their "just reward" and "market worth." Their song-poems regularly invoked the cultural heritage, calling for "justice," "rights," "honor," "manhood," "honest toil," "independence," "true wealth," "noble souls," and "just reward." Such emotionally charged language recalled the major social movements of the previous hundred years—the American Revolution, anti-Federalism, Jacksonian working-men's democracy, antislavery, and even the international fight for liberal democracy from the French Revolution to the revolutions of 1848. Workers' more immediate encounter with an ascending industrial capitalist order, however, infused the slogans with additional meaning. With the most heinous injustice—slavery—abolished, justice for the workers seemed a priority. Boston's printers, therefore, not only acted as precursors of nation-wide collective effort but also exemplified an outlook characteristic of that effort. The fight for specific working-class gains would be an adjunct to the wider battle over the nation's future.

Workers who believed participation in the war would bring "just reward" felt sorely deceived. No sooner had peace been made than the Republican party began finding excuses for not living up to its promises.[2] Republicans chose a conservative interpretation of the party's founding principles and cemented a firm alliance with business in the postbellum decades. Not that the Democrats proved the workingman's friend to any great degree. While the party sometimes delivered a prolabor package on the local level, the package contained few "gifts" to labor. Whatever workers got from either party they earned themselves.[3]

The same might be said of workers' relations with the federal government. Few workers suffered from delusions that the state functioned as a neutral third party. The federal army and the legal system often acted as state-funded instruments to protect business interests. The federal government's land distribution and tariff policies, sometimes excessive and corrupt, amounted to a direct subsidy to business. Even the government's Indian policy meant clearing obstacles from capital's path and ensuring a stable environment for the cultivation and extraction of resource-intensive staples vital to the development of industry.

The ultimate success of industrial capitalism, nevertheless, derived from capital itself, which demonstrated remarkable powers for geometric self-generation. Figures for amount of capitalization, wage bill, value of product, and number of workers employed exhibited marked increase in major and minor industries. To many this scenario promised more for less, as the dollars expended declined relative to the value of output. Growth was phenomenal: the gross national product increased sixfold between 1869 and 1899.[4]

Such information concealed the ambiguity of expansion, however. Economist David Wells knew that growth had its cost and in 1889 offered insight into capitalism's destructive powers.

> Thirty or forty years ago the tinman, whose occupation was mainly one of handicraft, was recognized as one of the leading and most skillful mechanics in every village, town, and city. His occupation has, however, well-nigh passed away. For example, a townsman or a farmer desires a supply of milk cans. He never thinks of going to his

corner tinman, because he knows that in . . . other large towns and cities there is a special establishment fitted up with special machinery, which will make his can better and fifty percent cheaper than he can have it made by hand in his own town. . . . And what has been thus affirmed of tinplate might be equally affirmed of a great variety of other leading commodities; the blacksmith . . . no longer making but buying his horseshoes, nails, nuts, and bolts; the carpenter, his doors, sash, blinds, and moldings; the wheelwright, his spokes, hubs, and wheels; the harness maker, his straps, girths, and collars; the painter, his paint, ground and mixed, and so on.[5]

Wells accurately perceived the sum total of the nation's economic changes may have been growth, but not everyone shared equally. Workers hardly got their fair share, or so it seemed to sympathetic observers. True, workers' real incomes rose on average over the period. But aggregate increase could be deceiving, since not all workers received steadily higher wages. Moreover, workers regularly faced a myriad of problems: harsh working conditions, long hours, minimal job security, layoffs, wage cuts, poor housing, substandard city services, and economic depressions.

Nevertheless, workers' chances for moderate economic advancement appeared real enough. Hard work rarely led to wealth, but for adult males it could lead to mobility within the job hierarchy. Generational mobility offered greater promise, as many second-generation workers moved beyond the economic standing of their parents. What's more, despite the abuse heaped upon it by ill-informed observers, the working-class community offered significant amenities. Family, saloon, neighborhood, fraternal order, church, and sports provided workers with important nonpecuniary rewards. They kept workers' and families' sense of dignity intact, where the workplace often destroyed them. "A life apart" may have checked workers' rebelliousness, but even a culture of consolation allows the human spirit to retain a rebellious potential.

Potential sometimes was realized. Between 1865 and 1895 workers persistently rebelled against employers. Emerging from the war with their organizations in shambles, skilled workers took the offensive. Iron molders, cigar makers, and typographers repeatedly organized and reorganized unions in their trades. They also joined other workers and reforms in various federations such as the National Labor Union, formed in the immediate postbellum years. The spirit of solidarity, however, found greatest expression in the Knights of Labor after 1869. Socialists and anarchists might fulminate against the Knights, but they could not deny that, particularly in the 1880s, the organization tapped a wellspring of discontent among workers. Not until the 1890s would another federation—the more conservative American Federation of Labor—eclipse the Knights of Labor.

From 1865 to 1895, however, defeats and setbacks could not dispel optimism. Tactical and ideological disputes might divide workers, but generally organized labor's fighting strength increased. In 1865, after all, workers had only just awakened from wartime doldrums and organized labor's presence was virtually nonexistent. Few would have guessed that workers would cripple the nation's rail system and shut down local industries throughout the country in 1877. A few years later the Knights provided organizational voice for protest and led hundreds of thousands, if not millions, of workers in the upheavals of 1884, 1885, and 1886. Bitter defeats followed and employers took the offensive, but not until the defeat of the American Railway Union at Pullman in 1894 did the movement lose momentum. At that point both leaders and rank and file alike lost their sense of inevitable progress and moved to reconsider strategies for individual and collective survival.

While not many workers (with the exception of certain radicals) gave it serious thought, the strength of the movement owed much to its cultural dimension. Nowhere near as extensive or influential as the "alternative culture" constructed by social democrats in Germany, American movement culture still should not be disregarded. Every major city where labor exerted a presence in the workplace counted a network of related cultural institutions, activities, and events. Men, women, and children could participate daily in some activity designed to bolster spirits, maintain and recruit members, and engender solidarity. Besides regular meetings one might attend a concert, a picnic, a dinner, a parade, a ball, a dramatic presentation, or an ice-cream social. In addition, one could hear a lecture or debate at the workers' hall, subscribe to the labor press, invest in a cooperative, stop by the prolabor saloon, spend time at the workers' library, join a study group, or chat with the grocer on the "approved" list. These cultural elements provided a separate way of life based on the intersection of workplace, community, class, and labor movement; the values of this lifestyle stood sharply at odds with those of the dominant cultural system. Although these values never were fully realized and never formed the basis of an autonomous working-class culture, workers offered a powerful challenge in this cultural alternative and created an energetic and vibrant movement culture.

In Detroit, for example, Richard Oestreicher discovered a "subculture of opposition" existed.[6] This subculture found its focus in its hostility to obvious particulars—the accumulation of wealth, grinding employers, and the grim conditions for workers—rather than in a clearly delineated ideology. Its concrete manifestations were sometimes explicit in their working-class message, as evidenced by the labor press, the "Dialectical Union" for debate, the distribution of scab and boycott broadsides, appeals to invest in cooperatives, street demonstrations, and worker militia groups. A more amorphous sense of solidarity, however, informed the more popular events such as dances, dinners, concerts, steamship excursions, and strawberry and ice cream festivals.

Similarly, across the border in Canada, the movement gave shape to a movement culture. Indeed, Gregory Kealey and Bryan Palmer see in this culture "an alternative hegemony" based on working-class values of "collectivity, mutuality, and solidarity" supplemented by contempt for elite culture.[7] In rituals, symbols, funerals, parades, festivals, poetry, journalism, religious ideas, demonstrations, and picnics, workers challenged capitalism, both in and out of the workplace. The Knights of Labor stood at the head of this challenge and for a brief moment spelled hope for those who dared to "dream of what might be."

Workers in other cities dared to dream as well. Pittsburgh's burgeoning working-class population turned the city into a "craftmen's empire" replete with a vibrant "plebeian culture."[8] Much of that culture was geared toward nothing more than libertarian leisure and entertainment, but it also crossed paths with the city's powerful labor movement. The latter put culture creation and dissemination to its own use, employing everything from saloons to parades to recruit and maintain its membership. Likewise, those workers and their families who populated Lynn and Fall River, Massachusetts, built a labor movement with its own movement culture.[9] In Lynn, a shoemaking center, the Knights of Saint Crispin "provided community and fellowship for their members through an intricate pattern of social functions, picnics, benefits, and lodge meetings."[10] Other unions followed suit, and the city's culture bore the mark of blue-collars workers until the turn of the century. And in Fall River, native and foreign-born workers, particularly from Lancashire, England, created a set of institutions that reflected and reinforced their class consciousness while promulgating an increasingly dim view of owners. Sports teams, taverns, fraternal orders, workingmen's clubs, benefit societies, and cooper atives all worked with organized labor and acted as "agents for maintaining proletarian culture."[11]

The Chicago anarchist movement, more attuned to cultural activities as a tool for raising consciousness than most groups, presided over "a secular and class culture it had created, adapted, and invented for itself" or what another historian dubbed anarchist "counterculture."[12] The sound of that culture could be heard at dances, grand balls, parades, holiday processions, pageants, and commune festivals. An even stronger voice, however, emanated from German Americans at the forefront of Chicago's labor movement.[13] For them indigenous working-class culture was judged a priority, an important part of creating one's identity. The city abounded with brass bands, orchestras, singing societies and choirs, book clubs, theatrical productions, militias, physical culture societies, women's groups, and original literature of all genres linked to the labor movement and the German element specifically. At the turn of the century, even as the working-class German community waned, a labor parade counted 107 marching bands in its ranks.

Perhaps the greatest testimony to the vitality of movement culture, however, comes not from an industrial center but from one of those thousands of smaller cities and towns that became labor strongholds, especially once the Knights of Labor captured the working-class imagination. Scranton, Kansas, was just such a place. In 1879 citizens chartered a local assembly of the Knights of Labor.[14] Organized as a trade assembly of coal miners, the local operated until 1893, along with a mixed assembly established in 1883 and another miners' assembly chartered in 1886. These locals established a visible presence for labor in Scranton, including cultural activities to strengthen their cause internally and to spread it to the larger community as well. Consider, for example, Jonathan F. Young's report to the *National Labor Tribune* in 1881 on his local's second anniversary celebration. Young informed readers that the Knights celebrated by hosting "an oyster supper and concert in the City Hall." The evening included an address by "Brother Linn" on the exalted principles of the Knights and the virtuous character of their local cooperative mining operation. Celebrants also heard a musical program, with Young's rendition of Osage County poet William Hastie's song-poem for the Knights and a piece entitled "The Knights of Labor" "declaimed to perfection" by a Miss Maggie Linn. Young concluded with an announcement for an upcoming benefit gathering for the local Irish Land League.[15]

Young thus captured Scranton Knights in the act of coming to grips with the meaning of class itself. Male workers might have learned the meaning of class as they hacked and hewed Osage County's coal veins, but they and their families learned as well where that world of work intersected with an oyster dinner, the city hall, a cooperative coal mine, a pro-Knight speech, a song, a poem, and the Irish Land League—a network of activities comprising the Knights' cultural arm and essential to their overall success.

As Maggie Linn stepped forth with her song-poem, she enlisted herself in the fight and became directly involved in cultural creation and in movement culture. She was hardly alone. Song-poems would be written, composed, sung, recited, declaimed, printed, and distributed throughout the country. Inferior by literary standards, they nonetheless spoke the language of class, addressed subjects important to workers, and served as vehicles for the expression of collective sentiment. Thus they became enmeshed in that complex maze of activities making up movement culture and a subsidiary of the labor movement as a whole.

Labor song-poets discovered a number of options for reaching their comrades. The most accessible was the labor press that had grown from a handful of publications in the 1860s to hundreds by the 1880s. Unlike the later labor press, these publications typically subscribed to unrestrictive policies regarding contributors and subject matter and established the press as a forum for debate on topics ranging from socialism, third-party politics, and anarchism to temperance, religion, and women's rights. Although editors occasionally complained about song-poems, they published just about every one sent to them, regardless of quality or subject.[16] Doubtless, they sometimes used them as filler—along with the poems of Whitman, Whittier, Pope, Shelley, and Byron—but they also expressed awareness of song-poetry's importance.

Almost without exception, only marginal, irregular publications, or those first published in the 1890s, excluded original song-poetry.[17] Otherwise, song-poems appeared in publications representing an array of occupations—typographers, coal miners, iron molders, machinists, coopers, seamen, granite cutters, railway carmen, saddle makers, cigar makers, printers, window-glass workers, brakemen, locomotive engineers, and bakers. These papers spoke for diverse organizations: the Knights of Labor, Socialists Labor party, Coopers' International Union, Omaha Central Labor Union, Iron Molders' International Union, National Labor Union, United Mine Workers, Sons of Vulcan, Coast Seamen's Union of the Pacific, Order of Railway Conductors, and the Brotherhood of Railroad Brakemen. Moreover, cities with such papers included Boston, San Francisco, Denver, Chicago, Omaha, St. Louis, Pittsburgh, Cincinnati, Cleveland, Detroit, Philadelphia, Baltimore, and Indianapolis, as well as smaller locations such as Elmira, New York; Rock Island, Illinois; Dayton, Ohio; Cedar Rapids, Iowa; Richmond, Virginia; Paterson, New Jersey; Haverhill and Fall River, Massachusetts; and Rockland, Maine. Not all of these publications printed the same number of song-poems. *The Carpenter, Painter, Saddle and Harness Makers' Journal, Railway Carmen's Journal* included no more than a handful, while the *Cooper's Journal, Iron Molders' Journal, Journal of United Labor, Truth, Critic,* and *Labor Enquirer* (Denver) made them a regular feature. *The Workingman's Advocate, John Swinton's Paper, National Labor Tribune, Railroad Brakemen's Journal* printed as many as two hundred over the span of a few years. Between 1865 and 1895 some forty-three English-language publications printed nearly 2,600 original song-poems.

Writers with fervent ambition and determination sometimes took special steps to locate an audience. Poet Mulhall, a Pennsylvania coal miner turned itinerant songster, printed his works as broadsides and hawked them in bituminous coal-field communities.[18] Railroad worker Patrick Fennell, better known as Shandy Maguire; Michael McGovern, the Puddler Poet; and journalist-activist George McNeill issued volumes of their writings.[19] B. M. Lawrence, James D. and Emily Tallmadge, and Karl Reuber wrote, collected, compiled, and published songbooks for labor gatherings.[20]

Song-poems found wide circulation among workers. Knights of Labor leader Terence Powderly knew the popularity of song-poetry; he received hundreds of song-poems from individuals searching for comments or a publisher.[21] He must have thrown most in the wastebasket, because his personal papers contained only a dozen or so.[22] Fortunately, others escaped this fate. Some turned up in books.[23] Some, like Maggie Linn's, surfaced in correspondent reports to the labor press. A number enjoyed such popularity that workers recalled them in the twentieth century when scholars retrieved them from oral tradition.[24] Although most song-poems disappeared after their immediate use, a conservative estimate based on printed English sources would number at least four or five thousand.

Such popularity stemmed from song-poetry's relevance for workers. Song-poets expressed everything from the most general to the most specific working-class concerns in this period. Not surprisingly, improving workers' collective lot and advancing the labor movement served as a standard point of reference. Karl Reuber, a German piano and furniture polisher in Pittsburgh, typified the spirit of song-poetry in his "Song of Labor."[25] Reuber delineated the principles of working-class political economy as he alternately exalted labor and chastised its oppressors:

> Now that want and distress doth Labor oppress,
> What shall we sing for Labor's song?
> What shall we plead against Mammon's greed,
> Base selfishness and grievous wrong?
> "Close the rank—close the rank, still closer ever,
> Let Union be our high endeavor!"

> For the coal and the ore earth's depths you explore,
> Your strong arm and courage make fruitful the soil,
> Yes, heroes all when King Labor doth call,
> And what reward have you for all your toil?
> Mammon all freemen slave would make;
> Then unite—unite, for Freedom's sake!

> In vain, church's preaching, in vain Christian teaching
> If manhood be nothing, and gold be all;
> And Humanity's claim is naught but a name,
> If while heaping up wealth we our brother enthrall.
> O brothers! O sisters! let speed the good cause,
> And inscribe on our flag—"Better life, better laws!"

> Labor's heroes, O ne'er in life's battle despair,
> For your cares and your toil behold Victory nigh:
> Together unite,—and be steadfast in right;
> Be ready to live,—and be ready to die!
> Be ready and steady to battle life's wrong,
> And "Union for ever!" be Labor's song!

Reuber's song-poem exemplified the genre. Its theme of labor's advance; its class-mediated restatement of the language of liberal political democracy; the labor theory of value, and New Testament morality; its social criticism; and its elevation of union principles became hallmarks of song-poetry. Nearly every song-poem recalled the language of Reuber's "Song of Labor."

While espousing workers' cause, song-poets also entertained more specific agenda.[26] Many composed song-poems praising particular organizations and enjoining others to heed the call. The Knights of Labor became an obvious choice for such drum-beating, but so too did the Iron Molders' International Union, the Order of Railway Conductors, the American Federation of Labor, the Coast

Seamen's Union, the Granite Cutters' Union, the Brotherhood of Locomotive Firemen, the Socialist International, the Coopers' Union, the Cabinet Makers' Union (Reuber's choice), various coal miners' unions, and a curriers' union. Everything from the Greenback–Labor party to the Chicago anarchists became a rallying cry. Members and nonmembers alike heard pleas for organizations and summons to join the noble fight.[27]

A wide range of subjects and topics also occupied the song-poets' attention. Writers issued, for example, strike song-poems, that reported on and encouraged support for striking workers.[28] Workers who crossed picket lines could be subjected to severe opprobrium: song-poems described scabs and blacklegs as loathsome creatures.[29] In contrast, certain labor leaders, from William Sylvis to unknown local officials, became subjects of praise.[30] Similarly. when describing trades such as shoe making or printing, writers exuded pride, sentimentalism, and nostalgia.[31] Elsewhere song-poets directed criticism toward economic exploitation forcing women into prostitution.[32] Others examined the impact of marginal wages on families, particularly those children who worked to ensure family survival.[33] Still others considered problems of the workplace—the degradation of labor, unspeakable working conditions, unemployment, substandard wages, company stores, discrimination based on age, and the hardships of miners, to name a few.[34]

Within these and other song-poems, writers labeled and criticized the culprits as well. John Thompson pointed the finger at the typical capitalist, whom he judged nothing more than a "robber anarchist."[35] Cornelius Vanderbilt, Andrew Carnegie, and other industrial magnates garnered criticism as rapacious exploiters of workers.[36] In juxtaposition to noble labor, capital emerged as a class of "non-producers," "parasites," "leeches," and "vampires."[37] Only the clergy generated as much hostility as the new class of lazy idlers.[38]

While song-poets uniformly covered the same issues, both specific and general, they did not always reach the same conclusions. All agreed that immigration policy, temperance, monetary reform, fiscal legislation, and political involvement rated high on workers' agenda. Their positions on third parties, labor candidates, greenbacks, free silver, taxation, tariffs, and immigration restrictions nevertheless remained as varied as those of differing strands in the movement.[39]

Despite disagreement on other issues, everyone allied with the labor movement reached consensus on the eight-hour day. Song-poets provided a host of eight-hour songs. I. G. Blanchard and Reverend Jesse H. Jones's "Eight Hours" captured the spirit of the campaign and quickly became one of the most popular song-poems in American history.[40] Its opening and closing stanzas, along with its rousing chorus, provide a hint of its attraction and power:

We mean to make things over, we are tired of toil for naught,
With but bare enough to live upon, and never an hour for thought,
We want to feel the sunshine, and we want to smell the flowers,
We are sure that God has will'd it, and we mean to have eight hours.
We are summoning our forces from the shipyards, shop and mill,
Eight hours for work, eight hours for rest, eight hours for what we will!
Eight hours for work, eight hours for rest, eight hours for what we will!

Hurrah, hurrah, for Labor! for it shall arise in might.
It has filled the world with plenty, it shall fill the world with light;
Hurrah, hurrah, for Labor! it is mustering all its powers,
And shall march along to victory with the banner of eight hours!
Shout, shout the echoing rally till the welkin thrill,
Eight hours for work, eight hours for rest, eight hours for what we will!
Eight hours for work, eight hours for rest, eight hours for what we will!

Even the authors must have been surprised by the wide circulation their song-poem achieved. Throughout the nation workers could be heard singing the song at rallies, demonstrations, and parades as the campaign reached a climax in 1886. Jesse Jones, the working-class preacher, had devoted his life to the workers' cause without much success, but the adoption of his song surely gave him some sense of accomplishment. Few could doubt the efficacy of song-poetry's collective function when thousands sang and marched to the refrain "eight hours for work, eight hours for rest, eight hours for what we will."

Other song-poems found service in similar settings. Workers in the 1880s needed little prompting to break into a chorus of "Hold the Fort."[41] With a working-class message and a melody borrowed from an evangelical hymn, "Hold the Fort" gained a warm reception among workers. A Knights of Labor variant of the song quickly became the most popular labor song-poem of the century. Although its heyday came in the 1880s at Knights of Labor gatherings, workers sang the work into the twentieth century. As they marched against "king capital," workers would raise their voices in fervent chorus:

Storm the fort, ye Knights of Labor;
'Tis a glorious fight:

Brawn and brain against injustice—
God defend the right![42]

Song-poems like "Eight Hours" and "Hold the Fort" strikingly illustrate the enthusiasm with which workers greeted song-poems. Few song-poems, however, found such dramatic service. Nonetheless, the most impressive aspect of song-poetry may be not the fact that certain works enjoyed movement-wide circulation but the way song-poetry generally permeated the movement and movement culture. In this regard, very little separates the song-poem of Blanchard and Jones from that of Maggi Linn or thousands of others. All had their function in the day-to-day business of building and maintaining the ranks of labor.

Not surprisingly, in this mundane business Chicago workers fully embraced song-poetry, whether Irish or German, Knights of Labor or anarchist. As early as 1870 a parade held in conjunction with the "labor brotherhood festival" included six bands and two choirs in the procession.[43] Thirteen years later at the annual Paris Commune celebration in 1883, Michael Schwab recited "In Memory of Karl Marx."[44] In addition, the funeral ceremony for the Haymarket victims in 1885 featured the LaSalle Music Band performing "La Marseillaise," the Southwest Side Men's Singing Society singing "Goodnight," and two other bands and some thirteen or more singing societies rendering song-poetry and music as well.[45] What's more, these were only the most visible offerings of song-poetry.[46] Chicago's labor press regularly featured original song-poems, and any time Chicago workers gathered to advance their cause, they placed a song-poem or song-poet on the program.

In fact, song-poetry followed the labor movement throughout the nation. Most of the time it did not get much beyond the labor press. The majority of song-poems undoubtedly had a small audience—probably no longer than those readers who cared to plod through the pages of any labor paper. In this context, the song-poem served as a means of expression not unlike a letter to the editor; they often appeared in the same section or were submitted with a note, letter, or report to an editor.[47] That so many workers employed song-poems to state their views and to try their hand at "versifying" indicates both the popularity of song-poetry and the vitality of movement culture in this era. Moreover, as quasi-letters to editors song-poems could generate a wider audience. Song-poet Shandy Maguire astutely exploited this potential to his advantage. He frequently contributed song-poems that addressed individual readers by name.[48] These song-poems did not contain much of a union message, but they spawned a lively exchange between Maguire and his readers and unquestionably helped create a cooperative spirit throughout the union.

Creating that spirit typically involved equally unspectacular but more direct action from song-poets. For example, when Mrs. Henry B. Jones appeared before Local 17 of the Brotherhood of Locomotive Engineers in 1884, she recited a song-poem to increase their sense of brotherhood and esteem.[49] Elsewhere the president of a local in the Amalgamated Association of Iron and Steel Workers cultivated similar sentiments in a song-poem he recited to his union's membership.[50] Likewise, a meeting of Local 251 of the Knights of Labor featured a "member worker" reading a song-poem in which he called on the audience to dedicate themselves to union principles and the labor movement.[51] A somewhat different approach emerged in Isaac Taylor's song-poem read before the national convention of the iron molders union in 1870. Taylor chastised fellow workers for indicting capitalism when union members shirked their duties.[52] Twenty-two years later, Michael McGovern also appeared before that union to recite his song-poem. The "Puddler Poet" recounted the triumphs and failures of the organization and reminded the audience to aid the union.[53]

Recitations like McGovern's became common in the Pittsburgh region, where song-poets frequently emerged from the ranks of iron and steel workers.[54] Recitations became common elsewhere as well and more than one song-poet gained recognition for their skill. However, song-poets also wrote works for audience participation and singing became a regular feature of the labor movement. German workers organized choirs and singing societies.[55] Evidence abounds for less formal group singing as well. Terence Powderly maintained that the Knights of Labor established group singing as a standard part of their functions: "Understand, no one member was selected to sing alone; all joined in; some one led, of course, but we all tried to sing and if all didn't do it right the volume of sound enabled us to escape detection and, being a forgiving lot of mortals, no effort was ever made to ferret out and punish the offenders against harmony."[56]

During the 1880s, song-poems often had a particular place on the union schedule. John Cotter, for example, wrote a song-poem that members sang as an initiation ode.[57] Sung to the tune of "America" the work welcomed strangers to the noble Knights of Local 2897 in Saginaw, Michigan. Organizer M. A. Dalbey of Ottumwa, Iowa, wrote an opening ode and closing ode, which locals around the country adopted.[58] Both advised commitment, spirit, harmony, and hard work in the name of organized labor. Moreover, J. J. Martin contributed an opening song and Isaac Kinley wrote "Goodnight," song-poems that members in their locals sang when they opened and closed meetings.[59] Less immediately popular was Tom O'Reilly's "Song of the Proletaire."[60] First printed in 1876 in a socialist publication, O'Reilly's "Song" was later presented at a general assembly of the Knights; thereafter, union members would enjoy its lyrics and melody on a regular basis.

O'Reilly was one of hundreds of individuals whose song-poems found use in the labor movement. From San Francisco to Eau Claire, Wisconsin, song-poetry became standard labor-movement fare. In itself it played a minor role in working-class struggle. In the context of movement culture, however, song-poetry assumes a greater role as an element of a labor movement culture, embodied in events, institutions, activities, and gatherings, that proffered a set of values and ideals increasingly at odds with, and distinct from, the dominant society. Song-poems were part of both an explicit challenge to industrial capitalism and labor's effort to chart an alternative path for the nation's future.

The nation's elites could have sensed a new spirit among the nation's workers, epitomized in one union member's report from St. Louis in 1884. Edward Reese reported in the *National Labor Tribune* that his union consisted of a "fine body of men" with "representatives" from many ethnic groups—English, Polish, Welsh, Irish, Scottish, German, Swedish, and American.[61] These "good men and true" formed a musical and literary group to complement and strengthen their local. They even purchased a "three-hundred dollar piano" for the group. According to Reese, the local's meetings thereafter took on the air of an enjoyable and entertaining social event with "songs, recitations, etc. . . ." that also deterred union members from frequenting saloons. Edward Reese possessed no radical inclinations and yet the implicit challenge in his report would have seemed clear to "king capital." Here were workers joining a union and a movement for social change based on their interests. Moreover, that union united, and the movement offered promise to unite, workers from ethnic groups often at loggerheads. In addition, these workers had begun to create their own social life as a subsidiary to their union. Here, then, were the ingredients of open challenge to domination by capitalism, of a union and a movement advancing labor's obvious economic agenda and a movement culture spreading the gospel of labor. For thirty years the challenge continued and for thirty years "songs, recitations, etc. . . . " would do their part.

## NOTES

1. Anon., "Appeal to Workingmen," *Workingman's Advocate*, 12 December 1863.

2. The relationship between the Republican party and labor in the Civil War era is described in David Montgomery, *Beyond Equality* (New York: Alfred Knopf, 1967). On Chicago labor reform, "republicanism," and politics, see John Jentz and Richard Schneirov, "Social Republicanism: A Multi-Ethnic History of Labor Reform in Chicago, 1848–1877" (Paper presented to Chicago Area Labor History Group, 1985).

3. On the Knights of Labor and politics, see Leon Fink, *Workingmen's Democracy: The Knights of Labor and American Politics* (Urbana: University of Illinois Press, 1983).

4. For a survey of the economic history of this period, see W. Elliot Brownlee, *Dynamics of Ascent: A History of the American Economy* (New York: Alfred Knopf, 1974).

5. David Wells, *Recent Economic Changes* (New York: Appleton, 1899), 107–8.

6. Oestreicher, *Solidarity and Fragmentation*.

7. Kealey and Palmer, *Dreaming of What Might Be*, and Bryan Palmer, *A Culture in Conflict: Skilled Workers and Industrial Capitalism in Hamilton, Ontario, 1860–1914* (Montreal: McGill-Queen's University Press, 1979).

8. Francis Couvares, *The Remaking of Pittsburgh: Class and Culture in an Industrializing City, 1877–1919* (Albany: State University of New York Press, 1984).

9. On Lynn and Fall River, respectively, see John T. Cumbler, "Labor, Capital, and Community: The Struggle for Power," *Labor History* 15 (Summer 1974): 395–415, and "Transatlantic Working-Class Institutions," *Journal of Historical Geography* 6 (July 1980): 275–90.

10. Cumbler, "Labor, Capital, and Community," 402.

11. Cumbler, "Transatlantic Working-Class Institutions," 288.

12. Bruce Nelson, "Dancing and Picnicking Anarchists? The Movement below the Martyred Leadership," in *Haymarket Scrapbook*, ed. David Roediger and Franklin Rosemont (Chicago: Charles H. Kerr, 1986), 76–79; and Paul Avrich, *The Haymarket Tragedy* (Princeton: Princeton University Press, 1984), 131–49.

13. German-American working-class culture in Chicago is explored in Heinz Ickstadt and Hartmut Keil, "A Forgotten Piece of Working-Class Literature: Gustav Lyser's Satire of the Hewitt Hearing of 1878," *Labor History* 20 (Winter 1979): 127–40; Hartmut Keil and John B. Jentz, eds., *German Workers in Industrial Chicago, 1850–1910* (DeKalb: Northern Illinois University, 1983), and *German Workers in Chicago: A Docu-*

*mentary History of Working-Class Culture from 1850 to World War I* (Urbana: University of Illinois Press, 1988); and Jentz and Schneirov, "Social Republicanism."

14. Information on the Scranton, Kansas, Knights of Labor may be found in Jonathan Ezra Garlock, "A Structural Analysis of the Knights of Labor: A Prolegomenon to the History of the Producing Classes" (Ph.D. diss., University of Rochester, 1974), 229.

15. Jonathan F. Young, "Letter from Kansas," *National Labor Tribune*, 21 March 1881.

16. See, for example, Martin Foran's comment, *Cooper's Journal* 3 (July 1872): 416.

17. A list of the publications surveyed for this study appears in the bibliography. Publications that did not feature original song-poetry included *Age of Labor, Cigar Makers' Official Journal, Furniture Workers' Journal, Garment Worker, Miners' National Record, Salt Workers' Journal, Vulcan Record, Workmen's Advocate.* Of these, only the *Cigar Makers' Official Journal* and the *Furniture Workers' Journal* appeared before 1893 or on a regular basis. The remainder began publishing after 1892 or were published sporadically.

18. On Poet Mulhall, see Korson, *Minstrels of the Mine Patch*, 294–95.

19. Patrick Fennell [Shandy Maguire], *Random Rhymes and Rhapsodies of the Rail* (Cleveland Printing Co., 1907), and *Recitations, Epics, Lyrics, and Poems Humorous and Pathetic* (Oswego, N. Y.: Patrick Fennell, 1886); Michael McGovern, *Labor Lyrics and Other Poems* (Youngstown, Ohio: Vindicator Press, 1899); and George McNeill, *Unfrequented Paths: Songs of Nature, Labor and Men* (Boston: James H. West, 1903).

20. B. M. Lawrence, *National Greenback Labor Songster* (New York: D. M. Bennett, 1878); James and Emily Tallmadge, *Labor Songs Dedicated to the Knights of Labor* (Chicago: J. D. Tallmadge, 1886); and Karl Reuber, *Gedanken über die neue Zeit* (Pittsburgh: Urben and Bruder, 1872), *Hymns of Labor: Remodeled from Old Songs* (Pittsburgh: Barrows and Osbourne, n.d.), and *Poems and Songs* (Pittsburgh: Louis Holz, n.d.).

21. Elizabeth Balch, "Songs for Labor," *Survey* (January 1914): 411.

22. Examination of Terence Powderly's papers yields a handful of song-poems.

23. Song-poems were also included in O. T. Hicks, *The Life of Richard F. Trevellick* (Joliet, Ill.: J. E. Williams, 1896); and John Swinton, *Striking for Life: Labor's Side of the Labor Question* (n.p.: American Manufacturing and Publishing, 1894).

24. See, for example, the nineteenth-century songs in Korson, *Coal Dust on the Fiddle, Minstrels of the Mine Patch*, and *Songs and Ballads*; and Duncan Emrich, "Songs of the Western Miners."

25. Reuber, *Poems and Songs*, 6.

26. For a survey of song-poetry from the nineteenth century, see Philip Foner, *American Labor Songs.*

27. Many song-poems could be included in a number of categories. For a sampling of song-poems that called on workers to support and join the Knights of Labor, and offered praise for the organization, see James Cain, "Answer to Gowen's Letter," *National Labor Tribune*, 29 March 1878; C. Drake, "Knights of Labor Call," *Journal of United Labor* 11 (13 November 1890): 3; J. F., "Verses for the Toiler," *Journal of United Labor* 9 (2 November 1888): 2575; Bertram Wilson Hoffman, "Hymn of the Knights of Labor," *Journal of United Labor* 13 (6 April 1893): 1; A. Member, "The Knights' New Year," *Journal of United Labor* 13 (4 January 1893): 1. On song-poems calling on coopers to join their respective union, see A. S. Farquaharson, "Acrostic," *Cooper's Journal* 3 (July 1872): 406. On molders, see S.D.B., "Union Forever," *Iron Molders' Journal* (September 1884): 3; Michael Conway, "Song of the Molders' Union," *Iron Molders' Journal* (March 1880): 4; Mrs. H.B.H., "Union," *Iron Molders' Journal* (January 1880): 6; and Rees E. Lewis, "March of the Rolling Mill Men," *National Labor Tribune*, 11 April 1878. On miners, see William Clark, "The Miners' Goal," *United Mine Workers Journal* 1 (3 September 1881): 2; Joseph Harris, "The Miners' Dream," *National Labor Tribune*, 11 April 1891; George Parker, "Fully Endorsed," *United Mine Workers Journal* 4 (28 June 1894): 2. On sailors, see Xavier Leder, "Union Song," *Coast Seamen's Journal*, 6 November 1887. On curriers, see P. P. Higgins, "Words of Cheer," *Fincher's Trades Review*, 6 February 1884. On railroad engineers, see Shandy Maguire, "Dedication Lines," In *Recitations*, 275–77. On railway carmen, see Matthew Quinlan, "When We're Fifty Thousand Strong," *Railway Carmen's Journal* (April 1894): 30.

Song-poems that sought to rally members in their struggles included, among others, Anon., "A Union Molder," *Iron Molders' Journal* (10 August 1880): 11; James Adolphus, "Knights of Labor," *Knights of Labor* 28 September 1880; A. E. Call, "Onward," *Journal of United Labor* 8 (12 November 1887): 2521; Dugald Campbell, "Keep a Stiff Upper Lip," *Fincher's Trades Review*, 27 February 1864; W. J. Durham, "Knights of Labor," *Journal of United Labor* 4 (December 1883): 608; T. C. Keleher, "Be Firm, Do Not Waver," *Granite Cutters' Journal* 15 (June 1892): 3; Thomas Naylor, "A Union Song," *Coast Seamen's Journal*, 16 April 1888; R. J. Preston, "Brotherhood," *Journal of United Labor* 3 (June 1882): 237; John Shelton, "Do What's Right," *National Labor Tribune*, 19 March 1881; and A. Sister, "Only the Working Class," *Journal of United Labor* 6 (April 1886): 2054.

Song-poems glorifying and praising unions included Anon., "Order of Railway Conductors," *Railway Conductor's Monthly* 1 (April 1884): 183–84; Hugh Cameron, "With Stamps as Measures," *Journal of United Labor* 8 (13 August 1887): 2471; Ellen Dare, "Knighthood," *Knights of Labor* 1 (5 February 1887): 13; J. F., "Laudatory Lines," *Granite Cutters' Journal* 11 (January 1888): 2; Dyer Lum, "International," *Alarm*, 3 October 1885; T. H. Mathias, "Lines on the Sixth Anniversary of the Coast Seamen's Union," *Coast Seamen's Journal*, 11 March 1891; Shandy Maguire, "Lines," *Railway Carmen's Journal* 2 (March 1884): 162–65; George

Miller, "Knights of Labor," in letter to Terence Powderly, 7 May 1887, *Powderly Papers*, Reel 16; E. Roots, "The A.F.L.," *Labor Leader*, 27 September 1890; and Van Ginkle, "Division 38," *Railway Carmen's Journal* 1 (January 1884): 37–38.

28. Anon., "The Charleston Navy Yard Strike," *Fincher's Trades Review*, 21 November 1863. See also Henry Gordon, "Mighty Men Are Watching," *Labor Leaf*, 2 March 1886; and Will Minnick, "Would We Strike?" *Journal of United Labor* 7 (10 May 1886): 2066.

29. Anon., "Dear Brother Coopers," *Cooper's Journal* 3 (October 1872): 614; Anon., "The Scab and the Ghost," *Cooper's Journal* 2 (18 September 1881): 356–57; C. Harry Ander, "On the Highway," *Critic*, 1 September 1888; John Cairns, "A Song for the Times," *National Labor Tribune*, 5 April 1879; Mr. Hardup, "A New Scab Shop," *Labor Leader*, 6 February 1892; Sam Leffingwell, "The Scab," *Our Organette*, 6 January 1883; Michael McGovern, "The Fall of Abel Cain," *National Labor Tribune*, 13 December 1890; William Mullen, "The Non-Union Chorus," *United Mine Workers Journal* 1 (25 June 1891): 4; J. J. Sullivan, "The Blackleg's Refrain," *United Mine Workers Journal* 4 (2 August 1894): 8; and A.D.T., "The Molders," *Iron Molders' Journal* (March 1877): 276. For an exception to the rule, see Albert Shrewsberry, "A Plea for the Scab," *Knights of Labor*, 4 May 1887.

30. On Debs, see Frank Foster, "To E.V.D.," *Labor Leader*, 5 January 1895. On Sylvis, see John James, "The Fallen Chieftain," in Life, *Speeches, Labors, and Essays of William Sylvis*, ed. James Sylvis (New York: Clayton, Remsen, and Haffelfinger, 1872). See also 'A Colored Worker,' "A Fruitless Mission," *National Labor Tribune*, 25 March 1882.

31. Song-poems praising workers' contributions to craft and country number in the hundreds. See, among others, Anon., "April First," *Locomotive Fireman's Monthly Magazine* 12 (June 1888): 434; Anon., "The Printer's Dream," *Labor Enquirer* (Denver), 2 August 1884; Enoch Bowley, "The Mines," *National Labor Tribune*, 14 June 1884; E.A.L., "The Workingman's the Noblest of His Kind," *Cooper's Journal* 4 (February 1873): 93; Ed Lambert, "The Puddler," *National Labor Tribune*, 22 April 1882; C. B. Lincoln, "The Workingmen," *Boston Daily Evening Voice*, 22 March 1865; F. Livingston, "The Dignity of Labor," *Journal of United Labor* 1 (November 1880): 70; Thomas O'Rourke, "The Knight of the Scoop," *Locomotive Fireman's Monthly Magazine* 3 (April 1879): 97; and Robertson, "Labor Day Reflections," *United Mine Workers Journal* 5 (September 1895): 8. On railroad workers and self-praise in song-poetry, see Norm Cohen, *The Long Steel Rail: The Railroad in American Folksong* (Urbana: University of Illinois Press, 1981).

32. Woodbury Fernald, "The Working Girls," *Fincher's Trades Review*, 19 December 1863. Fernald's much reprinted song-poem was exceptional in linking women's economic exploitation with the need for unionization. See also railroad worker Joseph Maize, "Degraded and Fallen," *National Labor Tribune*, 25 February 1888.

33. C. A. Chatfield, "Only a Miner's Child," *United Mine Workers Journal* 5 (October 1895): 3; Charles Cheesewright, "The Factory Girl," *Labor Enquirer* (Denver), 16 July 1887; Robert Hume, "Labor Lyrics—No. 8 Modern Heroism," *Boston Daily Evening Voice*, 5 March 1867; Frederick Lennon, "The Little Miner Boy," *United Mine Workers Journal* 5 (October 1895): 2; George Taylor, "A Christmas Story," *National Labor Tribune*, 21 December 1878; and Jonathan Wickers, "The Miners Child," *National Labor Tribune*, 3 July 1875.

34. On degradation and working conditions, see Clara Dixon Davidson, "Who Will Pay the Rent," *Labor Enquirer* (Chicago), 3 March 1888; B. J. Hall, "The Workman's Song," *Granite Cutters' Journal* 7 (November 1883): 6; Robert Hume, "Labor Lyrics, No. 3," *Boston Daily Evening Voice*, 19 December 1866; D. H. Ingham, "The Five O'Clock Whistle," *Journal of United Labor* 9 (6 June 1889): 2851; Victoria Lyons, "Routine and Duty," *Advance*, 2 March 1889, and "The White Slaves of Today," *Advance*, 6 April 1889; J. G. Malcom, "The Poor Man's Soliloquy," *Journal of United Labor* 3 (January 1883): 394; Si Slocum, "Song of King Capital," *John Swinton's Paper*, 24 February 1884; and Henry White, "Year after Year," *Labor Leader* 30 March 1889.

On wages and unemployment, see Anon., "Keep Off the Grass," *Journal of United Labor* 13 (May 1891): 1; Frank Foster, "The Unemployed," *Labor Leader*, 15 January 1894; Mrs. J. Jasper, "To Workingmen," *United Mine Workers Journal* 1 (May 1891): 8; John McIntosh, "Out of a Job," *Iron Molders' Journal* (February 1877): 237; Dyer Lum, "Out of Work," *Alarm*, 20 February 1886; and Henry White, "A Procession," *Labor Leader*, 30 December 1893.

On company stores and age discrimination, see Isaac Henna, "The Company Store," *United Mine Workers Journal* 5 (May 1894): 8; and Henry White, "Counted Out," *Labor Leader*, 3 February 1894.

On the mining hardships, see A Digger, "The Miner's Doom," *National Labor Tribune*, 5 June 1881; Mrs. Henry B. Jones, "Coal Miner's Song," *Locomotive Fireman's Monthly Magazine* 8 (December 1884): 7; Mrs. Alice Peacock, "The Worth of a Miner's Life," *United Mine Workers Journal* 4 (November 1894): 8; and Wishful, "The Miners' Bewail," ibid. 1 (October 1891): 2.

35. John Thompson, "The Robber Anarchist," *Knights of Labor*, 23 October 1886.

36. James Laviers, "Vanderbilt's Dream," *National Labor Tribune*, 3 May 1884; J. H. E. Partington, "Honest Andrew's Prayer," ibid., 29 October 1892; Alfred Morton, "To the Employees of Andrew Carnegie," ibid. 16 February 1893; and William Mitchell, "The Coal Operator," ibid., 7 February 1891.

37. This sort of criticism pervades song-poetry. See, for example, Clara D. Dixon Davidson, "Suffering Reflexive," *Truth*, September 1884; Laurene Gardner, "Trifles," *United Mine Workers Journal* 1 (December 1891): 3; Frederick Lennon, "The Boozing Aristocracy," ibid. 5 (September 1895):

9; James Jeffrey Roach, "For the People," in Swinton, *Striking for Life*, 428–29; George Sloan, "A Mystery," *Labor Enquirer* (Chicago), 21 April 1888; and Suture "A Merry Christmas," *Alarm*, 3 January 1884.

38. Chapters 5 and 6 below explore anticlericalism.

39. For song-poems urging workers to vote in order to influence politics, see John Brophy, "Mike Mechanic's Relatives," *John Swinton's Paper*, 21 September 1884; W. H. Hanford, "To My Laboring Brothers," *Journal of United Labor* 3 (March 1883): 377; and J. M. Lenahan, "Turn the Rascals Out," n.d., *Powderly Papers*, Reel 23.

On political parties, see Anon., "General Cary," *Workingman's Advocate*, 12 September 1868; T.H., "Song," *John Swinton's Paper*, 14 September 1884; H. Mount James, "We'll Battle for the Noble Cause of Labor," 24 October 1886, *Powderly Papers*, Reel 19; B. M. Lawrence, "Poll Your Vote," in *Greenback Songster*, 4; Walter Nelbeb, "Capitalism," *Cleveland Citizen*, 24 September 1892; Samuel Stokes, "Take Your Choice," *Knights of Labor*, 20 November 1886; and John Thompson, "Hail Milwaukee," *Knights of Labor*, 4 December 1886.

On financial matters, see Anon., "Home of Our Own," n.d., *Powderly Papers*, Reel 26; Anon., "Remodeled Rhymes," *Workingman's Advocate*, 6 February 1869; Anon., "Resumption Day," *National Labor Tribune*, 3 November 1877; Anon., "Ten Per Cent," *Workingman's Advocate*, 24 April 1869; J. H. Fairchild, "Silver and Gold," *St. Louis Labor*, 24 May 1895; C. M. Maxon, "When John Gets the Bond," *Journal of United Labor* 13 (1 March 1894): 1; Lee Redgod, "The Muse of Chicago," *Workingman's Advocate*, 19 June 1869; Thomas Shell, "The Greenbacker's Declaration," *National Labor Tribune*, 23 October 1880.

On immigration, see Anon., "Thirty Cents a Day," *Workingman's Advocate*, 19 November 1872; Frank Foster, "Restricted Immigration," *Labor Leader*, 20 February 1893; R. W. Hume, "Chow-Chow and His Friends," *Workingman's Advocate*, 1 January 1870; R. W. Hume, "John Chinaman," *Workingman's Advocate*, 12 April 1869; and Waldron Shear, "Boycotting," *Truth*, 9 August 1882.

40. The Blanchard-Jones song-poem first appeared as a poem by Blanchard in the *Boston Daily Evening Voice*, 7 August 1866, and in the *Workingman's Advocate*, 18 August 1866. Later, Jesse Jones added the music. See *Labor Standard* (Paterson), 21 July 1878. On this and other eight-hour song-poems, see Foner, *American Labor Songs*, 217–34.

Other eight-hour song-poems include Anon., "Eight-Hour Song," *Workingman's Advocates*, 7 March 1868; Anon., "On Viewing the Eight-Hour Question," *Journal of United Labor* 4 (April 1884): 676; William B. Creech, "Eight Hours a Day," *Iron Molders' Journal* (November 1880): 10; J. Harden, "Eight Hours Is the Measure by Law," *Knights of Labor*, 27 November 1886; Charles Haynes, "Eight Hours," *Fincher's Trades Review*, 18 November 1865; Thomas Kesson, "All Honor to the Chicago Boys," *Granite Cutters' Journal* 13 (September 1890): 4; and John McIntosh, "Eight Hours a Day," *National Labor Tribune*, 15 December 1877.

41. On "Storm the Fort" (or "Hold the Fort"), see Foner, *American Labor Songs*, 154. See also "Storm the Fort," *John Swinton's Paper*, 7 June 1885; Anon., "Storm the Fort," *Labor Leaf*, 30 September 1885; and Tallmadge, *Labor Songs*, 15.

42. This particular chorus is from the Tallmadge version of the song. See Tallmadge, *Labor Songs*, 15.

43. "Labor Brotherhood Festival," *Der Deutsche Arbeiter*, 4 June 1870, reprinted in Keil and Jentz, *German Workers in Chicago*, 208–9.

44. Michael Schwab, "In Memory of Karl Marx," *Fackel*, 18 March 1883, reprinted in Keil and Jentz, *German Workers in Chicago*, 269–70.

45. "Final Salutations: The Five Victims of Their Humanity Are Accompanied on Their Final Journey," *Chicago Arbieter-Zeitung*, 14 November 1885, reprinted in Keil and Jentz, *German Workers in Chicago*, 190–95.

46. For additional information on German song-poetry and cultural activities, see Keil and Jentz, *German Workers in Chicago*, particularly "Culture of the Labor Movement," 221–99, and "Literature," 300–346.

47. Examples of letters to the editor that contain song-poems include O. M. Robbins, "To the Senate Committee on State Prisons," *Granite Cutters' Journal* 14 (April 1891): 6; John James, "From Braidwood," *Workingman's Advocate*, 18 January 1868; G. Parker, "Fully Endorsed," *United Mine Workers Journal* 4 (June 1894): 2; and Edward T. Morgan, "From Pennsylvania," *Workingman's Advocate*, 18 June 1870.

48. For examples of Shandy Maguire's individualized song-poems, see *Random Rhymes and Recitations*, as well as *Locomotive Engineer's Monthly Journal*, 1873–92, and *Locomotive Fireman's Monthly Magazine*, 1876–95.

49. Mrs. Henry B. Jones, "Old Post Lodge," *Locomotive Fireman's Monthly Magazine* 8 (August 1884): 499.

50. Anon., "Ivory Lodge," *National Labor Tribune*, 21 June 1884.

51. "A M.W.'s Impromptu Talk," *Journal of United Labor* 4 (March 1884): 661.

52. Isaac Taylor, "Who Is My Foe, Is It Capital? No!" *Iron Molders' Journal* (December 1870): 16.

53. Michael McGovern, "Again We Meet," *National Labor Tribune*, 13 June 1892.

54. On Pittsburgh labor song-poetry, see Jacob Evanson, "Folk Songs of an Industrial City," in *Pennsylvania Songs and Legends*, ed. George Korson (Baltimore: Johns Hopkins University Press, 1949), 423–66.

55. German workers' fondness for choirs and group singing is revealed in the documents in Keil and Jentz, *German Workers in Chicago*. In addition, see the references to choirs and musical gatherings reported in the *Socialist Alliance* (Chicago), 1896–99.

56. Powderly, quoted in Balch, "Songs of Labor," 41. Evidence refutes his claim that "no one member" sang alone.

57. John Cotter, "Initiation Ode," in letter to Terence Powderly, 26 February 1886, *Powderly Papers*, Reel 13.

58. M. A. Dalbey, "Opening Ode" and "Closing Ode," *Journal of United Labor* 1 (15 March 1880): 102.

59. J. J. Martin, "Opening Song," *Labor Enquirer* (Denver), 29 January 1887; and Isaac Kinley, "Goodnight," *Journal of United Labor* 5 (25 February 1885): 918.

60. Tom O'Reilly, "A Labor Song," *Socialist*, 6 May 1876, and "The Song of the Proletaire," *Journal of United Labor* 8 (October 1887): 1. See also Foner, *American Labor Songs*, 159–61.

61. Edward Reese, "Ivory Lodge," *National Labor Tribune*, 12 June 1884. Shoe lasters in Lynn, Massachusetts, also reported the use of a piano for singing at union gatherings. See John T. Cumbler, "Labor, Capital, and Community," 402.

# 2

# Labor Song-Poems and Song-Poets

AMERICAN workers could count many victories and defeats during the Gilded Age. Everyone agreed, however, that 1885 had been a banner year. Twenty years of resentment found an outlet as workers went on the offensive. Strikes erupted throughout the country and workers joined organized labor by the hundreds of thousands. Thomas Selby joined this Great Upheaval and voiced his support in a song-poem. Waxing enthusiastic, Selby called on other workers to support the cause, particularly that of the organization spearheading the movement—the Knights of Labor:

> Knights of Labor stand for action,
> Never let an outside faction
> In our ranks to cause distraction.
> Listen to the call.
>
> Shoulder stand to shoulder
> Then we'll march the bolder,
> The air is free, and we must be
> No longer bond, but freemen.
>
> 'Tis our noblest aspiration,
> To improve our generation,
> Raise the standard of our nation
> And defend our cause.
>
> Men from every land and nation
> Join our ranks and take your station.
> If you're toilers of creation
> Join our noble band.

> We are fighting, not for glory,
> Our land is famed in story,
> The land is free by God's decree
> That we might all have plenty.

> Equal rights for self and neighbor
> Honest pay for honest labor,
> 'Knights of Labor' wants no favor,
> Only truth and right.[1]

Selby's song-poem hardly differed from thousands of others—perhaps more spirited than some but similar in form, style, and language to many. Unfortunately, Selby's song-poem shared another all-too-typical characteristic of song-poetry—a dearth of information on its author. Song-poems were commonly published anonymously, under a pseudonym, or with the author's name only. Even when the name and union local appear, as in the case of Selby, additional information on the author can be impossible to trace. And yet if song-poems are to be examined for insight into more than the song-poems themselves, information on the authors is a necessity. In particular, we need to know the occupational and class background of song-poets. Otherwise we might surmise that song-poets came predominantly from the middle class or labor officialdom and that the character of movement culture derived wholly from such individuals as well. Without information on a sample of song-poets, we might deny Selig Perlman's charge that the individual workman leaves no historical records, but the labor movement does without having the evidence to disprove him.

Fortunately, despite the paucity of evidence, enough exists to compile a sample of song-poets. In some cases song-poets carried enough weight in the labor movement to be included in various accounts of the movement. A few occupied positions in the upper echelons of labor officialdom. More often, names and residences listed with song-poems lead to additional information in union directories, local histories, city directories, newspapers, obituaries, and census data. Such a sample has an obvious bias toward those most likely to be included in such reports—prominent labor leaders and officials, elites, skilled workers, and males. Lower-level leaders and officials, nonelites, semiskilled workers, and women will be underrepresented, and the working-class character of the sample will be understated. Nevertheless, information gathered on ninety-three song-poets yields important findings.

Even after accounting for biases, the sample still evokes a strong working-class presence. The majority of writers earned their live-

lihoods in working-class occupations. Also, if labor leaders from
working-class backgrounds are included, then the sample even
more convincingly demonstrates song-poetry's ties to the working class. By contrast, it also documents a sizable contingent of
"producer" or "worker" song-poets who had professional-type occupations. Itinerant salesmen, small farmers, grocers, musicians,
saloon keepers, small job printers, clerks, and a host of others fell
into this marginal group. Although less prone to the vagaries of
direct economic exploitation in the workplace, this group justifiably felt squeezed by advancing industrial capitalism, and some
openly sided with the labor movement. Until the twentieth century, many such Americans described themselves as "workers"
and "producers," and their consciousness and culture intertwined
with that of people commonly associated with the term "working
class" today.[2] Their active role in song-poetry serves as a reminder
that the labor movement and movement culture—particularly
the mainstream strand represented by the Knights of Labor—still
counted significant support from an old element of the producing
classes. Moreover, even though the vast majority of song-poets
held working-class occupations, they typically came from the more
skilled ranks in their class.

Not surprisingly, few of the nation's elite can be found among
labor song-poets. Indeed, only three song-poets had any claim to
the title "upper class" and two of the three cases stretch the definition. Only the Ohio native Donn Piatt died assured that his obituary would be included in the national press in 1891. Born in
1819, Piatt began his career as a lawyer and judge before gaining
appointment to the American diplomatic corps in France in 1853.
After a tour of duty in the Civil War, Piatt embarked on a newspaper career and founded the publication *Capital* in 1871. That paper
gained a national reputation in the 1870s for repeated attacks on
government corruption. After Piatt achieved financial and political security, he spent much of his time writing history, fiction,
biography, and poetry, including a few song-poems of temperate
concern for the downtrodden. Piatt's mugwump convictions nevertheless set definite limits on his sympathy for workers.[3]

T. R. Magill's upper-class status paled in comparison to Piatt's.
Magill, the son of Irish immigrants, was born in South Carolina in
1826. Prior to his enlistment in the Confederate Army, Magill
served as a local postmaster. He established a wholesale-retail gro-
cery business in Charlotte after the war and until his death in
1903 took an active role in regional politics. Like his father and

brother, Magill found poetry a serious avocation. He even wrote one song-poem praising workers' contribution to society.[4]

Outspoken support for workers and the labor movement came from only one elite song-poet, Hugh Cameron. A more unlikely candidate for a career in reform and the labor movement would be unimaginable. Born to a prominent Pennsylvania family in 1826, Cameron spent his youth learning the requisite skills for life among the eastern political and social establishment. He committed class treason, however, by moving to Kansas in 1854 and enlisting in the Emigrant Aid Company's antislavery cause. He fought for that same cause during the Civil War as a lieutenant colonel in the Union cavalry. Thereafter he championed alternate lifestyles, social reform, and organized labor. His personal eccentricity escaped few residents: Cameron refused to eat meat, wear shoes, cut his hair, date women, or sleep long hours. His passionate devotion to politics and labor, manifest in his work for the Grange, Farmers' Alliance, Populist party, and Knights of Labor, earned him respect among state and national reformers. In reward he held several positions in the labor and reform movement: he served on the executive committee of the state's central labor body in 1879, he represented Kansas at the Knights of Labor general assembly in 1886 and sat on its national cooperative board, and he acted as a Knights organizer in the late 1880s. He also found time to write strongly worded prolabor song-poems. Clearly, Cameron was an anomaly, more in the tradition of those men and women attached to utopian reform after the Second Great Awakening. Among his upper-class peers, his commitment to workers marked him as an oddity.[5]

Labor leaders, by contrast, regularly voiced strong class sentiments in song-poems. Eleven song-poets in the sample held positions in national labor organizations or had national reputations as activists. All but two also grew up in working-class families or spent much of their lives in working-class occupations. Three are names recalled easily—Terence Powderly, Eugene Debs, and Albert Parsons.[6] Others never achieved the same degree of recognition but were known in labor circles. George McNeill, for example, started his career in the harsh confines of the woolen mill but eventually became one of the movement's most respected journalists. He also became a prolific song-poet.[7] He would be joined by individuals of similar standing—Richard Trevellick, the ship carpenter who gave his life to every labor cause from the National Labor Union to populism; Frank Foster, the printer-journalist-editor who once sat on the executive board of the Knights of Labor but also aided in the formation and growth of the American Federation of Labor; August Spies, the socialist upholsterer turned anarchist who was executed with Albert Parsons; and Burnette Haskell, the well-born California lawyer who vigorously but erratically worked as an activist-journalist for socialism, anarchism, and the Knights of Labor before Powderly expelled him in 1887.[8]

Equally devoted but among the least well-known of labor official song-poets was Samuel Leffingwell. Leffingwell helped establish the typographers' union as well as serving both the Knights of Labor and the AFL in critical roles. He acted as president at the second convention of the Federation of Organized Trade and Labor Unions, became president of the Indianapolis Trades Assembly in the early 1880s, and appeared as an integral figure at the founding convention of the AFL in 1885. Despite such efforts, Leffingwell spent most of his life on the brink of financial disaster. His obituary read: "Mr. Leffingwell had a varied career." He was born in 1830 in Chillicothe, Ohio. He learned the printer's trade while very young but did not become an established printer until after his fiftieth birthday. Following stints in the Mexican War and the Civil War, and various jobs, Leffingwell moved to Indianapolis to work as a printer for *The People* in 1876. He was employed as a carpenter and boxmaker from 1877 to 1882, however, and only gained a full-time position in his trade when he became editor-proprietor of *Our Organette*, the official printers' union publication. Later he served as reporter, editor, and printer for the Indianapolis *Sentinel*. On one occasion he also took time to express his views on "The Scab" in song-poem form.[9]

Leffingwell's career pattern distinguished him only slightly from numerous song-poets. Alternating between wage labor, self-employment, and white-collar tasks, he followed a path reminiscent of other writers who operated marginal businesses, had low-status professional positions, and did time at wage labor as their fortunes dictated. The petit bourgeois and even so-called professionals came and went in an age of economic concentration, anarchic competition, and periodic economic collapse. Leffingwell and people like him never entirely escaped the shadow of the working class and remained dependent upon the resources and patronage of the working-class community for survival.

Appropriately, song-poets sprang from their ranks in significant proportions—thirty of ninety-three song-poets. Almost none ever achieved any degree of financial security or stability. Many changed businesses, locations, or professions at an alarming rate but rarely were upwardly mobile. Some proved difficult to locate because they never stayed in any city for too long. A few employed suspicious, if not contrived, titles for their professions, as "M.D." and "manufacturer of food cure" testify. As a whole they appear somewhat out of place in the late nineteenth century, a group whose backgrounds, livelihoods, and thoughts mark them a dying and wayward breed of "old" Americans. They also offer testimony to pervasive hostility to industrial capitalism among people of similar ilk. What's more, their appearance reveals the ability of the labor movement to generate widespread support and to maintain a trans-class foothold. Until economic changes created a "new middle class" with clear allegiance to the corporation and made such values and language irrelevant, the labor movement captured a wide audience.

Thirteen of this group of thirty, for example, operated small businesses. Among them, Patrick Maloney, a brickyard owner from Saint Tammany Parish, Louisiana, wrote to Terence Powderly in 1886 to ask him to consider a song-poem for publication. Maloney's fortunes were then at their apex. Prior to the Civil War, however, he had been simply one of millions of Irish émigrés to the United States. Young and single, he made Boston his temporary home and secured employment as a laborer. Inexplicably, he later enlisted as a private in the Louisiana Infantry of the Confederate Army, fought at Gettysburg, and spent a year and a half as a prisoner of war. Still in his twenties, Maloney settled in Saint Tammany Parish, where he lived until his death in 1886. Perhaps nothing more than southern hostility to Yankee capitalism explains his prolabor stance. More likely, he remembered his youthful encounters with exploitation in Boston, felt kinship with those many Irish-Catholics sympathetic to the labor movement, and perhaps had ties with the Irish Land League, whose members, including Powderly, often belonged to the Knights. Additional incentive may have come from the tribulations of small business in an age of industrial capitalism. Were it any of these, he would not have been alone.[10]

He was joined by James and Emily Tallmadge, who resided in Chicago for more than twenty-five years and operated a small printshop for much of the period. The city's labor movement did not escape their notice. They cast their lot with the Knights of Labor and used their shop and skills to advance its cause. In 1886 they published a sizable songbook of labor song-poems.[11]

Shopkeepers of similar background throughout the nation also contributed. Dyer Lum—Albert Parsons's mystical replacement as editor of *Alarm* in 1887 and an important anarchist in his day— spent most of his adult life operating a small bookbindery when not railing against the evils of capitalism in essays and song-poetry.[12] J. G. Schonfarber, an occasional song-poet, owned a printing shop in Baltimore, maintained ties with both the Knights of Labor and local socialists, and served as editor for the *Critic*, a local labor paper, from 1888 to 1893.[13] Years earlier, John McIntosh also edited a labor paper. McIntosh left his native Rochester, New York, his tobacco shop, and his numerous antilabor enemies behind, and took over the editorial reins of Cincinnati's *National Socialist*. Rochester's elites admittedly breathed a sigh of relief, but Cincinnati's found him an irritation for years to come. He proved a deft song-poet and an adroit social critic.[14] McIntosh's outlook found expression in his paper's motto: "The Earth is the Lord's and the fulness thereof."[15]

Others less radical, less skilled, or less prolific at song-poetry also sided with labor. San Francisco laundry operator, part-time journalist, and real estate agent Waldron Shear wrote a song-poem supporting the boycott tactic and belonged to the Knights of Labor.[16] Mrs. S. E. Lenfest, who owned a cigar and confectionary shop in Aspen, Colorado, expressed song-poem support for labor while enrolled in a miner's assembly of the Knights.[17] Finally, Patrick Morrow, a grocer and tavern operator in a neighborhood adjoining Pittsburgh's iron and steel mills, contributed a song-poem celebrating the triumph of the city's striking boilermakers in 1879.[18]

In addition to those thirteen shopkeeper song-poets, seven individuals with white-collar occupations also pursued a prolabor path. None served more zealously than Eau Claire, Wisconsin, insurance agent C. L. James. He unswervingly devoted himself to advancing the working class in his community, region, and nation. James joined the Knights in his hometown and acted as their spokesperson while serving as alderman from 1887 to 1888. An avowed anarchist, he regularly contributed to the *Alarm* and kept close ties with Chicago anarchists. His essays on economics established him as an important figure in anarchism.[19]

Others showed less zeal but wrote a song-poem or two for labor. J. W. Howe, a Chicago postal clerk and carrier; William Stockman, an agent, medicine manufacturer, and "manufacturer of Food Cure" from Detroit; and A. H. Nunemacher, an agent for a Paducah, Kentucky, express agency each wrote a labor song-poem.[20] An assorted lot of similarly employed clerks, agents, and salesmen did the same.[21]

The remaining nine song-poets in the group of thirty distinguished themselves from the others by their education and training. That did not keep them from supporting labor: six of them had direct links to labor organizations. Two earned their livings as musicians—Charles Haynes of Chicago and Henry Butler of St. Louis. Haynes, a working-class musician, rented a small downtown studio and spent more than twenty years as a blind, obscure musician-teacher in the city. The only surviving reminder of his passion for music and labor is a piece he wrote for early eight-hour efforts in the 1860s. Haynes gauged his audience accurately, borrowing his melody from the Civil War ballad "Tramp, Tramp, Tramp." His text and tune combination proved successful; when *Fincher's Trades Review* published it in 1865, the editor remarked that of all the eight-hour compositions he believed Haynes's "without exception, the best yet received, and will soon become popular."[22]

In contrast, Butler had credentials that equaled those of any nineteenth-century American musician. Born in Massachusetts in 1831, he served his apprenticeship under Lowell Mason and George Root, two of the century's most famous composers and hymnologists. That background helped Butler locate a position as supervisor of music in St. Louis and St. Joseph schools from the 1860s through the 1880s. He established himself as a major composer in the state and his works became standards there. Perhaps influenced by the struggles of workers, the wide following of the Knights in the state, or the evangelical temper of his background in hymnology, Butler moved into open support of the Knights of Labor. In the height of the Great Upheaval, he wrote to Powderly expressing an interest in the eight-hour movement and in placing his musical talent at the disposal of the organization. Powderly apparently never wrote back.[23]

Self-proclaimed M.D., B. M. Lawrence wrote his song-poems prior to the ascendance of the Knights of Labor. Lawrence joined Butler, Hugh Cameron, and C. L. James as one of those odd characters attached to the labor movement. Scant information about Lawrence's life survives, but he seems to have resembled others who embraced a variety of antebellum reforms—homeopathology, women's rights, temperance, abolition—and eventually supported the labor movement. With working-class comrades who had fought for labor prior to the war, they provided a critical link between antebellum reform and the Gilded Age labor movement. Lawrence first appeared in 1860–61 as an itinerant lecturer-doctor of spiritualism and natural health. Later he surfaced at labor gatherings offering his expertise and song-poems. For more than two decades he traversed the country, campaigning for labor, female suffrage, greenbacks, and temperance. He took added measure by compiling the *National Greenback Labor Songster* in 1878.[24]

Clerics like T. L. Drury of Rutland, Vermont, or Woodbury Fernald of Boston also perceived the labor struggle as one for all humanity and one closely akin to the struggle for a world based on the moral precepts of the New Testament.[25] Nothing less than that motivated the Reverend Jesse Jones. A Methodist minister, labor journalist, and union member, Jones spread the gospel of labor solidarity, Christian socialism, and the social gospel long before most ministers bothered to notice the plight of the working class. Although he wrote other song-poems as well, his song-poem "Eight Hours" became the official song of the eight-hour movement.[26]

Jones and similar individuals may have contributed their energy and song-poems to the movement.[27] However, workers comprised the majority of song-poets. Of ninety-three in the sample, forty-nine (or 53 percent) labored in working-class occupations. That did not mean that most song-poets came from the lower levels of the job hierarchy. In an era when capitalism still needed vast quantities of skilled workers, most song-poets worked in skilled trades. Song-poet Edward Lambert, for example, was one of only three song-poets listed in an unskilled occupation. He appeared in the Pittsburgh city directory in the 1880s as a laborer. However, Lambert's song-poem makes numerous references to the intricacies of puddling—a highly skilled occupation—suggesting detailed personal knowledge of the craft. The person collecting the data likely knew nothing of the trade.[28]

On the other hand, Mary Agnes Sheridan, a carpet mill operative in New York City and a member of a Knights of Labor assembly in that occupation, probably does qualify as unskilled, given the state of her trade.[29] Xavier Leder might also, since he spent most of his life as a seaman shipping out of California ports. Only much later did he earn the position of editor of the seamen's union publication and allow himself to write song-poetry.[30]

The examples of Lambert, Sheridan, and Leder ought to caution us against generalization about the ability of workers to create culture. Despite the most difficult circumstances, workers found the time and learned the skills to write song-poems. In fact, song-poetry sometimes flourished in occupations that were physically taxing and dangerous. Of the remaining forty-six song-poets, for example, the largest single group—eleven—represented coal mining. Those high numbers indicate the vitality of song-poem traditions in this craft and the legacy of conflict and solidarity among coal miners. Seven worked in the Pennsylvania coal fields where George Korson later collected labor song and lore. From Coal Bluff came the union message of Enoch Bowley and John Barnett in the 1880s and from Roscoe came a similar message from Irish immigrant John Cairns in 1893.[31] At about the same time, pro-union sentiments also emerged in the work of East Leinsenring miner William Mullen, George Parker of Nowerytown, and Samuel Simon of New Castle.[32] Much earlier, in 1870, a Pennsylvania miner also provided one of those rare song-poems that entered oral tradition. Seventy years after Thomas Morgan wrote "The Sliding Scale" during a strike of the Workingman's Benevolent Association against Frank Gowen's company, a resident of the famous Schuylkill County still recalled the lyrics. When the work first appeared in the Chicago *Workingman's Advocate*, an added note read: "Composed in the Mines. Lost Creek District #7 W.B.A. of Schuylkill County." As George Korson discovered, miners sometimes took the occasion of work breaks to perform and compose music, even in the mines themselves.[33]

Miners outside Pennsylvania also wrote song-poems. Song-poems and song-poets surfaced in tipple towns like Oskaloosa, Iowa, home of numerous Knights of Labor assemblies, and Glouster and Corning in Ohio's Hocking Valley.[34] Illinois produced one of the most interesting coal miner song-poets. John James from Braidwood became a key figure in the Illinois labor movement. From his arrival in the United States in 1865 until his peculiar exit from labor affairs in 1878, James fiercely defended miners' interests. Indeed, his contribution began long before he settled in this country. Born to a Scottish mining family in 1839, James began mining at age nine. At fourteen he met British miners' leader Alexander MacDonald, helped establish a miners' benevolent association, and lost his job for championing a mine inspection bill. He mined in numerous communities for the next twelve years and each time lost his job for his labor activism. At about the same time as the American Civil War, his reputation made finding employment difficult, so he and his wife sailed for America.

James quickly made enemies among this nation's mine operators by quitting his first job after he discovered he had been duped into being a scab. A brief bout with farm labor and membership in the American Miners' Association led James to Braidwood and increased activism. In 1867 he met Andrew Cameron of the *Workingman's Advocate*, became one of its correspondents and song-poets, formed a local in the A.M.A., and directed their unsuccessful strike in 1868. Blacklisted and evicted, he kept up the fight. He founded miners' temperance groups and a state-wide benevolent and protective association, and secured passage of mine safety legislation. His horizons expanded to the national level when in 1873 he aided John Siney in the formation of the Miners' National Association; he continued to support Siney until 1876. He withdrew from labor activism around 1878 and found employment as clerk and manager in various mining operations until his death in 1902.[35]

Few occupations had traditions of muse and bard akin to those of coal miners, but among skilled workers as a whole, song-poem writing thrived. In our sample, thirty-five skilled workers—representing nineteen different occupations—also wrote song-poems. A miscellaneous group of twelve writers labored in twelve different occupations, six of which would seldom be associated with organized labor in this period. James Norris worked as the driver, helper, and coachman for a Cleveland doctor at the time he beckoned "freedom's day" in song-poetry.[36] T. H. Norton, secretary for Local 3423 of the Knights of Labor in Bolivar, New York, served as a rig builder.[37] And Boston's George Davenport regarded himself as a gilder.[38] Elsewhere, a Wheeling, West Virginia, nailer, a Chicago locksmith and Knight, and Mrs. S. E. Olmstead, the wife of a Marlboro, Massachusetts, tinsmith, wrote song-poems in the decade from 1877 to 1887.[39] Those six other occupations, counting one song-poet each, reflected organized labor's recognized strength in certain trades. Included were a shoemaker, a machine woodworker, a baker, a carpenter, a painter, a metal worker, and a piano-furniture finisher from, respectively, Roxbury, Massachusetts; Toledo, Ohio; New York City; San Francisco; Keene, New Hampshire; South Bend, Indiana; and Pittsburgh, Pennsylvania.[40]

Occupations producing any number of song-poets also mirrored those exhibiting a strong organizational presence. As early as 1866 machinist George Eddy of Bloomington, Illinois, saw his song-poem published in the *Workingman's Advocate*.[41] In the thirty years that followed, four other machinists could do the same. One of them, M. A. Dalbey of Ottumwa, Iowa, a machinist-organizer for the Knights of Labor, wrote the "Opening Ode" and "Closing Ode" which locals throughout the order adopted for regular use.[42] Dalbey's work, however, never equaled the quality of seasoned union veteran and Chicago stonecutter John Thompson. Thompson's adept mixture of the language of the American Revolution, evangelical Protestantism, and class anguish resembled, but vastly surpassed, that of almost any writer, including two other "cutters." Thompson's zeal in word and action won the respect of fellow cutters, who elected him delegate to the granite cutters' congress in 1881.[43]

Thompson's ardor complemented that of union printers. Six printers working their craft in Galveston, Texas; Saginaw, Michigan; San Francisco; and Indianapolis authored song-poems in the 1880s and 1890s. Only Saginaw's John Cotter, however, wrote the "Initiation Ode" that secured him a regular spot on the agenda of many Knights of Labor meetings. No doubt Cotter and Saginaw's Knights put the song-poem to practical use in their arduous battles against lumber barons for shorter hours.[44]

A more conservative spirit typified the mood of the railroad trades between 1865 and 1895. Skilled railroad workers shared a legacy of song-poetry surpassing almost every other occupation, with the possible exception of coal miners and molders and puddlers. Rarely, however, did that tradition manifest itself in labor song-poems. Instead, railroading song-poets composed works that spoke to those baptized in the work culture of the fraternity.[45] Nonetheless, railroad workers sometimes did compose song-poetry pertaining to the grievances of workers. Irish immigrant, railway carman, union member, and Ottumwa, Iowa, resident Matthew Quinlan, for example, wrote "When We're Fifty Thousand Strong," advocating solidarity across occupational boundaries on the rails.[46]

The railroad trades also produced one of the most widely known song-poets, Patrick Fennell. Better known as Shandy Maguire, a name taken from an Irish folk hero, Fennell wrote thousands of song-poems from the 1870s onward. They established him as a regular feature at conventions of railroad unions in the United States and abroad. At the 1889 convention of the Brotherhood of Locomotive Engineers, he received formal recognition—a floral harp, the emblem of his avocation and his native land. So great was the demand for his work that volumes were published in 1886 and 1907. None matched Fennell's output and few displayed his talent.

Fennell's own experiences provided ample subject matter. He was born in Ireland in 1841. His family emigrated and settled in Oswego, New York, in 1849. He first worked in a tannery, but left at age sixteen for the adventure of sailing on the Great Lakes. When the romanticism of the sailor's life dissipated, he returned to Oswego and began a railroading career. Initially a brakeman, he advanced to engineer and dispatcher. Active in community affairs, especially education, he served as president of the school board and as commissioner of schools. He also supported temperance and remained a devout Catholic, although a vocal critic of the church. Through all he stood by the unions of railroad workers.[47]

Such sentiment more frequently found its voice among iron and steel workers, particularly molders and puddlers. Union molders from Louisville, Kentucky; New Haven, Connecticut; and Lawrence, Kansas, contributed works.[48] Moreover, Chicago socialist molder William Creech composed song-poems that the city's socialists sang at their gatherings.[49] As early as the 1860s, iron molder Dugald Campbell was writing song-poems too. At the time he was a young molder in Jersey City, New Jersey, and had recently attracted the attention of National Labor Union and Iron Molders International Union president William Sylvis. Sylvis recruited the song-poet molder as an organizer and cemented Campbell's ties to organized labor. Years later Campbell turned up in Troy, New York, as a saloon keeper who led the 1878 strike among textile workers. Few knew he wrote song-poems on labor topics throughout these years. His romantic sentiments also found an outlet in his song-poems. Even the most dedicated labor song-poets such as Campbell or Fennell sometimes felt compelled to write imitations of the popular sentimental works of the day.[50]

Campbell, however, never generated the song-poems or the attention that Fennell did. Among molders and puddlers, that honor fell upon Michael McGovern. His song-poems earned him enormous popularity among Pittsburgh's workers and among iron and steel workers throughout the country. With Fennell he shared honors as the premier working-class song-poet of the day, unbeknownst to the middle class, and workers conferred upon him the title the Puddler Poet.

McGovern also traced his ancestry to Ireland and Catholicism. He was born in Ireland in 1848 and spent his youth as a shoemaker's apprentice before fleeing his harsh master to work in England's iron mills. Sometime before 1880 he and his wife left for the United States, where he secured a job in the mills of Bucks

County, Pennsylvania. Not long after, the labor movement and song-poetry gained much of his energy, and he began receiving invitations to recite his work at union gatherings. Workers appreciated his dedication and in 1890 elected him secretary of the Ferndale local of iron and steel workers. McGovern soon migrated to the Youngstown, Ohio, area, however, and spent most of his puddling career in the infamous "Siberia Mill." This proved an ideal environment for an aspiring worker song-poet, providing subject matter and access to the region's song-poem history. After the Civil War, local iron and steel workers created such a lively subculture of song-poetry that one scholar remarked: "Virtually every union had its own bard who made up ballads upon request or to mark special occasions, such as strikes, lockouts, and disasters."[51] McGovern quickly discovered workers receptive to his song-poems, and he maintained their support for over forty years. On his death in 1933 he had written over a thousand song-poems, appeared at countless union assemblages, published in numerous labor publications, and issued a compilation of his work. Perhaps the most appropriate compliment for the immigrant puddler and union song-poet came from those workers who memorized McGovern's song-poems.[52]

McGovern surpassed his comrades in his literary adeptness and volume of output. Yet he never separated himself from fellow puddlers or the workers' cause. In this regard he hardly differed from those other forty-eight song-poets employed at wage labor. More than 50 percent of song-poets had working-class occupations. Moreover, if the occupations of labor leaders are considered, that proportion increases considerably. Discounting Albert Parsons and Burnette Haskell, all labor leader song-poets spent significant portions of their lives at wage labor. When they are included, nearly two-thirds of all song-poets qualified as workers.

This composite portrait of song-poets, however, needs some qualification. Black workers are conspicuously absent from the sample, an indication of their exclusion from most of organized labor. In addition, as in the labor movement itself, women performed a subordinate function in song-poetry relative to their role in industry. Song-poetry bears the obvious stamp of men and reflects the masculine temper of public life and of movement culture as well. With some notable exceptions too complex to be taken up here, song-poems have to be judged as part of the preserve of white males.

Historians would not be surprised by these biases. That most worker song-poets had skilled occupations may not surprise anyone either. Specifically, the sources from which the sample was drawn include an obvious bias toward skilled workers. For a number of reasons, less skilled workers were less likely to be reported. More generally, skilled workers possessed the skills necessary to write song-poems and to find and utilize outlets for their compositions. More than that, the dominance of skilled workers reflected their importance in the workplace and the labor movement. Skilled workers continued to maintain a foothold in industry, even though employers worked to usurp what they perceived as the inordinate control of workers over production. Skilled workers hardly deluded themselves into thinking that employers felt content in their dependence on workers' skills and correctly understood that the move toward deskilling yearly became stronger and more systematic. In response, skilled workers moved to protect their own interests while also making attempts to unite with other workers. They brought to the labor movement an understanding of the world that drastically shaped the language and character of labor protest and the movement as well. Song-poetry and movement culture reflect skilled labor's influence as well as its understanding of the world and the impact of that understanding on the era's labor protest. That the majority of song-poets were white, male, and skilled must therefore be judged important, not just for what it says about song-poets and song-poetry but also for what it suggests about the character of labor protest and the labor movement of the time.[53]

Cursory examination of song-poets reveals that not all these skilled workers traced a long ancestry in the United States. Data on the entire sample cannot be located, but information suggests that a significant number immigrated to the United States. Writers such as Fennell, James, and Reuber hailed from Ireland, Scotland, and Germany, to name a few. On occasion these writers might be moved to compose works reflecting on their homelands and the particular meaning of their own ethnic background. That did not necessarily keep them divided from fellow workers; in fact, the presence of immigrant song-poets suggests that, despite antagonism, workers of varied ethnic backgrounds might also be led to cooperate. In addition, they remind us that the character of labor protest and the labor movement in this era owed something to shared sentiments among varied workers. Finally, they suggest that much of what historians have described as emanating from American and native-born workers in the Gilded-Age labor movement may have had a more international tenor to it than previously thought. That Michael McGovern and Karl Reuber found so wide an audience meant that in their song-poems they spoke a language that could be understood by more than just their Irish or German brothers and sisters in the working class. Obviously these immigrants came from traditional European labor markets rather than those of Eastern and Southern Europe. Even so, their contribution to song-poetry should caution historians against assuming that immigrant workers, skilled though they may be, could not contribute directly to an ethnically expansive labor movement and movement culture.[54]

Besides these immigrant bards, song-poetry received considerable impetus from people who would be judged lower middle class today. Thirty writers, comprising 32 percent of the sample, fall into this group. Most owned small shops of one sort or another or held some moderately professional status in the employment hierarchy. Yet they were a far cry from the "new middle class" that would populate the executive-managerial ranks of industry and government after 1900 and stand at the head of "progressive" reform. In truth, this group of song-poets bespoke an earlier era for capitalism, when small shopkeepers and individuals with a modicum of education formed the majority of the middle class and counted themselves among those who "produced." In contrast, the new middle class of the progressive era wore white collars as a class badge and owed its existence and allegiance to a bourgeoning corporate infrastructure. Few would be moved to support the labor movement. The Gilded Age was different: a "clerk," a "manufacturer of food cure," a cigar shop operator, job printers, a self-proclaimed M.D., and a hymnologist might still proclaim themselves allies of labor. Many from the old middle class had no trouble supporting a movement that drew a line from the American Revolution to the plight of labor. Until the rise of monopoly capital and a new middle class, labor counted support beyond "workers," narrowly defined.

If song-poets are indicative, some continuity thus existed between antebellum reform and postbellum organized labor. For that reason the Gilded-Age labor movement appears less reformist or middle class than it does heir to the nation's and other nations' reform traditions. Until the economy literally changed the rules of the game, individuals such as B. M. Lawrence might side with labor. As a self-proclaimed M.D. who barnstormed for spiritualism and homeopathy in the antebellum years, Lawrence seems a bit odd among labor. Lawrence, however, saw no contradiction in advancing spiritualism, women's rights, and the labor movement.

All represented the struggle for a better social order. After 1900 such reformers became less common, and Lawrence's holistic view of social reform soon disappeared from the scene. Doctors formed the American Medical Association, barred individuals like Lawrence from practice, and moved steadily toward the elitist professionalism that marked them part of the new middle class.

## NOTES

1. Thomas Selby, "Knights of Labor," *Journal of United Labor* 6 (November 1885): 1122.

2. On this phenomenon, see Gutman, "Class, Status, and Community Power," as well as his other essays in *Work, Culture, and Society*. See also Alan Dawley, *Class and Community: The Industrial Revolution in Lynn* (Cambridge: Harvard University Press, 1976), and Paul G. Faler, *Mechanics and Manufacturers in the Early Industrial Revolution: Lynn, Massachusetts, 1780–1860* (Albany: State University of New York, 1981).

3. Donn Piatt's song-poems include "Poem by Don Piatt," *National Labor Tribune,* 11 November 1885, and "The Rich and Poor They Pass Me By," *John Swinton's Paper,* 18 October 1885. Biographical information on Piatt may be found in Charles Grant Miller, *Donn Piatt: His Work and His Ways* (Cincinnati: R. Clarke, 1893); David O. Anderson, "The Remarkable Piatt Brothers of Logan County," *Ohioana* 5 (Summer 1962): 34–38; and *Death of Donn Piatt* (n.p., 1891). For examples of Piatt's writing, see his *The Lone Grave of the Shenandoah* (Chicago: Belford, Clarke, 1888), *Memories of Men Who Saved the Union* (New York: Belford, Clarke, 1893), *Poems and Plays* (Cincinnati: R. Clarke, 1893), and *Sunday Meditations and Selected Prose* (Cincinnati: R. Clarke, 1893). I am indebted to Gary Arnold, assistant archivist, Ohio State Historical Society, for much of my information on Piatt.

4. T. R. Magill's labor song-poem was "I Sing to the Honor of Labor," *Journal of United Labor* 15 (November 1894): 1. Biographical information on Magill may be found in Mrs. Sam Presson, "Reminiscences of Charlotte: Career of Thomas R. Magill," *Charlotte Observer,* 9 February 1930; Hazell Parker Jones, *Descendants of James Boyd Magill* (n.p., n.d.), 38–39, 152–59; "Thomas Magill," 21 May 1904, *Mecklenburg County Records: U.S. Census 1900,* Charlotte, North Carolina, Sheet 10, 237a. I am indebted to Mary L. Phillips, local history librarian, Public Library of Charlotte and Mecklenburg County, and Frank D. Gatton, assistant state archivist, North Carolina, for information on Magill.

5. For examples of Hugh Cameron's song-poems, see "With Stamps as Measure," *Journal of United Labor* 8 (August 1887): 2471; "Kansas Valentine," 20 February 1889, *Powderly Papers,* Reel 31; and "Battle Hymn," in "H.P.C. Circular, No. 1," 1 May 1889, *Powderly Papers,* Reel 31. See also Susan Levine, *Labor's True Woman: Carpet Weavers, Industrialization,*

*and Labor Reform in the Gilded Age* (Philadelphia: Temple University Press, 1984), 135. For a biographical sketch of Cameron, see Montgomery, *Beyond Equality*, 138. In addition, see Cameron to Terence Powderly, 24 September 1889, *Powderly Papers*, Reel 31; "H.P.C. Circular No. 1," *Proceedings, General Assembly of the Knights of Labor*, delegates, 1886; John Samuel Papers, Mss 7a, State Historical Society of Wisconsin, Madison, Wisconsin; Kansas State Historical Society to General Hugh Cameron, 28 September 1892; and "A Kansas Character," *Boston Transcript*, n.d. I am indebted to the Kansas State Historical Society for providing me with copies of these last two pieces of information.

6. In his personal papers Powderly occasionally refers to his song-poems, but none appear. See *Powderly Papers*, Reels 1–38. The only surviving song-poem of Powderly's that I located appears in his autobiography, *The Path I Trod* (New York: Columbia University Press, 1940), 42.

For an example of Eugene Debs's song-poems, see E.V.D., "To the Friend of My Bosom," *Locomotive Fireman's Monthly Magazine* 1 (June 1877): 201.

For examples of Albert Parsons's song-poems, see "Freedom," reprinted in Roediger and Rosemont, *Haymarket Scrapbook*, 29. See also Avrich, *Haymarket Tragedy*.

7. For examples of George McNeill's song-poems, see his *Unfrequented Paths*. On his life and career, see the short biographical description in his own *The Labor Movement: The Problem of Today* (New York: M. W. Hazen, 1887), 623–24.

8. For examples of Richard Trevellick's song-poems and a biographical overview, see Hicks, *Life of Richard Trevellick*.

For examples of Frank Foster's song-poems, see "Restricted Immigration," *Labor Leader*, 20 February 1892; "The Slaughter of the Innocents," *Labor Leader*, 27 August 1887; and "To E. V. Debs," *Labor Leader*, 5 January 1895. A brief biographical description of Foster appears in McNeill, *The Labor Movement*, 619–20. See also George Bernard Cotkin, "Working-Class Intellectuals and Evolutionary Thought in America, 1870–1915" (Ph.D. diss., Ohio State University, 1978), and Norman Ware, *The Labor Movement in the United States, 1860–1895* (New York: D. Appleton, 1929). Biographical information on Spies appears in Roediger and Rosemont, *Haymarket Scrapbook*, and Avrich, *Haymarket Tragedy*. Spies's song-poems and essays appeared in the *Alarm* from 1884 to 1886.

For an example of a Burnette Haskell song-poem, see "To Liberty," *Truth*, 10 January 1883. Biographical information on Haskell appears in Avrich, *Haymarket Tragedy*, and Vincent J. Falzone, *Terence V. Powderly: Middle-Class Reformer* (Washington: University Press of America, 1978).

9. See Leffingwell's song-poem "The Scab," *Our Organette*, 6 January 1883. Information on Leffingwell's occupational history may be traced in the Indianapolis *City Directory* for the years 1876 to 1900. I am indebted to Ms. Linda Lambert, Genealogy Library, Indiana State Library, for addi-

tional information on Leffingwell. See also Stuart B. Kaufman, *The Samuel Gompers Papers* (Urbana: University of Illinois Press, 1986–88), 1:165–66, 210–11, 243, 248.

Another song-poet and labor leader whose life followed a pattern similar to Leffingwell's was E. H. Belknap, born in 1836 in Springfield, New York. Belknap's childhood and early adult life had been particularly arduous. An orphan, Belknap went to work on a farm at age seven. At twenty-one he found himself in Elgin, Illinois, doing odd jobs. Eventually he located a full-time job on the railroad as a brakeman and later a conductor. Belknap became head of the Galesburg, Illinois, local of the Order of Railway Conductors in 1883 and was appointed to the union's executive committee in 1885. He was also named editor of the order's journal in 1884 and served in that capacity for many years. His labor and nonlabor song-poems appeared in the pages of the *Railway Conductor's Monthly*. Biographical information on Belknap may be located in "Erwin H. Belknap," *Railway Conductor's Monthly* 4 (October 1887): 508–10, and "Erwin H. Belknap," in *Portrait and Biographical Album of Knox County, Illinois* (Chicago: Chapman Brothers, 1886), 824–25.

In addition see the information on Mrs. Henry B. Jones. An English immigrant and the wife of a coal miner, Jones edited the "ladies" section of the *Railroad Brakemen's Journal* and earned the nickname "Mother Jones" in the mid-1880s. Apparently she and her readers had no knowledge of another labor supporter who became well known as "Mother Jones." For examples of her song-poetry, see "But Jesus Said," *Railroad Brakemen's Journal* 6 (June 1886): 262; "Coal Miners' Song," *Locomotive Fireman's Monthly Magazine* 8 (December 1884): 740; "The Monopolist's Dream," *Locomotive Fireman's Monthly Magazine* 9 (September 1885): 546; "Old Post Lodge," *Locomotive Fireman's Monthly Magazine* 8 (August 1884): 499; and "When I Am Dead," *Railroad Brakemen's Journal* 6 (September 1889): 398. For biographical information on Jones, see *Railroad Brakemen's Journal* 4 (July 1887): 298–99.

10. Patrick Maloney's song-poem, "On Freedom," appears in Maloney to Terence Powderly, 24 March 1886, *Powderly Papers*, Reel 14. Information on Maloney may be gleaned from "Obituary: Patrick Maloney," *St. Tammany Farmer* (St. Tammany Parish, Louisiana), 21 August 1886; "Obituary: Evidences of Christianity," *St. Tammany Farmer*, 24 July 1886; "Jennie Maloney," *St. Tammany Parish Marriage Records*, 1884; "John P. Maloney," *St. Tammany Parish Marriage Records*, 1888; and "Patrick Maloney," in *Records of Louisiana Confederate Soldiers and Louisiana's Confederate Prisoners* (n.p., n.d.), 885. I am indebted to Mrs. Doris Holden and H. Callahan, Covington, Louisiana, for information on Maloney.

An individual who shared Maloney's sentiments and whose background was somewhat similar was Abraham Stedwell. His song-poem "The Modern Mills of Money Gods," in Swinton, *Striking for Life*, 434–35, mixed evangelical Christianity with republicanism to attack the nation's money power. In 1894, when the song-poem was published,

Stedwell was an apiarist in Kearney, Nebraska. He was born in 1826 in Cuyahoga, New York, where his father labored as a wheelwright. In 1829 hardship led the family to Lee County, Iowa, where his family farmed unsuccessfully for a few years before moving to Peoria, Illinois, for another farm. Young Stedwell worked that farm also, before striking out on his own as a farmer and carpenter. In 1860 he settled in Henry County, Iowa, where he remained until 1875 with the exception of his stint with the Union Army. In 1875 financial difficulties led him to Cage County, Nebraska. Grasshoppers ruined his crop and forced him to move once more. With twenty dollars and a few livestock, he took up farming on a small parcel in Buffalo County, Nebraska. Disaster struck again: drought and grasshoppers left him deeply in debt after his first season. Stedwell went to work hauling wood and working as a blacksmith's helper while his wife took in laundry. For the next dozen years, the couple barely survived. But by 1889 they had enough money to move to Kearney and purchase a home. Eventually, he purchased a number of homes and set up a successfull apiary business. He held a number of minor political offices prior to 1890. From 1882 to 1884 he also served in the legislature of Nebraska as a representative of the Farmers' Alliance in Buffalo County. Biographical information on Stedwell can be found in *Biographical Souvenir of the Counties of Buffalo, Kearney, Phelps, Harlan, and Franklin, Nebraska* (Chicago: F. A. Battey, 1890), 273–74; "Abram Stedwell," *Records, Prairie Center Cemetery* (Thorton Township, Buffalo County, Nebraska); and *City Directory* (Kearney), 1892. I am indebted to the Kearney City Library for making this information available to me.

11. The Tallmadges' song-poems can be found in their *Labor Songs*. James Tallmadge appeared in the Chicago *City Directory* as "printer" (1873), 921; (1880), 1087; (1881), 1162; (1884), 1285; (1885), 1345; and (1887), 1552. Emily Tallmadge appeared as "editor" (1882), 1162.

12. For examples of Dyer Lum's song-poetry, see his collection, *In Memoriam: Chicago, November 11, 1887* (Berkeley Heights, N.J.: Oriole Press, 1937). Texts of many of these works are reprinted in Roediger and Rosemont, *Haymarket Scrapbook*. They originally appeared just after the Haymarket affair. See also "Caste Rule—A Dream," *Alarm*, 27 December 1884, and "Harvest," ibid., 22 August 1885. The *Alarm* published Lum's song-poems from 1884 to 1886. He took over as editor of that publication after Parsons and the others were executed. Information on his life must be gleaned from a variety of sources. See fellow anarchist Voltairine de Cleyre's biographical introduction to *In Memoriam*. For a reference to Lum's early spiritualist activity, see Dyer Lum, *Banner of Light*, September 26, 1868.

13. See Schonfarber's song-poem "Shams and Humbugs," *Critic*, 27 December 1890. Schonfarber was listed in the Baltimore *City Directory* as "printer" and "editor" (1885), 1180; (1887), 1048; (1890) 1078; (1891), 1115.

14. On McIntosh's song-poems, see "Eight Hours a Day," *National Labor Tribune*, 15 December 1885; "Out of a Job," *Iron Molders' Journal* (February 1877): 235; and Foner, *American Labor Songs*, 124–25, 128,

299–300. He appears in the Rochester *City Directory* (1876), 223, as "tobacconist," In 1878, the directory indicated he "removed to Cincinnati, O." (226). A short description of his labor career appears in the *Rochester Union and Advertiser,* 9 May 1878. I am indebted to Lawrence Naukam, Rochester Public Library, for the latter piece of information.

15. Other shopkeepers writing song-poems included Harry Burns, Harry Flash, and Ralph Hoyt. Burns's song-poem "Labor Shall Be King" appeared in the *National Labor Tribune,* 1 February 1879, the same year that Burns appeared in the Pittsburgh *City Directory* as "cigar merchant" (141). A Harry Burns, "moulder," appears in the 1878 directory (128). The transition from molder to shopkeeper was a common one. Flash and Hoyt offer a somewhat different pattern. Flash's song-poem, "The Gold Bugs," was published in the *Labor Leader,* 3 January 1891, while Flash listed his occupation in the Los Angeles *City Directory* as "capitalist" (267). Three years earlier the directory also had listed Flash as "capitalist" (277). In subsequent years an H. L. Flash appears as "capitalist" as well. This may have been his son, Harry Flash, Jr. Hoyt's song-poem " America" appeared in the *Journal of United Labor* 11 (July 1890): 1, while the Los Angeles *City Directory* listed him as "President, California Cooperative Colony" (379). The listing was the same for 1888 (374). In 1891 the directory listed Hoyt as "President Illinois Association" (354). Finally, in 1893 he appears as "real estate dealer and journalist" (289).

16. Waldron Shear's song-poems include "Boycotting," *Truth,* 9 August 1892, and "Labor," ibid., 25 October 1882. Shear's occupation listings in the San Francisco *City Directory* include the following: "laundry" (1882), 860, and (1883), 944; "proprietor National and Saturday local" (1886), 1063; "journalist" (1888), 1066; "laundry" (1889), 1182; and "real estate" (1891), 1248. Interestingly, for each listing the address of the establishment did not change, indicating that Shear may have tried any number of enterprises at that location or that he simultaneously operated a number of businesses out of the same office. The assembly of the Knights of Labor to which he belonged, Local 1760, was a mixed local, organized in 1882, the year he wrote his song-poems. Information on that local appears in Garlock, "Prolegomenon," 254. Shear's song-poem "Boycotting" contained anti-Chinese sentiments, in addition to support for the Knights. Anti-Chinese feelings ran high among white laundry owners and fellow Knights of Labor.

17. Sarah Lenfest's song-poem "Then Onward" was printed in the *Journal of United Labor* 15 (January 1895): 3. Lenfest appeared in the Aspen, Colorado, *City Directory* as "cigar, confectionary" in 1892. I am indebted to Vera Haberman of the Aspen Historical Society for providing me with this information. Lenfest belonged to Local Assembly 4401 of the Knights of Labor. According to Garlock, Local 4401 was established in 1885 and lasted until 1896. A mixed assembly, it was predominately coal miners. See Garlock, "Prolegomenon," 256.

18. For Patrick Morrow's song-poem, see "The Boilers Have Triumphed," *National Labor Tribune,* 28 June 1879. In the Pittsburgh *City*

*Directory* Morrow was a "grocer" (1877), 410, and (1878), 426. His address was listed as "Second Ave." in both. In other directory listings he appears as "saloon" on "Second and Soho" (1880), 462, and (1881), 523.

19. For an example of C. L. James's song-poetry, see "Voltaire," *Alarm,* 23 January 1886. Articles and correspondence by James were a regular feature in the *Alarm* from 1886 to 1888. He appears in the Eau Claire *City Directory* as "collector" (1882), 100; as "insurance" (1885), 174; and as "sixth ward alderman" (1887), 181.

20. For J. W. Howe's song-poem, see "Nobody Really Cares," *Knights of Labor* (Chicago), 23 April 1887. As early as 1865, a J. W. Howe appeared in the Chicago *City Directory,* but not until the 1880s did the address agree with that given in his 1887 song-poem. Howe appeared in the *Directory* as "cigars" (1882), 611; as "carrier," (1884), 661; as "P.O. clerk" (1885), 687; as "carrier" (1886), 732; and as "engraver" (1887), 765.

For William Stockman's song-poem, see "Our Rights," *Labor Leaf,* 29 September 1886. Stockman appears in the Detroit *City Directory* as "traveling agent" (1884), 1161; and "agent" (1890), 1042. He also was listed as "medicine manufacturer" (1886), 1223, and "manufacturer of Food Cure" (1889), 1288.

For A. H. Nunemacher's song-poem, see "Oh Master of the Commonweal," *Locomotive Fireman's Monthly Magazine* 14 (June 1889). He was listed in the Paducah *City Directory* as "agent—Southern and Adams Express Co." (1881); and as "agent—Southern Express Co" (1890). I am indebted to Barbara W. Riley, Interlibrary Loan Division, Paducah Public Library, for information on Nunemacher.

21. See, for example, Ellen Dare's song-poem, "Knighthood," *Knights of Labor,* 5 February 1887. Like most women Dare does not appear in the Chicago *City Directory.* At her address, however, a Benjamin F. Dare appears in the directory as "clerk" (1886), 404.

Writers D. R. Lewis and S. Robert Wilson are no more easily identified. For Lewis's song-poem, see "A Song," *National Labor Tribune,* 27 August 1892. Listings for both D. R. Lewis and a Daniel R. Lewis appear in the Pittsburgh *City Directory* from 1877 onward, under diverse occupations, including puddling, clerk, and book agent. However, in 1892 the directory lists one as "book agent" and the other as "salesman" (551). We may conclude that at least for the year the song-poem was written, D. R. Lewis held a white-collar occupation. S. Robert Wilson's song-poems include "A Song," *Truth,* 14 April 1883; "Mammon," *Alarm,* 17 December 1887; "Murder Most Foul," *Alarm,* 17 December 1887; "Revolution," *Alarm,* 4 April 1885; and "She Is Not Dead," *Labor Enquirer* (Denver), 18 April 1885. He wrote a book entitled *Socialism: Being a Brief Statement of the Doctrines and Philosophy of the Social Labor Movement* (New York: Lovell, 1884). I am indebted to Anthony S. Bliss, rare book librarian, Bancroft Library, University of California, Berkeley, for pointing out this publication by Wilson to me. All that can be definitely established about Wilson's occupation is that he held a white-collar job, since the San Francisco *City Directory* lists a Samuel R. Wilson, "commercial traveler," and a Samuel R. Wilson, Jr., "clerk" (1888), 1231.

22. For Haynes's song-poem, see "Eight Hour Song," *Fincher's Trades Review*, 18 November 1865. Haynes was listed as "musician" and "music teacher" in the Chicago *City Directory* from 1863 to 1886. See, for example, (1863), 207; (1865), 392; (1869), 392; (1872), 433; (1884), 807; and (1886), 672.

23. Butler referred to his compositions in a letter to Terence Powderly, 16 March 1886, *Powderly Papers*, Reel 14. They do not appear in the *Powderly Papers*. Biographical information on Butler may be found in Ernst C. Krohn, *Missouri Music* (New York: DeCapo, 1971), 21, 105.

24. Lawrence's song-poems appear in a number of places, including his *Labor Songster*. See also "Hope for the Toiling," *Boston Daily Evening Voice*, 10 January 1867; "The Temperance Workingman," *Workingman's Advocate*, 9 April 1870; and "What We Want," *Workingman's Advocate*, 18 April 1868. Biographical information on Lawrence is difficult to locate, other than the scant information included with his song-poems. On 1 September 1860, B. M. Lawrence of Chicago appeared in the *Herald of Progress*, a spiritualist and reform publication, with a notice on a lecture he was giving. In 1868 he appears as a spiritualist "lecturer" in the *Banner of Light*. See the listings for 26 September 1868, for example. Also see the announcement on 10 October 1868, in the *Banner of Light*. Lawrence was named as a contributor to the *Spiritualist Harp* songbook.

25. For T. L. Drury's song-poem, see "The Thought and the Pen," *Journal of United Labor* 10 (April 1889): 2827. He appeared in the Rutland *City Directory* as "minister—Hope Advent Christian Church" (1884–89); as "journalist" (1889–97); and as "minister" (1897). I am indebted to the Vermont Historical Society for this information on Drury.

For Woodbury Fernald's song-poems, see "The Uprising of Labor," *Boston Daily Evening Voice*, 27 June 1866, and "The Working Girls," ibid., 22 October 1866. He appeared in the Boston *City Directory* as "reverend" (1864), 130.

26. For examples of Jesse Jones's song-poem, see "Eight Hours," *Labor Standard*, 9 June 1878, and the work in his labor publication *Labor Balance* from 1877 until 1879. For biographical information, see Charles H. Hopkins, *The Rise of the Social Gospel in American Protestantism, 1865–1915* (New Haven: Yale University Press, 1940), 42–49.

27. Two song-poets with education and training beyond most wage workers are Charles Chatfield and A. J. H. Duganne. Chatfield, the blind son of an iron worker, became a newspaper editor and later a lawyer in Murray City, Ohio. He supported labor, particularly coal miners, and joined with Populism in the 1890s. Later he became an ardent Republican. For a brief overview of song-poems by Chatfield and other song-poets from the Murray City region, as well as an account of the region's labor history, see Ivan Tribe, "An Empire of Industry: Hocking Valley Mining Towns in the Gilded Age" (Ph.D. diss., University of Toledo, 1976). I am indebted to

Professor Tribe for sharing his knowledge of Chatfield and the Hocking Valley with me. For examples of Chatfield's song-poems, see "Among the Poor," *United Mine Workers Journal* 4 (January 1895): 2; "The Curbstone Politician," *United Mine Workers Journal* 5 (August 1895): 7; "Only a Miner's Child," *United Mine Workers Journal* 5 (October 1895): 3; and "The People's Prayer," *United Mine Workers Journal* 5 (August 1895): 3. See also his book *Buds That Never Bloom* (Glouster, Ohio: Press Publishing Co., 1897).

A. J. H. Duganne's poetry became popular with reformers and labor even before the Civil War and was reprinted continuously from 1850 until the 1890s. For examples of his work, see his compilation *The Poetical Works of Augustine Duganne* (Philadelphia: Parry and McMillan, 1855). Duganne also supported the Knights of Labor—not to mention the Masons—and in November 1882 contributed the song-poem "Under Three Great Lights" to the *Journal of United Labor*. That work is reprinted in Kealey and Palmer, *Dreaming of What Might Be*, 288. On his life, see "Augustine Joseph Hickey Duganne," in *Dictionary of American Biography* (New York: Scribners, 1930), 5: 492–93.

28. For Edward Lambert's song-poem, see "The Puddler," *National Labor Tribune*, 22 April 1882. The only Edward Lambert to appear in the Pittsburgh *City Directory* during these years was a laborer. See, for example, (1878), 364; (1880), 398; and (1881), 449.

29. For examples of Sheridan's song-poems, see "Song of the Carpet Weavers," *Journal of United Labor* 5 (January 1885): 883, and "The Writing on the Wall," *Journal of United Labor* 6 (September 1885): 1086. Sheridan did not appear in the listings of the New York *City Directory*. However, she belonged to Local Assembly 2985 of the Knights of Labor, a female assembly of carpet mill operatives organized in 1883 and continuing in existence until 1889. See Garlock, "Prolegomenon," 346, on this local. On the history of these workers, see Levine, *Labor's True Woman*.

30. See Leder's song-poem, "Union Song," *Coast Seamen's Journal*, 6 November 1887. Leder appears in the San Francisco *City Directory* as "seaman" (1886), 729, and (1888), 723. He served as editor of the *Coast Seamen's Journal* during its first year and a half of publication from November 1887 until April 1889.

31. For Enoch Bowley's song-poem, see "The Mines," *National Labor Tribune*, 14 June 1884. For John Barnett's, see "Union and Reform," *National Labor Tribune*, 13 April 1889. Coal Bluff was a coal mining center, and according to Leatrice Miller, librarian, Byers Memorial Library, Monongahela, Pennsylvania, Bowley and Barnett appear to have been miners in the camp. For John Cairns's song-poem, see "A Song for the Times," *National Labor Tribune*, 31 August 1893. Cairns worked as a coal miner in the Coal Bluff region; his name was mentioned in a report on the Republican party in Coal Bluff for 1884. See "Coal Bluff," *Daily Republican* (Monongahela City), 2 November 1884. I am indebted to Leatrice Miller for information on Cairns.

32. For examples of William Mullen's song-poems, see "Doings in the Coke Region," *National Labor Tribune,* 22 August 1885, and "Non-Union Chorus," *United Mine Workers Journal* 1 (June 1891): 4. Mullen's residence and union affiliation were indicated in his song-poems. His efforts on behalf of the Miners and Mine Laborers' Amalgamated Association were often reported in the *National Labor Tribune.*

For George Parker's song-poem, see his letter to the editor, "God Bless Our Union," *United Mine Workers Journal* 4 (June 1894). Parker belonged to Local 649 of the United Mine Workers. George Korson included Parker's song-poem in *Coal Dust on the Fiddle* and described Parker as a bard "worthy of mention." See Korson, *Coal Dust on the Fiddle,* 409–10, 451.

For examples of Samuel Simon's song-poems, see "Salaries Unwarranted," *United Mine Workers Journal* 2 (August 1892): 6; and "The True Man," *National Labor Tribune,* 22 February 1890. See also his letters "Traitors," *United Mine Workers Journal* 2 (August 1892): 3, and "Why So Few Attend Church," *United Mine Workers Journal* 3 (July 1893): 3. Simon appears in the New Castle *City Directory* as "miner" (1889), 391. I am indebted to Helen Roux, director of New Castle Public Library, for this bit of information.

33. Morgan's song-poem appears in "From Pennsylvania," *Workingman's Advocate,* 18 June 1870. For an account of the events surrounding the strike and the song-poem, see Korson, *Minstrels of the Mine Patch,* 207–9, 222. A variant of the song-poem also appears in Korson, *Songs and Ballads,* 165. Korson collected the song in 1938.

34. Oskaloosa, Iowa, coal miner William H. Minnick wrote "Would We Strike?" *Journal of United Labor* 7 (May 1886): 2066. Minnick belonged to Knights of Labor Assembly 1403. On that local, see Garlock, "Prolegomenon," 283. According to Garlock, 1403 was one of four locals organized in Oskaloosa between 1880 and 1888. Local 1403 was the first to be organized (1880) and continued to operate longer than the others (1888). The local included coal miners. J. McInaw was a miner from Glouster, Ohio. See his song-poem, "The Hocking Leader's Address," *National Labor Tribune,* 5 December 1885, and "The Hocking Strike," ibid., 4 July 1885. From Corning came miner Joseph Siemer. See his song-poem, "After the Strike," *United Mine Workers Journal* 4 (May 1894): 8. For more on McInaw and Siemer, and other song-poets of the Hocking Valley, see Tribe, "An Empire of Industry."

35. For examples of James's song-poems, all published in the *Workingman's Advocate,* see "An Appeal," 22 February 1868; "Come, Join the Labor Party," 4 April 1868; "From Braidwood," 18 January 1868; "The Fallen Chieftan," 2 August 1869; "Labor's Champion," 15 May 1869; "Labor's Demands," 29 May 1869; and "Tribute," 9 May 1868. The most useful source of information on James is Richard Joyce, "Miners of the Prairie: Life and Labor in the Wilmington, Illinois, Coal Field, 1866–1897" (M.A. thesis, Illinois State University, 1980). I am deeply indebted to Mr. Joyce for sharing his knowledge of James with me.

36. For James Norris's song-poem, see "Freedom's Day," *National Labor Tribune*, 1 July 1882. Norris was listed in the Cleveland *City Directory* as "coachman" and "driver" for a doctor: (1879), 372; (1880), 390; (1881), 403; (1882), 421, (1883), 466.

37. For T. H. Norton's song-poem, see "A Level Head," *Journal of United Labor* 15 (January 1885): 883. Norton indicated that he belonged to Knights of Labor Local Assembly 3423. He appears in that union's directory as the recording secretary for that local. The local was an assembly of unskilled workers throughout its existence. See Garlock, "Prolegomenon," 368. According to the Bolivar Oil Field *City Directory* (1882), Norton worked as a rig builder. Apparently, he was employed in the region's oil fields. He was undoubtedly involved in the Bolivar Knights of Labor boycott of 1886. Whether he and fellow oil-field workers were really "unskilled" is questionable. I am indebted to the Bolivar Free Library for providing me with information on Norton and the 1886 boycott.

38. For examples of George Davenport's song-poems, see "A Psalm of Life," *Boston Daily Evening Voice*, 25 October 1865, and "Equal Rights for All," ibid. 21 March 1866. Davenport appeared in the Boston *City Directory* as "gilder" (1864), 100; (1865), 117, (1866), 129.

39. For an example of Albert Wells's song-poetry, see "My Country 'Tis of Thee," *National Labor Tribune*, 20 October 1877. Wells appeared in the Wheeling, West Virginia, *City Directory* as "nailer" (1877), 342. For James Adolphus's song-poem, see "Knights of Labor," *Knights of Labor*, 28 September 1886. Adolphus appeared in the Chicago *City Directory* as "locksmith" (1887), 120. The Knights of Labor listed him as a member of Local Assembly 508. However, no such local existed in Chicago. More likely he belonged to Assembly 5805, a trade assembly of skilled workers in the secondary metal trades organized in 1886. See Garlock, "Prolegomenon," 257. For the song-poems of Mrs. S. E. Olmstead, see "Bells of the Year," *Laborer*, 20 February 1886; "The Golden Bell," *Labor Leader*, 8 January 1887; "Song," ibid., 5 March 1887; and "The Writing on the Wall," ibid., 4 June 1887. Olmstead was born in 1839 and died in 1924. Her husband, Israel, was a tinsmith in Marlboro, Massachusetts, for many years prior to his death in 1909. See Marlboro *City Directory* (1885), 77; (1897), 110; (1909), 156; and (1921), 37. See also "Obituary: Israel Olmstead," *Marlboro Enterprise*, 1909, and "Mrs. Olmstead Passed Away This Morning," *Marlboro Enterprise*, March 1924. I am indebted to Margaret M. Grassby, assistant director, Marlboro Public Library, for providing me with occupational and biographical information on Olmstead.

40. The shoemaker was C. B. Lincoln. For Lincoln's song-poem, see "The Workingmen," *Boston Daily Evening Voice*, 22 March 1865. Lincoln appears in the Boston *City Directory* as "shoemaker" (1864), 150; (1866), 115. The woodworker was John Rector. For his song-poem, see "Save the Children," *Machine Woodworker*, 2 May 1892. Rector belonged to the Machine Woodworkers' International Union, Local 92. He appears in the Toledo *City Directory* as "cabinetmaker" (1891), 789; and as "machine

hand—Union Mfg. Co." (1893), 907; (1894), 923. The baker was Thomas Walsh. For his song-poem, see "The Claims of Labor," *Bakers' Journal*, 20 July 1886. Walsh indicated that he belonged to Local 63 of the Journeymen Bakers' National Union. He appears in the New York *City Directory* as "baker" (1885), 1996. The carpenter was B. F. French. For French's song-poem, see "The Workingman's Hope," *Workingman's Advocate*, 12 February 1870. He appears in the San Francisco *City Directory* as "carpenter" (1869), 247; (1871), 261. The painter was Thomas Leahy. For an example of his song-poetry, see "Come Join the Knights of Labor Boys," 19 May 1886, *Powderly Papers*, Reel 16. Leahy told Powderly that he belonged to Local Assembly 5545 of the Knights of Labor in Keene, New Hampshire. He appeared in the Keene *City Directory* from 1874 to 1910 as "painter," "carriage painter," "carriage painter and repairer," and "painter, carriage, house, and sign." He apparently died around 1910, while his wife lived into the 1940s. Leahy served in the Union Army in the Civil War. I am indebted to Ardis Osborn, reference librarian, Keene Public Library, for providing me with occupational and biographical information on Leahy. The metal worker was W. J. Hanford. For his song-poem, see "To My Laboring Brothers," *Journal of United Labor* 3 (January 1883): 377. Hanford indicated that he belonged to Local Assembly 2066 of the Knights of Labor in South Bend, Indiana, and the union's directory listed him as the local secretary. Local 2066 was a "secondary metal trades" assembly, operating from 1882 until 1892. See Garlock, "Prolegomenon," 276. Since two agricultural implement factories dominated the local economy and many of their employees worked in the metal trades, Hanford likely was employed by one of them. I am indebted to Martha Mullin, curator, Discovery Hall Museum, South Bend, Indiana, for providing me with information on the Knights of Labor and industry in the region. The piano-furniture polisher and repairer from Pittsburgh was Karl Reuber. Reuber's work appears in three volumes: *Gedanken, Hymns of Labor, Poems and Songs*. See also Foner, *American Labor Songs*. 117–19.

41. For George Eddy's song-poem, see "Onward Freedom," *Workingman's Advocate*, 11 August 1866. Eddy appears in the Bloomington *City Directory* for 1866 as "machinist." I am indebted to Greg Koos of the McLean County History Society in Bloomington for this information.

42. For M. A. Dalbey's song-poems, see "Opening Ode" and "Closing Ode," *Journal of United Labor* 1 (March 1880): 102. Dalbey indicated that he belonged to Local Assembly 1626 of the Knights of Labor and in 1881 appeared in the *Journal of United Labor* as an organizer for this region. Dalbey was listed in the Ottumwa *City Directory* as "machinist" (1882–85). I am indebted to Hilda Wilson, researcher, Ottumwa Public Library, for locating this information on Dalbey.

Three others machinists who wrote song-poetry were C. N. Brown of Providence, Rhode Island; Joseph Lee of Cleveland; and William R. Shaw of Buffalo, New York. For Brown's song-poem see "Eight Hour Song," *Socialist*, 27 May 1876. He appears in the Providence *City Directory* as "machinist" (1876), 60. For Lee's song-poems, see "The Warning," *Cleveland Citizen*, 20 May 1893, and "If Christ Came," *Cleveland Citizen*, 25 August 1894. Lee appears in the Cleveland *City Directory* as "machinist" (1891), 537; (1892), 551. For Shaw's song-poem, see "The Present," *Locomotive Engineer's Monthly Journal* 5 (September 1871). Shaw appears in the Buffalo *City Directory* as "machinist" (1872), 512.

43. For examples of John Thompson's song-poems, see "America," *Knights of Labor,* 18 December 1886; "Anarchist in a Coop," ibid., 20 November 1886; Cookgustycuss," *Labor Enquirer* (Chicago), 16 April 1887; "Gideon Is Coming," *Knights of Labor,* 30 October 1886; "Hail Milwaukee," ibid., 4 December 1886; "In Hoc Signes Vinces," ibid., 20 November 1886; and "The Red Flag," ibid. 2 October 1886. In "Trades Congress," *Granite Cutters' Journal* 5 (December 1881):1, Thompson appears as a delegate to the convention. He appears in the Chicago *City Directory* as "cutter," "stonecutter," "calciminer," and "carver" (1878), 1024; (1880), 1098; (1884), 1298–1299; (1885), 1359; (1886), 1462.

Two other stone or granite cutters to write song-poems were Thomas Kesson and T. C. Keleher. For Kesson's song-poem, see "Chicago, Ill: All Honors to the Chicago Boys," *Granite Cutters' Journal* 13 (September 1890): 4. Kesson belonged to the Chicago local of the Granite Cutters' National Union. For Keleher's song-poem, see his letter and song-poem, "Jersey City, N.J.: Be Firm Do Not Waiver," ibid. 15 (June 1892): 3. Keleher belonged to the Jersey City local of the Granite Cutters. He appears in the *City Directory* as "cutter" (1890), 303, and as "stonecutter" (1891), 289. In 1893, the directory listed him as "conductor" (372).

44. For John Cotter's song-poem, see "Initiation Ode" in Cotter to Terence Powderly, 2 February 1886, *Powderly Papers*, Reel 13. Cotter appears in the Saginaw *City Directory* as "printer" (1868), 236; (1884), 93; (1886), 509. Cotter sometimes did work for his brother's printing shop, since the 1884 and 1886 entries list him as an employee of his brother. Cotter belonged to Local Assembly 2897 of the Knights of Labor, and in 1886 he served as its master workman. That local appeared in a city directory (1886) listing with six other locals in the city. Cotter's local was a mixed assembly. See Garlock, "Prolegomenon," 314. As a master workman and a printer, Cotter undoubtedly played a part in the struggle of lumber workers in the region for the ten-hour day in 1886. The loss of the strike may explain why Cotter's local disappeared in the months after the strike. For an account of this strike, see Doris B. McLaughlin, "Ten Hours or No Sawdust," in *Michigan Labor: A Brief History from 1818 to the Present,* ed. Doris B. McLaughlin (Ann Arbor: University of Michigan—Wayne State University, Institute of Labor and Industrial Relations, 1970), 24–49.

The five other printers who wrote song-poems were Daniel T. Riordan and R. J. Preston of San Francisco, Alexander Spencer of Chicago, Frank Dinsmore of Galveston, and Tim Harrington of Indianapolis. For Riordan's song-poem, see "Strive on," *Typographical Journal,* 1 December 1894. He appears in the San Francisco *City Directory* as "printer" or "compositor" (1889), 1108; (1891), 1169; (1894), 1203. For Preston's song-poem, see "Brotherhood," *Journal of United Labor* 3 (June 1882): 237. He indicated that he belonged to Local Assembly 1580 of the Knights of Labor and in 1882 appeared as its recording secretary. Preston also appears in the San Francisco *City Directory* as "copyist" (1882), 785; (1883), 863. For Spencer's song-poem, see "Labor's Awakening," *Typographical Journal*, 1 September 1894. He appeared in the Chicago *City Directory* as "printer" (1893), 1545; (1894), 1586. For Dinsmore's song-poem, see "Western Union and Usury," *Typographical Journal*, 5 January 1894. Dinsmore appeared in the Galveston *City Directory* as "printer" (1890), 163; (1893), 170; (1897), 59. For Harrington's song-poem, see "A Sleek Little Error," *Typographical Journal*, 1 November 1894. Harrington was listed in the Indianapolis *City Directory* as "printer" (1893), 421; (1894), 398.

45. On railroad songs, see Cohen, *Long Steel Rail.*

46. For Matthew Quinlan's song-poem, see "When We're Fifty Thousand Strong," *Railway Carmen's Journal* (April 1894): 30. Available information on Quinlan is confusing because two men in Ottumwa (probably father and son) shared the same name. One Matthew Quinlan died in 1898 at the age of seventy, while the other died in 1946 at eighty-five. Although the former would appear to be a more likely candidate for being a song-poet, the latter was known to have worked as a railway carman. What's more, the "carman" was born in Ireland in 1861 and still was employed on the railroad in 1938. Indeed, an entry for Quinlan appears in the *City Directory* of 1943 as "car inspector" for the St. Paul Railroad. I am indebted to Hilda Wilson, Research Department, Ottumwa Public Library, for this information.

47. Between 1873 and 1892 more than two hundred Patrick Fennell song-poems appeared in the *Locomotive Engineer's Monthly Journal*, and between 1876 and 1895 over fifty were published in the *Locomotive Fireman's Monthly Magazine*. Hundreds were printed in his two volumes, *Random Rhymes* and *Recitations*. The most useful sources of biographical information on Fennell are "Patrick Fennell," *Railroad Brakemen's Journal* 7 (June 1890): 322–24, and "Obituary: Patrick Fennell," *Palladium Times* (Oswego, New York), 3 August 1916. See also Norm Cohen, "The Persian's Crew," *New York Folklore Quarterly* 12 (December 1969): 289–97.

48. For an example of Louisville, Kentucky, song-poet Isaac Taylor's work, see "Who Is My Foe, Is It Capital? No!" *Iron Molders' Journal* (December 1870): 16. He appeared in the journal directory as a member of Local 18 of the Iron Molders' International Union. He is listed in the Louisville *City Directory* as "molder" (1870), 343; (1871), 457. For an example of New Haven, Connecticut, song-poet Michael Conway's work, see "Song of the Molders' Union," *Iron Molders' Journal* (March 1880): 4. He indicated that he belonged to Local 77 of the union. He is listed in the New Haven *City Directory* as "molder" (1879), 69. For an example of Lawrence, Kansas, song-poet P. H. Dillon's work, see "The Pioneer Molder," *Iron*

*Molders' Journal* (February 1884): 6. Dillon indicated that he belonged to Local 162 of the union. He is listed in the Lawrence *City Directory* as "molder" (1886), 52.

49. For examples of William Creech's song-poetry, published in the *Iron Molders' Journal*, see "Eight Hours" (October 1880); 10; "Help One Another" (March 1880): 10; "In Union Lies Our Strength" (October 1879): 9; and "Suggested for the Iron Molders' Ball" (January 1880): 9. Creech appeared in the Chicago *City Directory* as "molder" (1865), 155; (1870), 193; (1878), 296; (1886), 383; (1887), 396. He also appears as "grocer" (1891), 568. A Chicago socialist named William B. Creech was regularly called upon to sing or recite his works at socialist gatherings in that city. See Foner, *American Labor Songs*, 297–98.

50. For examples of Dugald Campbell's song-poems, see "Centennial Lines," *Iron Molders' Journal* (May 1876): 694; "Keep a Stiff Upper Lip," *Fincher's Trades Review*, 27 February 1864; and "We Come, We Go," *Iron Molders' Journal* (January 1877): 202. Nonlabor song-poems of Campbell include "Come Nearer to Me Willie," *Fincher's Trades Review*, 21 November 1863, and "I Know Thou Art Changed," ibid., 26 September 1863. Campbell appeared in the Jersey City *City Directory* as "molder" (1864), 94. He appears in the Troy, New York, *City Directory* as "saloon" (1875), 43; (1877), 42. The only source on Campbell is Daniel Walkowitz, *Worker City, Company Town: Iron and Cotton-Worker Protest in Troy and Cohoes, New York, 1855–1884* (Urbana: University of Illinois Press, 1981), 1–3.

51. Evanson, "Folk Songs of an Industrial City," 426.

52. For examples of McGovern's song-poems from the 1890s, all published in the *National Labor Tribune*, see "Again We Meet," 13 June 1892; "Blacklisted," 30 April 1892; "The Fall of Abel Cain," 13 December 1890; "The Rolling Mill," 30 August 1890; and "When the Changing Whistle Blows," 24 September 1892. See also his compilation *Labor Lyrics*. For examples of his later song-poems, see "All Countries Have Their Reprobates," *Vindicator* (Youngstown), 22 November 1922; "Halloween," ibid., 25 October 1925; and "The Banker and the Mortgage," *Amalgamated Journal*, 30 March 1933. For information on McGovern, see "Michael McGovern," *Vindicator*, 3 April 1933; "Michael McGovern," photocopy of obituary notice (n.p., n.d.); and "McGovern's Poems Reveal Kindly Philosophy of Life," *Vindicator*, 9 April 1933. I am indebted to O. Marie McCurdy, reference librarian, Public Library of Youngstown and Mahoning County, for providing me with information on McGovern. In addition, see Evanson, "Folk Songs of an Industrial City."

53. The role of skilled workers in organized labor in Europe and North America has recently been the subject of considerable study. See, for example, David Bensman, *The Practice of Solidarity: American Hat Finishers in the Nineteenth Century* (Urbana: University of Illinois Press, 1985); Cumbler, "Transatlantic Working-Class Institutions"; Russell Hann, "Brainworkers of the Knights of Labor: E. E. Sheppard, Phillips Thompson,

and the Toronto News, 1883–1887," in *Essays in Canadian Working Class History*, ed. Gregory Kealey and Peter Warrian (Toronto: McClelland and Stewart, 1976), 35–57; Oestreicher, *Solidarity and Fragmentation*; Bryan Palmer, "Most Uncommon Common Men: Craft and Culture in Historical Perspective," *Labour/Le Travailleur* 1 (1976): 5–31; I. J. Prothero, *Artisans and Politics in Early Nineteenth-Century London: John Gast and His Times* (Baton Rouge: Louisiana State University Press, 1979); and Sewell, *Work and Revolution*.

54. A thorough study of internationalism and labor protest in the Gilded Age has yet to be written. However, see Cumbler, "Transatlantic Working-Class Institutions"; Jentz and Schneirov, "Social Republicanism"; Oestreicher, *Solidarity and Fragmentation*; and Clifton K. Yearley, Jr., *Britons in American Labor: A History of the Influence of the United Kingdom on American Labor, 1820–1914* (Baltimore: Johns Hopkins University Press, 1957).

# 3

# The Form and Style of the Labor Song-Poem

B ROWSING through the *Denver Labor Enquirer,* a Knights of Labor paper, on 18 June 1887, readers noticed a song-poem titled
"Fling to the Breeze Our Banner." The anonymous author pleaded
with workers to fight for labor and freedom, borrowing the tune of
a popular Protestant hymn to rouse them and reminding them of
their duty as guardians of the Revolutionary heritage:

> Come, brothers, come, our country calls you;
>   Dare you your dearest right maintain?
> Let us dethrone presumptuous leaders,
>   Let labor and true Brotherhood reign.
> Fling to the breeze our glorious banner,
> Fill up the ranks both young and old;
> Stand by your friends, united freemen—
> Freedom's grand host against the world.
>
> Back to your dens, ye base-born traitors!
>   Down to your degraded spheres;
> Ye cannot crush the Labor Movement,
>   Though you should live a thousand years.
> Fling to the beeze . . .

From its opening line to its closing refrain, "Fling to the Breeze
Our Banner" displayed characteristics common to song-poems
from the period. Workers regularly sang song-poems to the tunes
of well-known songs, particularly folk songs, hymns, and minstrel
tunes. Opening lines pleading for workers' attention had long been
familiar to working-class gatherings. Portrayals of workers and the

labor movement as the defenders of republican principles had become cliché. Hundreds stirred workers with appeals to patriotic duty by enumerating labor's grievances, and equating capitalists with disloyalty and workers with democracy.

These musical, poetic, and ideological devices permeated labor song-poems. In fact, even a superficial reading of a large group of song-poems reveals formulaic composition. Although the most talented writers might transcend this formula, the majority utilized recognizable and commonplace devices—devices that could be readily understood by an audience. Quite literally, song-poets spoke the same language as their audience.

On one level, the recurring use of formulaic devices underscores the influence that pre-industrial traditions, both Western European and American, exercised on writers and workers. We need not equate the term "pre-industrial" with "pre-capitalist" or contrast it to "industrial" to appreciate its meaning. In a technical sense these traditions antedated an industrial base and more properly belong to that amorphous stage sometimes labeled merchant capitalism. Frequently trans-class rather than class specific, certain traditions exerted profound impact on worker consciousness and protest after the Civil War.

Neither writers nor workers, however, acted only as passive recipients and carriers of cultural baggage. The term "traditional," when applied to Gilded-Age workers, is a misnomer, since no single worker remained "traditional." Song-poems indicate that workers felt the shaping influence of more contemporary social and cultural trends. Traditional devices mingled with elements of evangelical Protestantism and antebellum reform. Song-poems also recall the influence of very early popular culture and elite culture. Minstrelsy and romanticism, representing the extremes of the cultural spectrum, rarely existed side by side in song-poetry, but their presence is unmistakable.

None of these influences, however, can be found in unadulterated form. The particular experience of workers in the Gilded-Age capitalist environment infused traditional and antebellum practices or devices with new meaning, leading workers to refashion and transform their inheritance to serve the needs of movement culture and the working class. While never entirely autonomous cultural creations—and therefore never entirely rid of their non-working-class history—labor song-poems have a distinct working-class character about them. As industrial capitalism increasingly dominated the national landscape and class conflict became the

norm, workers moved toward an increasingly class-specific interpretation and vision of America. However, tradition continued to
wield influence, as skilled workers and the old middle class clung
to their place in the economy, and as skilled workers and their
allies continued to stand at the helm of organized labor. Labor
song-poems thus reflect a particular brand of class consciousness—one nurtured by the specific environment of Gilded-Age
capitalism.

Nowhere does the imprint of the past seem more marked than
on the form and style of the song-poem. Song-poets did not invent
an original musical or poetic style or form; nor did they merely
mimic the best-sellers of their day. Originality and mimicry existed, but more often song-poems display traits rooted in folk and
plebeian cultures of Western Europe and early America.

Broadside traditions, for example, proved especially useful to
song-poets. In varied form broadsides, the street literature of pre-
industrial and early industrial Europe, performed an important
function: among pre-literate Europeans street literature "created
an urban folklore, and printed non-books for poor people."[1] Victor
Neuberg claims that the chapbook, a particular form of broadside
provides "An indication of behavior and assumptions by which
men lived their lives in the past. This is all an important part of
what Edward Thompson has called 'the mental universe of the village.' . . . These little books more than any other evidence we have
open a window on the world of the eighteenth century poor.' "[2]

From their emergence in the seventeenth century until their
displacement by other printed forms in the nineteenth century,
broadsides occupied center stage in street literature. Initially, ballads mingled with advertisements, proclamations, religious and
political discussions, and reports on current events—all on single-
sheet broadsides.[3] Later, sermons, temperance tales, conversion
stories, and Christian didactics appeared.[4] Despite their uneven
quality, the ballads generated the largest following. They offered
spirited accounts of witchcraft, heroic deeds, murders, supernatu-
ral phenomena, biblical tales, the exploits of thieves, and the chi-
canery of the nobility.[5]

Over the years both broadsides and ballads changed noticeably.
Multiple-sheet broadsides containing more than one ballad developed concurrently with the older single-sheet format. Large sheets
of paper containing songs and poems, and other material were
folded several times to form pamphlet-like publications known as
chapbooks.[6] Publishers also issued garlands—small compilations

of ballads and songs.[7] Finally, around 1800 pocket-sized collections of traditional ballads, folk songs, and popular songs—songsters—began gaining favor.[8] These modifications did not alter the broadsides' status as street literature. Small back-street printers of limited means and itinerant street hawkers still formed the system of publication and distribution.[9] What's more, they retained an unsophisticated literary formula and musical simplicity in which recognition counted for more than innovation.[10]

The endless repetition of similar lines and the constant borrowing of familiar tunes won the favor of plebeian audiences. Contemporaries commented on the popularity of broadsides, particularly the ballads, and thousands of surviving copies offer testimony to public favor. No stronger evidence of approval exists, however, than the appearance of elements of broadside form and style in labor song-poems. Song-poets seem to have been steeped in broadside tradition, since they borrowed from it habitually.

The practice began even before the Civil War. The nation's first trade union song-poem—"Address to the Journeymen Cordwainers L. B. of Philadelphia," issued during the strike of 1799—bears close resemblance to a broadside. A single sheet printed by a small job printer, the work included the familiar bold-faced title without indicating the tune or providing notation. The opening lines summoned workers in typical broadside fashion: "Cordwainers! Arouse! The time has come! / When our rights should be fully protected." In addition, the text invoked terms well known to those who read broadsides from the nation's fight for independence, as the anonymous author called upon unions "one to thirteen" to protect their "rights."[11]

Postbellum song-poets also labored under the broadside's sway. Inspired by the labor uprising of 1877, Andrew Wall contributed a futuristic portrayal of "The General Strike" that quickly found large distribution as a broadside.[12] Shortly thereafter, E. R. Place's "The Workingman's Train" appeared in the Paterson, New Jersey, *Labor Standard* and circulated as a broadside in labor circles.[13] More spectacular for sheer volume of output were those Knights of Labor song-poems distributed like broadsides throughout the ranks. Some, like Budd Harris's "Knights of Labor," became a regular feature at meetings.[14]

Labor broadsides frequently surfaced during the struggles of coal miners, among whom song-poetry enjoyed a long history and song-poets commanded great respect. The intensity of class conflict in Pennsylvania's collieries encouraged one miner to desert the mines for a career as itinerant singer, writer, minstrel, and hawker of ballads. Upon witnessing the hanging of the Molly Maguire defendants, sixteen-year-old collier Martin Mulhall felt moved to compose a song-poem for each victim. A local printer offered them in broadside form and Mulhall sang and hawked them as he wandered the state's coal camps. Mulhall rapidly established his reputation as singer-composer and his talents earned him the title Poet Mulhall. Until he died hopping a freight train in the early twentieth century, Mulhall earned his income by selling broadsides in coal towns.[15]

The song-poems of Mulhall, Wall, Place and Harris owed much to the broadside. They were printed on single sheets or cards by small job printers who employed the standard bold-face title and did not include music.[16] And, like the European street hawkers, workers peddled their wares at gatherings where comrades or potential converts assembled. Although their subject and message reflected workers' concerns—a point that sharply distinguished them from early broadsides—such song-poems harked back to the broadsides of an era long past.

So, too, did collections of song-poems. Labor songsters compiled by B. M. Lawrence, James and Emily Tallmadge, and Karl Reuber closely resembled the chapbooks, garlands, and songsters that evolved from the broadside. Like their predecessors, Lawrence's *National Greenback Labor Songster,* the Tallmadges' *Labor Songs Dedicated to the Knights of Labor,* and Reuber's *Poems and Songs* and *Hymns of Labor* exhibited those pocket-size measurements popularized by chapbooks. Their small size belied the wealth of materials contained in such publications. The Tallmadges' thirty-one-page songster included twenty song-poems, and Lawrence's forty-eight pages gave readers thirty-three of the author's lengthy selections and compositions. Reuber's *Poems and Songs* counted seventy-four pages crammed full of original song-poems and essays in both English and German. His twenty-three-page *Hymns of Labor,* on the other hand, featured twenty-five original English song-poems.

The ten-cent price on the Tallmadge songster strongly suggests that these songbooks sold for a minimal amount. Obviously the authors worked with marginal publishers: the Tallmadges printed the work themselves, and Reuber enlisted a small fellow-German printer for *Poems and Songs* and the printer for the glass workers' union for *Hymns of Labor.* Lawrence tapped his spiritualist connections and relied on D. M. Bennet's Liberal and Scientific Publishing House in New York City. Bennet's confident claim to specialization in "Liberal, Oriental, Radical, Anti-Theological, Scientific, Reformatory, Progressive, and Spiritualist Works" recalls Gilded-Age labor's links to antebellum reform but does not disguise an operation as inconspicuous as the Tallmadges' humble printery.

Musically they all depended on time-worn practices as well. Only a handful of songs among them included musical notation or original score. Most gave the name of a familiar "air" or tune to which the text might be sung. Many appeared without any tune. In fact, among Reuber's many "songs and poems" not a single tune is listed.

By outward appearance, then, broadside influence weighed heavily on song-poets. Whatever the broadside's general external format, however, the broadside ballad—with its detailed narrative account—remained the center of the broadside. The product of the interchange of folk culture and a growing urban plebeian population, the ballad's influence extended into nineteenth-century America and Gilded-Age labor song-poems.[17]

On the surface the ballad form suggests little applicability to the labor movement or its song-poets. After all, the labor movement aimed primarily to rouse and maintain support for labor's cause, not to recount events in labor history. Nonetheless, writers sometimes found that balladry's narrative format well suited works critical of scabs and blacklegs. In 1879 Johnny Cash's "The Blacklegs" told the tale of Charlie Brough, an Irish emigré to America. In his new home, Brough rose rapidly through the ranks of a coal mining operation, ingratiating himself with the owner, marrying his employer's daughter, and gaining considerable financial standing. These accomplishments gained little respect from fellow miners, however, who felt Brough advanced at the expense of his working-class mates. Brough began as a strikebreaker—a scab—and violated union principles thereafter. The author advised workers not to follow the blackleg's path and betray their workmates, but rather to join unions and to forego economic advance.[18]

Song-poets chronicling mining disasters also employed the ballad format, which proved ideal for giving extended detailed descriptions of these events and the community's response. Two ballads, for example, materialized after the catastrophic Avondale mining disaster in 1869. That calamity left 110 miners dead, some of them children; convinced many of owners' disregard for human life; and remained a vivid collective memory for decades to come. Miners and their families regularly recalled the event by singing "The Avondale Mine Disaster" or the "Avondale Disaster," both of which described the accident and detailed the reaction of mothers, children, bystanders, and community residents.[19]

A similar ballad format could also be adapted for recounting strikes. During the 1875 strike of the Miners' and Laborers' Benevolent Association an anonymous writer issued a broadside:

> Come all you jolly colliers, wherever you may be,
> I pray you will attention give and listen unto me,
> I have a doleful tale, and to relate it I will strive—
> About the great suspension in Eighteen seventy-five.

Appropriately titled "The Long Strike," the song-poem continued by briefly explaining the miners' plight and their betrayal by "blacklegs."[20]

While "The Long Strike" recorded events of meaning for participants, its opening lines bear remarkable likeness to broadside openings centuries before. More than a century earlier English audiences heard hawkers sing the opening for "The Courtier and the Jovial Tinker":

> All you that jovial tinkers are,
>   Come and listen unto me;
> I dream'd a dream that was so rare,
> That none to it can e'er compare,
>   No tinker such did see.[21]

Literally hundreds of early European broadsides began similarly, establishing the "come all ye" opening as a standard device in broadside ballads.[22]

It became a recognizable feature of many labor song-poems as well. The first stanza of "The Avondale Mine Disaster" petitioned the audience:

> Good Christians all, both great and small,
> I pray ye lend an ear,
> And listen with attention
> While the truth I will declare;
> When you hear this lamentation,
> It will cause you to weep and wail,
> About the suffocation,
> In the mines of Avondale.[23]

Even non-narrative labor song-poems featured the "come all ye" address. An anonymous didactic that counseled iron molders to be thrifty began

> Come all you hardy molders, who work along the floor
> To keep the howling wolf from humble cottage door,
> And listen to a brother, who with kind intent
> Presumes to offer you advice, and take it as 'tis meant.[24]

Finally, when on worker sought to garner support for a single industrial union of railroad workers, he elicited others' attention with a clichéd opening:

> Come all ye men of the O.R.C.
>    And listen to my lay
> I represent the other crowd
>    The house across the way.[25]

In broadside ballads and folk songs the borrowing of phrases had a musical counterpart in the practice of taking the melody of one song and applying it to another. Tunes, like some texts, passed from one generation to the next, sometimes entering oral tradition. They might become identified with one song; transferred to another, or several other, songs; or evolve into a number of variant tune forms. In an era that had no copyrights, tunes moved freely.

Song-poems proved unexceptional in this regard. Song-poets seeking tunes for their works took them from folk songs, hymns, and a variety of other sources. During the 1880s, for example, the authors of the labor song-poem "Friends of Freedom" borrowed the tune of "Bruce's Address," a popular folk song in England and the United States and the melody for a number of folk hymns. The tune's immediate origins date to Robert Burns's famous poem "Bannockburn," also referred to by the titles "Wallace's Address" or "Bruce's Address." Appropriately, Burns modeled his poem after a traditional Scottish bagpipe air known as "Caledonia," which had surfaced in Scotland as early as 1500. By adapting a folk tune that had long been part of oral tradition, the authors of "Friends of Freedom" perpetuated, though perhaps unconsciously, cultural traditions.[26]

T. H. Walton employed a tune with a similar history for "My Safety Lamp." The tune, "Let Us Haste to Kelvin Grove," first appeared in print as the tune for "Kelvin Water" in R. A. Smith's 1824 songster *The Scottish Minstrel*. Smith's lyrics celebrated the beauty of Kelvin Grove, located near Glascow. However, neither tune nor text could have been wholly original: a song by the same name had circulated in Scotland for decades to the tune of the folk song "O the Shearin's No for You," which, with its own text, had been in oral tradition even longer. Walton had obviously been no more original than R. A. Smith, and both had served as agents of tradition even as they transformed it.[27]

Among floating tunes, hymns enjoyed great popularity. Hymn tunes could serve diverse texts, both sacred and secular, including labor song-poems. For example, when the Tallmadges and two other writers used "The Wearing of the Green" as the tune for their song-poems, they had chosen one of America's best-known folk songs. The "Wearing" originated in Ireland, quickly entered oral tradition, and spawned numerous variants. Long before the Civil War it became established in the U.S. and its tune was adopted for folk spirituals, some of which had already been in oral tradition for some time.[28] Likewise, "O That Will Be Joyful" had been so popular as an evangelical hymn that one scholar recently located versions of the hymn's chorus in forty-seven different antebellum songbooks. Fittingly, the hymn's tune made its way to M. A. Dalbey's Knights of Labor standard "Opening Ode."[29]

Dalbey and many others adapted traditional tunes because few had formal music training. Song-poets such as Charles Haynes or Henry Butler, both of whom earned their livelihoods as musicians, were rare. For that reason writers who desired to hear workers sing discovered a simple but effective method: borrowing familiar tunes. Moreover, listeners benefitted by not having to spend time learning a new melody. However, the technique could not have been used had song-poets and workers not been steeped in broadside and folk song traditions.

Neither workers nor song-poets, however, lived in a historical vacuum. Song-poets' contemporary environment, including the workplace itself, exerted great influence on song-poetry, illuminating some of the forces acting on the working class as a whole in the Gilded Age.

Of the more contemporary influences, a few are very specific. For example, in the decades after 1840 the middle class increasingly chose sentimental parlor songs, performed in a private space, as a badge of class identity, but workers lent their support to the unabashedly public music of the minstrel show.[30] As if the embodiment of the working-class "life apart," minstrelsy stood midway between folk music and tin pan alley, promulgating an urban, democratic, libertarian message; reflecting working-class anxieties and racial prejudices; and simultaneously subverting and reinforcing the existing order.[31] No doubt workers accepted the racial ideology minstrelsy disseminated as it lampooned bourgeois values at the expense of black Americans. Certainly minstrelsy received a warm welcome from the nation's working-class population, whose first taste of consumerism often came with the minstrel show.

The use of minstrel tunes for labor song-poems therefore cannot be considered surprising. Song-poets borrowed traditional and religious tunes in greater numbers, but minstrel songs proved adaptable too. The anonymous writer of "South Halstead Street Strike" in 1880, for example, took the tune of George Knauff's 1851 minstrel hit "Wait for the Wagon."[32] Also, the tune from "De Boatman's Dance," written by the famous Daniel Decatur Emmett in 1843, served as the tune for an 1878 B. M. Lawrence song-poem.[33] Lawrence and others also found the tunes of Stephen Foster's 1848 classic "Oh! Susanna" and his famous 1852 composition "Massa's in de Cold, Cold Ground" useful for a number of labor song-poems.[34] In addition, in 1873 William Joice borrowed the tune of the minstrel favorite "Josiphus Orange Blossom" for his "That's So."[35]

No less conspicuous than minstrel tunes were the tunes of Civil War songs.[36] Workers comprised the majority of Union troops during the war and came into contact daily with songs written to capitalize on the market created by the war. Moreover, workers absent from the battle zones found themselves bombarded by these songs since new ones appeared almost daily to fill demand. In fact, during the war, publishers made record profits, which provided the necessary impetus for the music business to lay the foundation of a mass culture industry that emerged later in the century.

Combining both martial and religious spirit, war songs made ideal candidates for labor song-poem tunes. The most famous song of the era, "John Brown's Body" (or "The Battle Hymn of the Republic"), for example, appeared as the tune for seven labor song-poems between 1870 and 1890.[37] George Root's "Tramp, Tramp, Tramp" proved even more popular. From 1865 to 1887 the song's tune became a standard choice for writers, who used it for eleven song-poems.[38] Three songs by anti-slavery, pro-northern composer Henry Clay Work had their tunes transferred to nine labor song-poems in the 1880s.[39] And the melody from Walter Kittredge's "Tenting on the Old Camp Ground" surfaced in an 1890 song-poem.[40]

Not all the specific influences on song-poetry claimed the plebeian status of war songs or the working-class credentials of minstrelsy. "High culture" left a mark on song-poetry also. Editors of

English-language labor publications regularly reprinted the works of Whitman, Whittier, Pope, Shelley, and Keats; and readers and writers could hardly escape their influence entirely. Some needed no prodding. Shandy Maguire, for example, occasionally felt compelled to write song-poems paying homage to writers he considered great masters and to mimic the language and style of Burns, Keats, and Shelley. His "Illustrious Guests" amounted to nothing more than name-dropping as Maguire informed readers of his literary debt to everyone from Moore to "Bobbie Burns" to Swift, Goldsmith, Dante, Cowper, Lowell, Milton, Hood, Poe, and Whittier, as well as Bret Harte, Eliza Cook, Leigh Hunt, Jean Ingelow, and Kipling![41] Unlike many British working-class song-poets, however, Maguire never severed his ties with fellow workers or organized labor.[42] Moreover, the fact that one of his song-poems—a work that reads more like a broadside ballad than "Bobbie Burns"—entered oral tradition cautions us against exaggerating the influence of high literature on worker song-poets.[43]

The Germans, whether socialist, trade unionist, or anarchist, were another matter altogether. Implicitly, and often explicitly, they sometimes supported a position akin to elitism supplemented by cultural chauvinism, as if German high culture offered an alternative to the one offered by American capitalism. No one could argue about a rich heritage of socially relevant German poetry. Poets Karl Beck, Georg Herwegh, Heinrich Heine, and Ferdinand Freiligrath mixed political themes and poetic skill in the social lyrics they popularized in Germany between 1830 and 1850.[44] Emigrés, especially "brainworkers" heading the labor movement, could thus hardly be blamed for choosing such mentors as models. What's more, Karl Marx himself had evoked scant sympathy for any work that evolved from folk roots and preferred that politically oriented writers look to Goethe, Shakespeare, Balzac, Heine, Dante, and Cervantes as exemplars.[45] German-American song-poets knew their audience better than Marx, however, and as much as they employed elements of elite writers in song-poems and other cultural endeavors—and sought to introduce workers to the best writers of the day, including American ones—they also regarded song-poetry as a tool for consciousness raising. Song-poets could be simple, direct, and unpretentious, as the song-poems of Gustav Lyser, Michael Schwab, Ludwig Lessen, and Robert Reitzel demonstrate. Such authors generated carefully written but easily understood works full of crafty sarcasm, wit, irony, allegory, and satire. At the same time, they might also call upon their knowledge of bourgeois literature, German or American, as well.[46]

Minstrelsy, war songs, and literary canons constituted important contemporary influences on song-poetry. Their influence, however, never compared with that of the antebellum reform movements. During those years, the spirit of reform soared to new heights, fueled largely by the evangelical energy and perfectionist enthusiasm of the Second Great Awakening. Reform groups proliferated, encompassing causes as diverse as aid to the impoverished, temperance, women's rights, antislavery, monetary reform, improved health and diet, and utopian socialism. Convinced of the ability of humans to change their lives and intent on mixing faith and activism, individuals in such groups set out to remake the world. Like all of the offspring of evangelical Protestantism and revivalism, they would sing as they did so.

Few Americans could escape the reformers or their music. Workers remained skeptical of reformers because they exuded a middle-class cant and anti-working-class overtones. However, the causes of reform and labor were not necessarily exclusive. Those who sought to build a new world often found themselves attracted to the working-class cause, viewing it as an opportunity to make a truly more just, equal, nonexploitative, democratic society. Their move into labor's camp seemed logical and the working-class cause the most promising effort toward perfectionism writ large on the world. Moreover, many workers who balked at supporting most antebellum reform did not go untouched by either its general message or its music. When organized labor regrouped at the end of the Civil War, more than one commentator noticed the continuity between antebellum reform and the movement for workers.

Certainly continuity existed in song-poetry. Labor song-poets, after all, had not been the first to establish original song-poetry as a vital element of social movements. Antebellum reformers provided ample precedent, making the singing and writing of song-poems a central feature of their activities. Within the spiritualist movement, the last major reform movement prior to the war and the most underrated and least understood, song-poetry occupied a key place. The two major publications of the movement, *Herald of Progress* and *Banner of Light*, featured original song-poems in almost every issue alongside the essays and reports on temperance, Owenism, clairvoyance, women's rights, homeopathology, spirit mediums, and social harmony. Song-poets such as Cora Wilburn, Lizzie Doten, Mary Davis, and Francis Osgood became recognized

figures in the movement and among the nation's most prominent song-poets. The *Herald of Progress* went so far as to include
a "New Music" column to report on recent compositions of use
to members. Advertisements and announcements commonly appeared on new spiritualist songbooks.

That spiritualists and the working-class cause had anything in
common would seem doubtful. Spiritualism had at its core an exaggerated faith in the power of the human mind to influence the
behavior of individuals and society. The *Herald of Progress* and the
*Banner of Light* featured columns in which readers recounted their
mentally transmitted correspondence with other spiritualists.
However, the movement had a more grounded side as well, as the
*Banner of Light*'s move toward criticism of capitalism and sympathy with organized labor testified. Many spiritualists came to
view capitalism as a source of injustice and a major obstacle to a
more humane world. Just as slavery, the established church, and
the liquor trade impaired social and spiritual progress, so too did
capitalism.[47]

Such logic no doubt propelled many reformers to support labor.
In the case of song-poetry clear links existed between the two.
Many reform song-poets, for example, had their works reprinted in
the labor press. The song-poems of Cora Wilburn and Lizzie Doten
appeared regularly. After the Civil War some spiritualist song-
poets moved directly into organized labor. In the 1860s, B. M.
Lawrence lectured and sang on Christianity and spiritualism, and
contributed song-poems to *The Spiritual Harp*. A decade later he
would be stumping the country for greenbacks and labor while
also writing labor song-poems.[48] Similarly, J. O. Barrett from Sycamore, Illinois, contributed song-poems to *The Spiritual Harp* and
edited the second edition of the spiritualist text, only to surface as
a labor song-poet in the 1870s.[49] Perhaps the most interesting and
surprising example, however, was Dyer Lum. Lum has long been
known for his role in the Chicago anarchist movement. Few would
guess that he cut his philosophical and political eye teeth in the
spiritualist movement, and by 1886 he probably never bothered to
disclose that part of his past. Lum's name appeared in the 1860s
attached to essays on spiritualism in the *Banner of Light*. The
mystical quality that pervaded his later song-poems can thus be
traced to spiritualism rather than to anarchist insight.[50]

The links of reform and labor song-poetry involved more than
spiritualism. A. J. H. Duganne never sympathized with spiritualism, but he did embrace social reform prior to the Civil War and
became a prolabor song-poet. Duganne's reputation as an Ameri-

can literary figure developed from his hyper-patriotic verse and his pulp adventure stories. Duganne's democratic sensibilities, however, led him to fight for organized labor. In the 1850s his song-poetry already enjoyed a large following among workingmen's organizations. Duganne's antebellum song-poem "Acres and Hands" became one of the most popular labor song-poems of the Gilded Age and editors would reprint the work continuously. He continued to support labor in the postbellum years, as he joined the Knights of Labor and wrote song-poems on their behalf.[51]

The reform-labor association extended to other areas as well. The tunes of reform song-poems, for example, might be borrowed by labor song-poets, as happened with the famed Hutchinson family's "The Good Time Coming" or A. Cull and R. P. Clark's "Marching Along," both of which emerged from abolitionism.[52] In addition, labor songbooks bear close resemblance to those of antebellum reform. Horace Waters's *Golden Harp* and *Harp of Freedom*, for example, can be distinguished from the songsters of Reuber and the Tallmadges only by lyrics.[53] The *Golden Harp*, ostensibly a revival-missionary songster, sold for twenty cents, counted two hundred songs and hymns, included original music by famous hymnologist Lowell Mason, employed Stephen Foster tunes, and sandwiched a host of antislavery songs in its pages. Similarly, his *Harp of Freedom* sold for five cents, included antislavery hymns and more narrowly religious hymns, and provided some accompaniment but often gave only tune title. Moreover, like the labor songsters, Waters's songsters could fit in someone's pocket. Their similarity to labor songsters indicates that labor song-poets did not rely only on archaic traditions when they wrote and compiled songsters. The songsters of antebellum reform probably served as a more immediate influence, a mediating device at the interface of broadside tradition and an emerging working class. If only on the level of song-poetry, Gilded-Age workers carried the legacy of antebellum reform even as a more distant intellectual past continued to wield its influence.[54]

The distinctive character of labor song-poetry, however, derived from the experience of song-poets within a capitalist society. Working-class song-poets altered traditions to conform to the needs of labor and thus refashioned the song-poem into a indigenous cultural creation. These creations never entirely lost those qualities gained from the transclass influences of tradition and reform, and never achieved the status of what some historians have termed "autonomous" culture. Labor song-poems and movement culture never became entirely self-generating or holistic. They did, however, offer an alternative that had a working-class flavor, a quality derived from the material reality of the lives of the nation's workforce.

Song-poets themselves offer evidence of song-poetry's class character. The majority of labor song-poets came from working-class backgrounds. In contrast, few who wrote folk songs or broadsides belonged to the working class because their society remained primarily rural and pre-industrial. Moreover, broadsides may have been street literature, but few who populated the streets contributed to their content. Not until the nineteenth century did broadside writers emerge from the working class—a reflection of improved education, literacy, and political organization among workers. Minstrelsy, war songs, and reform song-poems differed somewhat in this regard: some workers became performers in minstrel shows. Few composers from the antebellum period, however, rose from the working class, and popular music remained the preserve of middle-class composers. The fact that workers commonly wrote labor song-poems must therefore be judged phenomenal. Observing a similar phenomenon among French workers, William Sewell described it as near miraculous, given the cultural and economic constraints workers faced.[55]

More than the class background of writers separates labor song-poetry from its predecessors. Those devices and elements adopted from broadsides and folk songs did not escape the impact of the working class and capitalism. For example, in labor ballads recounting strikes, disasters, and scabbing, writers employed a working-class setting and perspective quite different from folk songs or broadsides. Song-poets described strikes as a form of working-class protest directed toward capitalist foes and portrayed protest as an action with special relevance for workers. Also, labor song-poets evinced scant interest in writing sensational stories with potential for broad appeal and mass sales. While broadside writers sought the widest possible market in order to increase sales, labor writers directed their accounts to the working-class community and reported certain events that held important consequences for the community.

This perspective extended to the distribution of song-poems as well. These works rarely circulated outside the labor movement or the working-class community. Labor papers, songsters, and broadsides—the primary mechanisms for distribution—reached a predominantly working-class market. Writers perceived this fact, so even talented writers such as Poet Mulhall never ventured to sell works outside coal camps. Mulhall's song-poems told stories and addressed issues important to miners and families with whom he had lived and to whom he gave his support. His reputation grew from his ability to write song-poems meaningful to workers. Mulhall's consciousness had been shaped by his own experiences as a miner and a member of coal-miner communities. Unlike the writer or hawker of broadsides, he saw no need to distribute his works among non-working-class groups.

Mulhall was no captive product of the heritage he drew upon; he became a skillful synthesizer of tradition and a mind-set formed in the Pennsylvania coal fields. "Thomas Duffy," written during the Molly Maguire affair, offers evidence of his adaptive and creative skills.[56] The work included many traditional features: a ballad account of the hanging and related events; a single-sheet broadside, containing neither tune nor score, printed by a local printer; and street-hawking as a means of distribution. Mulhall even employed the clichéd come-all-ye opening:

> Come all ye true-born Irishmen wherever you may be
> I hope you will pay attention and listen unto me,
> Concerning ten brave Irishmen, all in their youthful bloom,
> Who died in Pennsylvania on the twenty-first of June.

The anthracite fields left their mark on Mulhall, however, and the song-poem reflected this fact as well. Obviously the author had no inclination simply to recall an event pertinent or salable to most Pennsylvania residents. The episode had the suspense, drama, and intrigue of a good broadside, but for Irish immigrants, miners, and organized labor, Mulhall's ballad touched an emotional nerve because the Maguire affair arose from the intense class conflict of the industry and the owners' cabalistic maneuvers to crush the nascent organization of Irish miners. Colliers and their families understood that the "true-born Irishmen" beckoned by Mulhall worked in the collieries and that the "ten brave Irishmen" hanged by the state had been murdered because they fought for miners' rights. Duffy, the central figure in the song-poem, earned the admiration of Mulhall and miners for his heroic deeds, and the song-poet portrayed him as valiant and courageous at death. Miners no doubt felt moved as Mulhall recounted Duffy's claim to innocence and divine favor, and his final words on the just character of the centuries-long struggle of the Irish.

A song-poem such as "Thomas Duffy" could not have been written prior to the rise of industrial capitalism and a large wage-earning class. Even the industrial revolution proved no guarantee that song poems sympathetic to labor would emerge. Broadsides from the nineteenth century reported murders, robberies, witchcraft, heroism, patriotism, and romance.[57] Sentimental and romantic ballads and song sheets about wars, heros, patriotism, gold miners, fires, immigration, and prize fighters proved popular between 1850 and 1870.[58] Finally, in the Gilded Age, the developing pop music industry discovered the parlor song, with themes of morality, death, and romance, and it soon became its staple.[59] Of course, broadsides addressing issues relevant to workers occasionally did appear outside labor circles. The major ideological debates of the revolutionary era found outlet in broadsides and pamphlets and even involved song-poems. Thomas Paine and others employed song-poems to state their case to the public, especially the increasingly politicized artisan sector.[60] Neither Paine nor less notable comrades, however, employed the perspective of the citizen worker. That waited until the rise of industry and the experiences of workers within the environment.

The largely public character of song-poetry distinguished it from most middle-class cultural music, poetry, and entertainment of the day. Mulhall, McGovern, or Maguire never imagined their works would be performed or enjoyed in a private setting akin to that of the middle-class parlor. While the daughters of the middle class tinkered away on the piano at the latest sentimental parlor song or lyric ballad—and the family sat in idle reverie—labor song-poets wrote for other audiences. Mulhall would walk the streets of coal camps singing his latest work and hawking his compositions; song-poets such as Maguire and McGovern would stand before countless audiences to declaim their work; Knights of Labor meetings around the country resounded to the strains of "Hold the Fort"; and countless labor groups featured vocal and instrumental labor music in their parades. This did not mean song-poets and song-poetry had a function exclusively public in nature. However, compared to the increasingly privatized forms of music and entertainment favored by the middle class, labor song-poetry appears boisterously public.

Whatever the origins of this public cant, certain general settings proved particularly conducive to song-poetry and the process whereby writers recast tradition in working-class garb and song-poetry took on a working-class life of its own. As Mulhall shows, the mining population of the eastern coal fields made song-poetry into a working-class art form. Miners detached song-poems from their ethnic roots and reshaped them to the colliery setting.

George Korson observed this fact while doing field work in the 1930s. Referring to ethnic traditions Korson said, "The bituminous miner did not merely transmit things learned in childhood." Rather, miners "created a culture of their own from inner resources playing upon everyday experiences."[61] Not that Korson denied the weight of ethnicity. He noted that black, Scottish, Slavic, and Mexican traditions shaped song-poetry and emphasized the "Celtic flavor" of song-poetry. Initially, according to Korson, miners found inspiration in their ethic past. Welsh miners turned to the melodies and meters of their native hymns and folk songs, and the works of Irish miners echoed the fiddle tunes, folk songs, and come-all-ye openings of Irish tradition.[62]

Welsh miners imported traditional musical events from the homeland. The *Gymnfa Ganu*, a gathering of the community for the singing of traditional hymns, surfaced in the United States at the beginning of the nineteenth century. At about the same time, miners also introduced the famous *Eisteddfod*. This event functioned as the pivot of Welsh communal life and tied miners to the ancient festival and competition in Wales. Massive crowds gathered to hear songs, poetry, prose, instrumental composition, and elocution at the local and regional levels. Only the best competitors advanced to international competition in Wales, but those who won even the local bard's crown gained tremendous status in the community.

Miners coveted the crown as more than an ethnic honor, however. In the United States, for example, the *Eisteddfod* turned into every bit as much a working-class and miners' festival as an ethnic one. Welsh miners in Pennsylvania established the event and became its chief organizers and competitors. For decades nearly all the competitions took place in anthracite and bituminous regions, and miners always wore the bard's crown. The title became synonymous with coal mining. Only when a significant portion of the Welsh population became middle class did the festival lose its class connotations, and when that happened—as in the massive *Eisteddfod* held at the Columbian Exposition in 1896 under the aegis of the Welsh National Cymrodorian Society—the festival's demise followed shortly.[63]

That workers might develop traditions of their own should not surprise us. As early as the eighteenth century, before gentlemen folklorists judged them quaint repositories of tradition, British workers counted "worker poets" in their ranks. Hardly immune from the influence of the printed word, these workers proved pragmatic synthesizers who borrowed from whatever songs and poems they heard, including the latest broadsides.[64] British miners held song-poetry in great esteem, elevating men like Tommy Armstrong to the status of "the pitman's poet," expecting them to compose song-poems for every disaster and strike, and organizing formal and informal competitions between bards. Such practices continued into the twentieth century and remind us of the distance between miners and the British bourgeoisie. Commentators spoke of the miners' near "mania for rhymes and nicknames," and in 1952 an octogenarian pitman recalled: "Making rhymes and songs used to run through the pit like a fever. Some of 'em seemed to go daft thinking up verses. Even us young lads used to answer back in rhyme."[65]

American miners, and workers in general, thus had ample working-class precedent for composition. By the postbellum years miners busily made up their own song-poems by adapting diverse traditions and utilizing the inspiration of their own surroundings. Among miners, the urge to compose, like their British predecessors, reached fever pitch—so much so that, according to Korson, "From the Civil War to the first decade of the present century, no patch or town escaped the fever of improvising or composing songs, ballads, ditties, and doggerel of some phase or another of the mining theme. Unlettered mine workers seem to have gone daft thinking, talking, writing, and singing in measured and rhymed sentences."[66]

Miners who composed had little training for the craft, but had keen eyes and ears and an instinct for subjects that appealed to the community. Most learned by doing, students of oral tradition. They borrowed tunes at random and performed wherever and whenever opportunity arose—spontaneous gatherings, front porches, saloons, mines, festivals, union meetings. The most gifted showed great proficiency in improvisation, while others labored over words and notes. No one denied the value of the effort, since coal camps from Virginia to Iowa referred to at least one resident bard whom they revered as if annointed. Miners judged these talents so special that they bestowed the coveted title on not only Anglos but Slavs and Afro-Americans also. The chosen bards served as the miners' voice, detailing the joys and sorrows of miners, including strikes and disasters, in song-poem form.

Local minstrels contributed to this process as well. They might even be called upon to serve as bards because they possessed both musical and compositional talents. As they traversed the countryside, offering tunes, songs, ballads, and stories to eager coal-camp audiences, the peripatetic minstrels often acted as the migrant voice of miners' consciousness. Many became regional favorites with reputations that lasted long after their deaths.[67] Their work, and that of more sedentary bards, might be recalled for decades to come. Thomas Morgan's 1870 composition "The Sliding Scale" was remembered by a miner's widow as late as 1938.[68] Similarly, in 1936 WPA collectors located coalfield residents who still recalled the strike song-poem "Coal Creek."[69] George Korson located legions of song-poems circulating in oral tradition among miners in the early twentieth century. As Korson aptly perceived, among American miners song-poets had long since transcended the limits of traditions and developed a vibrant song-poetry of their own.[70]

Nor were miners the only ones gone daft with song-poetry. Readers of the *Cooper's Journal* apparently suffered a similar mania, for editor Martin Foran threatened to send song-poems to authors' sweethearts if they did not stop submitting so many to his office.[71] Many years later, Terence Powderly informed one interviewer that Knights of Labor headquarters were deluged with verse sent from member workers.[72] No doubt some of it came from iron molders and puddlers, who, between 1865 and 1890, became among the most skilled song-poets. With Pittsburgh as their center, iron and steel workers developed a thriving community of worker song-poets and a welcome audience. Undoubtedly, like other occupations nurturing song-poetry, iron and steel workers rooted their works in traditions; song-poets could not have escaped the influence of Pittsburgh's countless ethnic groups. And yet these song-poems' fundamental working-class character grew out of workers' everyday experiences. Pittsburgh song-poems were born of the city's bitter wage and class conflict, and song-poets spoke as representatives of workers and their union lodges.

Jacob Evanson observed the city's song-poets in a capacity not unlike that of coal-miner bards.[73] Almost every union local had its own song-poet who composed strike, disaster, and lockout ballads as well as work on more mundane topics. Molder and puddler bards gained respect and adoration from rank-and-file workers and were repeatedly called upon to write and present new works. A host of song-poets—Billy Jenkins, Reese Lewis, Sylvester Sullivan, and Ed Lambert—became recognizable features at local labor gatherings. None, however, matched Michael McGovern, the Puddler Poet, as workers affectionately dubbed him. McGovern symbolized the strength of indigenous worker song-poetry in his adopted hometown. No one ever referred to him as a Catholic or Irish poet, despite the unmistakable influence of both on his work. Instead, he received a title indicative of his working-class background and reminiscent of the most critical factor in his work. Only a body of workers with their own dynamic brand of working-class song-poetry could have conferred such an honor on a song-poet. Evidence of that fact can be found in the comment of a workmate on McGovern's death in 1933. McGovern's former union and workplace comrade Roger Evans remarked that his friend's song-poems circulated in the city's mills until their pages became tattered and illegible. According to Evans, "Many were those who memorized the poems and could repeat them as readily as the author himself."[74]

Evans's comments reveal the deep commitment and attachment that workers might feel toward labor song-poems and song-poets. They reveal as well that labor song-poems became more than the sum total of the influence of traditional elements plus minstrelsy, war songs, high culture, and the antecedent reform song-poetry. Certainly the labor song-poem was a hybrid creation. This combination in itself, however, would have had only limited appeal, touching workers' non-working-class emotions only and never speaking to their own class concerns. Such works would have read like imitations of the best-sellers of the day or the traditional works of the past. McGovern and other song-poets, however, contributed works with a working-class imprint.

Figuratively, their works were built on a foundation of traditional and transclass elements and a more contemporary superstructure of working-class experience. The traditional elements imparted some essential features to the labor song-poem—everything from folk tunes, to ballad form, to pocket-size songbooks. From the contemporary working-class experience, song-poetry derived its unique and distinguishing features—from the large percentage of working-class song-poets, to the settings or contexts in which song-poems were sung, recited, and declaimed, to transformation of traditional and antebellum song-poetry elements into tools to advance workers' causes, to the topics and subjects reflecting workers' concerns, to a general perspective that bore faint resemblance to earlier reform song-poetry or the popular works of the day.

## NOTES

1. For a useful review of such materials, see Leslie Shepard, *The History of Street Literature* (Devon, England: David and Charles, 1973); quote on 50.

2. Victor Neuberg, Introduction to John Ashton, *Chap-Books of the Eighteenth Century* (Welwyn Garden City, Hertfordshire, England: Seven Dials Press, 1969), 6, 7-10.

3. Leslie Shepard, *The Broadside Ballad: A Study in Origins and Meaning* (Hatboro, Penn.: Folklore Associates, 1962), 22.

4. Harry B. Weiss, *A Book About Chapbooks: The People's Literature of Bygone Years* (Hatboro, Penn.: Folklore Associates, 1969), 31-34.

5. A sampling of broadside-ballad texts appears in John Ashton, *Chap-Books.*

6. Shepard, *Broadside Ballad,* 26; Wilgus, *Anglo-American Folksong Scholarship,* 430-31.

7. Shepard, *Broadside Ballad,* 27.

8. Wilgus, *Anglo-American Folksong Scholarship,* 437. See also G. Malcolm Laws, Jr., *American Balladry from British Broadsides* (Philadelphia: American Folklore Society, 1957), 39-48.

9. On printers, publishers, and hawkers, see Shepard, *Street Literature,* 51-106.

10. Ibid., 21.

11. Foner, *American Labor Songs,* 11-13.

12. Andrew Wall, "The General Strike," in Foner, *American Labor Songs,* 130-32.

13. E. R. Place, "The Workingman's Train," *Labor Standard* (Paterson), 28 July 1878. See Foner, *American Labor Songs,* 132-34.

14. Budd Harris, "Knights of Labor," in Foner, *American Labor Songs,* 148-49.

15. For a brief biographical sketch of Poet Mulhall, see Korson, *Minstrels of the Mine Patch,* 294-95. Three of Mulhall's song-poems also appear in that volume: "Thomas Duffy," 254, 265-67; "Muff Lawler, the Squealer," 267-68; and "Lost Creek," 42, 53-54.

16. Only E. R. Place provided the tune for his song-poem. His 1871 work borrowed the tune from the popular song "Old Dan Tucker."

17. David Vincent has recently argued the case for the impact of "literature" on workers throughout the eighteenth century and for the interaction between oral and written forms among workers from 1700 onward. Long before the collectors discovered the "folk," according to Vincent, chapbooks and "worker poets" enjoyed popularity among workers. See David Vincent, "The Decline of the Oral Tradition in Popular Culture," in Storch, *Popular Culture and Custom,* 20-47. For a similar argument, though for a somewhat later period, see Diane M. Dugaw, "Anglo-American Folksong Reconsidered: The Interface of Oral and Written Forms," *Western Folklore* 43 (April 1984): 83-103.

18. Johnny Cash, "The Blacklegs," *National Labor Tribune,* 5 April 1879. For a similar ballad, see Michael McGovern, "The Fall of Abel Cain," *National Labor Tribune,* 13 December 1890. The biblical allusion in the title, and the main character, seems clear. See also Anon., "The Scab and the Ghost," *Cooper's Journal* 2 (September 1871): 356-57. The song-poem recounts the story of a disreputable scab cooper named Sandy

McGee who begged to join the union after union coopers subjected him to a charivari. On workers and charivaris, see Bryan Palmer, "Discordant Music: Charivaris and Whitecapping in Nineteenth-Century North America," *Labour/Le Travailleur* 3 (1978): 5-62. Among British miners anti-scab broadsides also appeared. See "First Drest Man of Seghill" (1831), in Martha Vicinus, *Broadsides of the Industrial North* (Newcastle upon Tyne: Frank Graham, n.d.), plate 20.

19. "The Avondale Mine Disaster" and "Avondale Disaster" both appear in Korson, *Minstrels of the Mine Patch,* 189-91, 191-93. For examples of similar disaster song-poems, see "The Sugar Notch Entombment," 193; "The Mines of Locust Dale," 193-96; "The Twin-Shaft Mine Squeeze," 97-98; "The Miner's Doom," 203; and "The Miners' Fate," 198-99.

20. "The Long Strike," in Korson, *Songs and Ballads,* 160-62.

21. "The Courtier and the Jovial Tinker," in Weiss, *Book about Chapbooks,* 96.

22. See, for example, "Dr. John Faustus," in Shepard, *Street Literature,* 196. On "come all ye" openings in American broadside ballads, see Laws, *American Balladry,* 88-89.

23. Korson, *Minstrels of the Mine Patch,* 189-91. Of the nine disaster song-poems in that work, five begin with the "come all ye" opening.

24. William Powers, "Come All You Hardy Molders," *Iron Molders' Journal* (May 1883): 6.

25. W. V. S., "The Striking Appeal," *Railway Conductor's Monthly* 6 (June 1888): 278.

26. Anon., "Friends of Freedom," *Labor Enquirer* (Denver), 18 June 1887. For another labor song-poem with this tune, see Tallmadge, "Friends of Freedom," in *Labor Songs,* 23. On the history of "Bruce's Address," see Robert Guy McCutchan, *Hymn Tune Names, Their Sources and Significance* (New York: Abingdon Press,1957), 50-51, and Dorothy Horn, *Sing to Me of Heaven: A Study of Folk and Early American Materials in Three Old Harp Books* (Gainesville: University of Florida Press, 1970), 32. For a text of "Caledonia," see Gavin Grieg, *Folk-Song in Buchan and Folk-Song of the North-East* (Hatboro, Penn.: Folklore Associates, 1963), plate 77. On the tune's use in folk hymns in America, see George Pullen Jackson, *Another Sheaf of White Spirituals* (Gainesville: University of Florida Press, 1952).

27. T. H. Walton, "My Safety Lamp," *Workingman's Advocate,* 8 January 1870. On "Kelvin Grove" and its long history, see Alfred Moffat, *The Minstrelsy of Scotland* (London: Augener, n.d.), 108.

Other labor song-poems had tunes with similar histories. See Maurice Enright, "Poverty and Wealth," *Granite Cutters' Journal* 18 (February 1894): 1. On the history of its tune, "The Pretty Girl Milking Her Cow," see Minnie Earl Sears, *Song Index and Supplement* (New York: Shoestring Press, 1966), 83, 454. See also Mrs. Jacief, "Come Brothers All," *Truth,* 13 December 1882. On the history of its tune, "Royal Charlie," see Sears, *Song Index,* 400. Another song-poem by Mrs. Jacief, "The Land of Our

Fathers," *Truth*, 25 October 1882, used the tune from "The Harp of Tara," which first appeared in Thomas More's (1799-1852) famous collection of *Irish Melodies*. More employed the tune from a much older folksong known as "Gramachree" and based his lyrics on an ancient Irish folktale. On the history of "The Harp of Tara," see Charles Hamm, *Yesterdays: Popular Song in America* (New York: W. W. Norton, 1979), 44-60, and Theron Brown, *The Story of Hymns and Tunes* (Grand Rapids, Mich.: Zondervan Press), 328.

Three labor song-poems employed the tune "Red, White, and Blue." See Anon., "The Miners' Bewail and Expected Triumph," *United Mine Workers Journal* 1 (January 1891): 1; B. W. Goodhue, "The Hope of the Nation," in Tallmadge, *Labor Songs*, 12; and John Harden, "Eight Hours Is the Measure," *Knights of Labor*, 27 November 1886. On the history of the tune "Red, White, and Blue" in England and America, see Duncan Emrich, *American Folk Poetry* (Boston: Little, Brown and Company, 1974), 430-32. Emrich points out that the tune rapidly entered oral tradition in the United States.

In addition, see Thomas Selby's song-poem, "Knights of Labor," *Journal of United Labor* 6 (October 1885): 1122. Its tune, "The Men of Harloche," is described in Maurice Willson Disher, *Victorian Song* (London: Phoenix House, 1955), 80. Charles Cheesewright's "The Factory Girl," *Labor Enquirer* (Denver), 16 July 1887, used the tune from "The Orphan Boy," a German song brought to the United States and adapted to a number of other songs. The most widely known version of the latter in this country was "O Where, O Where." On the history of the latter, see Sigmund Spaeth, *Read 'Em and Weep* (Garden City: Doubleday, Doran, 1935), 28-29. B. M. Lawrence employed the tune from "Cork Leg," for his song-poem "The Greenback Yankee Medley," in *Greenback Songster*, 43. "Cork Leg" derived from an Irish song and became the tune for a number of popular nineteenth-century songs. On "Cork Leg," see Florence E. Brunnings, *Folk Song Index: A Comprehensive Guide to the Florence E. Brunnings Collection* (New York: Garland Publishing Co., 1981), 61.

28. James and Emily Tallmadge, "Our Ship of State," in Tallmadge, *Labor Songs*, 28. See also Anon., "Thirty Cents a Day," *Workingman's Advocate*, 19 November 1872, and Anon., "The Shout for Liberty," *Trades*, 13 September 1879. On the history of the tune "The Wearing of the Green," see Jackson, *Another Sheaf*, 75, 101.

29. On the tune "O That Will Be Joyful," see Ellen Jane Lorenz, *Glory Hallelujah: The Story of the Campmeeting Spiritual* (Nashville: Abingdon Press, 1978), 88. M. A. Dalbey, "Opening Ode," *Journal of United Labor* 1 (March 1880): 102.

30. For a review of minstrelsy and its relation to economic and social change in the United States, see Alexander Saxton, "Blackface Minstrelsy and Jacksonian Ideology," *American Quarterly* 27 (March 1975): 3-28.

31. For a sampling of minstrel songsters and compositions, see *The Comic Forget-Me-Not Songster* (New York: Philip Cozans, 1845) and *Fattie*

*Stewart's Comic Songster* (New York: Dick and Fitzgerald, 1863). Both evoke an obvious racist message mixed with a libertarian, anti-elitist, democratic one. The influence of "tradition" and of Irish-Americanisms seems clear as well.

32. Anon., "The South Halsted Street Strike," *Iron Molders' Journal* (February 1880): 8. On George Knauff's song "Wait for the Wagon," see Julius Mattfield, *Variety Music Cavalcade, 1620-1969* (Englewood Cliffs, N.J.: Prentice-Hall, 1971), 84, and Nicholas Tawa, *Sweet Songs for Gentle Americans: The Parlor Song in America, 1790-1860* (Bowling Green, Ohio: Bowling Green State University Popular Press, 1980), 99.

33. B. M. Lawrence, "Waiting for the Morning," in Lawrence, *Greenback Songster*, 44. On "De Boatman's Dance," see Mattfield, *Variety*, 63. Emmett's career and his contribution to music is best described in Nathan, *Dan Emmett*.

34. Labor song-poems with the tune "Oh, Susanna" include G. W. Drinkard, "The Bondholder and the Soldier," in Lawrence, *Greenback Songster*, 14; B. M. Lawrence, "Oh, Gold Gamblers," in Lawrence, *Greenback Songster*, 7; and T. H., "Song," *John Swinton's Paper*, 14 September 1884. "Massa's in de Cold, Cold Ground" is the tune for B. M. Lawrence, "Sleeping in the Cold Camp Ground," in Lawrence, *Greenback Songster*. Stephen Foster's music is surveyed in Charles Hamm, *Yesterdays*. On "Oh, Susanna" and "Massa," see Mattfield, *Variety*, 75, 87.

35. Locating information on "Josiphus Orange Blossom" is difficult. Minnie Earl Sears, *Song Index*, 164, lists it as a minstrel song. The tune surfaced in William Joice, "That's So," *Cooper's Journal* 4 (August 1873): 383.

36. The music industry and the Civil War's impact upon its development are described in Hamm, 232-39. See also Gilbert Chase, *America's Music: From the Pilgrims to the Present* (New York: McGraw-Hill, 1966), 179-80. For an indication of the tremendous number of broadsides distributed during the war, see Edwin Wolf II, *American Song Sheets, Slip Ballads and Poetical Broadsides 1850-1870: A Catalogue of the Collection of the Library Company of Philadelphia* (Philadelphia: Library Company of Philadelphia, 1963).

37. The origins of "John Brown's Body" and "The Battle Hymn of the Republic" are described in Mattfield, *Variety*, 109-11, and Hamm, *Yesterdays*, 236. Labor song-poems employing these tunes include Anon., "Interesting Meeting," *Critic*, 4 August 1888; Anon., "The March of the Workers," *Labor Leader*, 22 November 1890; Anon., "The New John Brown," *Labor Enquirer* (Denver), 10 April 1886; Beulah Brinton, "All Hail Labor Knights," 10 March 1886, *Powderly Papers*, Reel 14; William Creech, "Suggested for the Iron Molders Ball," *Iron Molders' Journal* (January 1880): 9; B. M. Lawrence, "Down with the Money King," in Lawrence, *Greenback Songster*, 13; and Tallmadge, "The Labor Battle Song," in Tallmadge, *Labor Songs*, 6.

38. The song "Tramp, Tramp, Tramp" and its authors are described in Mattfield, *Variety*, 118; Chase, *America's Music*, 179-80; and Hamm, *Yes-*

*terdays,* 232-34. The labor song-poems using the tune include Anon., "The Eight Hour Song," *Workingman's Advocate,* 7 March 1868; Anon., "The March of Labor," *Journal of United Labor* 8 (September 1887): 2482; Anon., "The Working Voters," *Workingman's Advocate,* 10 September 1870; E. A. Bacon, "Labor's Chorus," *Labor Enquirer* (Denver), 2 July 1887; C. N. Brown, "Eight Hour Song," *Socialist* (Fall River), 27 May 1876; H. A. Coffeen, "Labor's Emancipation," in Tallmadge, *Labor Songs,* 10; William Creech, "Eight Hours," *Iron Molders' Journal* (November 1880): 10; Charles Haynes, "Eight Hour Song," *Fincher's Trades Review,* 18 November 1865; H. Mount James, "We'll Battle for the Noble Cause of Labor," 24 October 1886; *Powderly Papers,* Reel 19; B. M. Lawrence, "Hope for the Toiling," *Boston Daily Evening Voice,* 10 October 1867; and Whitefield, "Workingman's Rallying Song," *Workingman's Advocate,* 9 November 1867.

39. Henry Clay Work's music and career is described in Hamm, *Yesterdays,* 232-34, and Chase, *America's Music,* 179-80. On the popularity of his music during this period, see the listings for "Battle Cry for Freedom" in Wolf, *American Song Sheets,* 7-8, 91, 131. Labor writers used the tunes of his "Battle Cry of Freedom," "Marching through Georgia," and "Kingdom Coming." Song-poems with "Battle Cry" as a tune include Charles Cheesewright, "Social Freedom," *Labor Enquirer* (Denver), 18 June 1887; Thomas Leahy, "Come Join the Knights of Labor," 19 May 1886, *Powderly Papers,* Reel 16; and James Tallmadge, "Labor Cry of Freedom," in Tallmadge, *Labor Songs,* 31. Song-poems using "Marching through Georgia" include J. O. Barrett, "Home Rule for Ireland," in Tallmadge, *Labor Songs,* 9; Edwin G. Brown, "The Workers Are Forming an Army," *John Swinton's Paper,* 31 July 1887; James Tallmadge, "The Battle Hymn," in Tallmadge, *Labor Songs,* 7; and W. Wiley, "Labor Free to All," in Tallmadge, *Labor Songs,* 20. The song-poem with "Kingdom Coming" as a tune was James Tallmadge, "The Runaway Banker," in Tallmadge, *Labor Songs,* 16.

40. On Walter Kittredge, an employee of the famous Oliver Ditson music publishing company, see Hamm, *Yesterdays,* 236-39, and Mattfield, *Variety,* 117. A labor song-poem using the tune "Tenting on the Old Camp Ground" was Anon., "Song of Brotherhood," *Labor Leader,* 22 November 1890.

41. Maguire, "Illustrious Ghosts," in his *Random Rhymes,* 398.

42. On British working-class song-poets in general, and the particular problems they had to endure when they achieved some success, see the informative study of Martha Vicinus, *The Industrial Muse: A Study of Nineteenth-Century British Working-Class Literature* (New York: Barnes and Noble, 1974).

43. Shandy Maguire's song-poem—not a labor song-poem, but a shipwreck song—entered oral tradition and was long considered a folk song. Norm Cohen, however, discovered Maguire as the author. See Cohen, "The Persian's Crew."

44. For a survey of early German poets whose work frequently dealt with social and political issues, see Solomon Liptzin, *Lyric Pioneers of*

*Modern Germany: Studies in German Social Poetry* (New York: Columbia University Press, 1928).

45. On Karl Marx's favorite writers, see Karl Marx and Friedrich Engels, *Literature and Art* (New York: International, 1947), 138-44.

46. For thoughtful analysis of German literature and song-poetry related to labor and socialism in Chicago and the United States, and a sampling of works from the period, see Keil and Jentz, *German Workers in Chicago*, "Culture of the Labor Movement" and "Literature," 221-99, 300-346.

47. By 1870 the *Banner of Light* regularly printed essays and editorials on the labor question in which it criticized capital, allied itself with workers, and expressed moderate support for organized labor.

48. On B. M. Lawrence's involvement in spiritualism, see the lecture notice, *Herald of Progress*, 1 September 1860; the lecturers list, *Banner of Light*, 26 September 1868; and notice for *The Spiritual Harp*, 10 October 1868. During the late 1860s and early 1870s his song-poems also began to appear in the *Workingman's Advocate* and *Boston Daily Evening Voice*.

49. On J. O. Barrett's spiritualist activities, see the *Banner of Light*, 13 March 1869. A notice for a new song he wrote appears and he is listed as a contributor to the *Spiritual Harp*. Also on 20 March 1869 in the *Banner of Light* he is listed as an editor for the second edition of the *Spiritual Harp*. One of his labor song-poems, "The Labor Battle Song," was regularly reprinted during the Gilded Age. See Tallmadge, *Labor Songs*, 6-7.

50. A Dyer Lum essay appeared in the *Banner of Light* at least as early as 26 September 1868, if not before, and thereafter Lum continued to write for that paper. According to Voltairine de Cleyre, in the introduction to Lum's compilation *In Memoriam*, Lum came from "an old Puritan family" and had been brought up a "strict" Presbyterian. In 1876 he supported Greenback-Labor efforts, then became a state socialist, and ultimately came to the side of anarchism. Lum also studied both the classics and Buddhism. That his interest in such matters as Buddhism and spiritualism never disappeared seems obvious from his song-poetry. See, for example, "On the Way to Jericho," in *In Memoriam*, 28-30. See also his *Social Problems of To-Day; or, The Mormon Question* (Port Jervis, N.Y.: Lum, 1886).

51. "Acres and Hands" originally appeared in A. J. H. Duganne's *Poetical Works*, 146. It reappeared in the labor press from 1860 to 1900. For a sampling of Duganne's work, see the following sections in his *Poetical Works*: "Year of the People—For the Heroes of '48 and the Martyrs of '49," 39-68; "The Gospel of Labor," 69-86; "The True Republic," 87-100; and "The Iron Harp," 101-156.

52. The Hutchinson family was a popular antislavery and reform singing group in the North in the antebellum and Civil War period. Unlike other antislavery or reform groups, they enjoyed a large working-class audience. No doubt their support of the working-class cause contributed to their popularity. "The Good Time Coming" was a regular part of their

repertoire for many years. The best source on the Hutchinsons is Joshua Hutchinson, *A Brief Narrative of the Hutchinson Family* (Boston: Lee and Shepard, 1874.) See the reference to "The Good Time Coming" on page 74 of that work.

"Marching Along" appears in the evangelical and antislavery songster by Horace Waters, *Waters' Golden Harp* (New York: Horace Waters, 1863), 34-35. Waters lists A. Cull as the composer of the music, and R. P. Clark as the lyricist.

53. Horace Waters, *Harp of Freedom*, pt. 1 (New York: Horace Waters, n.d.), and *Waters' Golden Harp*.

54. See also William Bradbury and Charles Sanders, *The Young Choir* (New York: Mark H. Newman, 1841); George Clark, *The Free Soil Minstrel* (New York: Martyn and Ely, 1848); and *The Clay Minstrel: or, National Songster* (New York: Greely and M'Elrath, 1844).

55. Sewell, *Work and Revolution in France*, 236-42.

56. Martin Mulhall's "Thomas Duffy" appears in Korson, *Minstrels of the Mine Patch*, 265-66.

57. On the topical orientation of nineteeth-century broadsides, see Emrich, *American Folk Poetry*; Laws, *American Balladry*; and Shepard, *Broadside Ballad*.

58. On the topical orientation of songs from 1850 to 1870, see Wolf, *American Song Sheets*, iii-vii.

59. The parlor song is discussed in Tawa, *Sweet Songs*, 141-48.

60. On broadsides of the American Revolution, see Bernard Bailyn, *Pamphlets of the American Revolution, 1750-1776* (Cambridge, Mass. Belknap Press, 1965). On Thomas Paine, see Eric Foner, *Thomas Paine and Revolutionary America* (London: Oxford University Press, 1976).

61. Korson, *Coal Dust on the Fiddle*, 20.

62. My discussion of the musical activities of miners derives largely from Korson, *Coal Dust on the Fiddle*, 3-28, and *Minstrels of the Mine Patch*, 1-12.

63. On the Welsh music festival held at the Columbia Exposition in 1893, see the program from the event: *Eisteddfod Gydenedlaethol* (Chicago: Cambria Printing Co., 1893). Little research has been conducted on Welsh mining-labor songs or the transfer of musical and other traditions from Wales to the United States. The most useful introduction to Welsh mining songs and poetry is the cassette recording of Walter Hayd Davies and Ivor Owen, *Mining Ballads and Pieces* (St. Fagans, Cardiff, Wales: Welsh Folk Museum, n.d.). I am indebted to D. Roy Saer, department head, National Museum of Wales, Welsh Folk Museum, for information on Welsh mining songs. Letter to author, 16 February 1981.

64. On early worker poets, see Vincent, "The Decline of the Oral Tradition." See also Vicinus, *The Industrial Muse*.

65. Colls, *Collier's Rant*, 51-52.

66. Korson, *Minstrels of the Mine Patch*, 5.

67. Korson, *Minstrels of the Mine Patch*, 389-402.

68. The original appears with Thomas Morgan's letter to the editor, "From Pennsylvania," *Workingman's Advocate*, 18 June 1870. See also "The Sliding Scale," Korson, *Songs and Ballads*, 165.

69. See "Coal Creek" in *Kentucky Folk Songs* (Louisville: Kentucky Federal Music Project—Works Progress Administration, 1936).

70. For example of the many works Korson found in oral circulation, see his three works, *Coal Dust on the Fiddle, Minstrels of the Mine Patch*, and *Songs and Ballads*.

71. Martin Foran in *Cooper's Journal* 3 (July 1872): 416.

72. Balch, "Songs for Labor," 11.

73. Evanson, "Folk Songs of an Industrial City."

74. Evanson, "Folk Songs of an Industrial City." 426.

# 4

# Song-Poems and
# the Republican Heritage

GILDED-AGE industry seemed to contemporaries to possess boundless powers of self-generation. Commentators in the popular press offered the public a cornucopic vision that industrial capitalism might realize. Yet even the most ardent cheerleaders sometimes felt slight misgivings—fears that industrial capitalists potentially threatened cherished democratic principles and institutions. Not only that, but some obvious intellectual maneuvering by apologists had to occur if capitalism's advance were to jibe with the popular belief that only those who worked for a living deserved the fruits of their labor. An uneasiness gnawed below the surface, as if the worlds of the Revolutionary forebears and Gilded-Age industrial magnates might not be compatible.

Mainstream commentators may have loathed to admit that capitalism did not measure up to the standards established by earlier generations, but some Americans equated such admission with patriotic duty. Farmers, for example, witnessed a precipitous decline in economic, political, and social status as the northern bourgeoisie triumphed. Many would not take their loss lightly and concluded that capitalism made a sham of the Republic and democracy, and robbed farmers of the wealth they had created. Strong criticism emerged from agriculture's ranks, particularly during the closing years of the century.[1]

Farmers were not the only ones to offer themselves as saviors of the Republic. Hundreds of thousands of workers—skilled, unskilled, native, immigrant—aided by a motley assortment of individuals who ran small businesses or drew meager salaries, joined together to halt capitalist injustice. Given the diverse character of industrial capitalism, their particular circumstances varied tremendously. Nonetheless, they shared the material reality of a specific era of capitalism and increasingly acknowledged those ties that bound them in opposition to industrial capitalism. What's more, as they protested capitalism's abuses, they discovered that many shared certain basic principles, which provided a common language, a guiding spirit, and a reference point as they sought to understand and improve their world. These principles formed the ideology of the mainstream of the labor movement and the foundation for movement culture's alternative vision for society.

At the heart of this ideology lay those values and ideals associated with republicanism and the mechanic ideology. Rooted in a variety of European and American traditions and the subject of debate among historians, republicanism and the mechanic ideology would be transformed and taken to their logical extreme as workers moved toward a sense of both solidarity and anticapitalism. Republicanism and the mechanic ideology would serve as the intellectual bulwarks of labor, losing their intellectual clout only after labor's defeat in the 1890s and the change in material reality generated by the rise of monopoly capitalism at the turn of the century.[2]

Patriotic prophets in their own right, song-poets continuously harped on the contradiction between those standards embodied in republicanism and the mechanic ideology and the reality produced by industrial capitalism. However, song-poets were not prisoners of the past, heirs to archaic values and beliefs. They and their comrades tested the limits of both traditions on the basis of their own working-class experiences. Aware of capitalism's power but convinced that the nation might yet be redeemed and the new tyranny destroyed, song-poets called on all Americans to join labor's crusade—a crusade to repudiate the degenerate values heralded by the moneyed aristocrats; a crusade to abolish the evils of the wage system, if not the system itself; a crusade to revitalize the nation in the name of brotherhood, cooperation, and humanity.

That song-poets assumed the guise of citizen defenders of the republic surprised no one at the time. Republicanism, after all, had deep roots in history. It first appeared in the colonial period among the "commonwealthmen" who formed England's unofficial opposition party in the eighteenth century. Commonwealthmen argued that England's unique qualities of freedom and liberty depended upon a political system that carefully balanced elements of monarchy, aristocracy, and democracy. They nonetheless believed that corruption and tyranny threatened to throw the system off balance and to jeopardize the freedom and liberty of its citizenry.[3]

Such reasoning had profound impact among colonial American politicos who concluded that events confirmed the common-wealthmen's predictions. Leaders who surveyed colonial policy saw nothing less than conspiracy: corruption grew rampant, officials harbored conspiratorial designs, and the rights of citizens became endangered. England would soon degenerate into complete despotism unless its citizens put the Republic back on a balanced course.[4] Men like Tom Paine grew convinced that England had succumbed to decadence and aristocracy and lost its trust in the republican mantle. He and sympathetic shopkeepers and artisans argued that American independence now offered the only assurance for the survival of liberty, freedom, and justice. Americans must sever their ties to England and establish a republic devoted to those rights and freedoms now imperiled by British action.[5]

Independence brought slight relief for those who counted freedom, liberty, democracy, equality, independence, and rights as their watchwords. The Republic remained in jeopardy from inception and demanded constant vigilance against assorted conspirators. From the 1780s onward any number of groups volunteered their services in the country's defense, proclaiming themselves heir to the revolutionary legacy. Jeffersonians challenged Federalists as a profligate class of idler aristocrats determined to reimpose monarchy. Jacksonian Democrats followed suit, hoisting the revolutionary-republican banner against parasite-aristocrat Whigs who preyed upon the freedom and wealth of the nation's citizen workers. Finally, abolitionists, free soilers, and Republicans incorporated the tenets of republicanism into the free soil ideology enlisted against the slavocracy that threatened democracy and free labor.[6]

In an era when industry's advance had only begun to be felt and class lines remained blurred, republicanism attracted Americans from diverse backgrounds. Indeed, as Sean Wilentz has demonstrated, republicanism continued to weld masters and journeymen together in the commonwealth tradition and revitalized the ties that bound Americans together across the economic spectrum. However, as the economy advanced, republicanism began to have a different meaning for employees than for masters. That meaning never became entirely class specific in the antebellum years, but workers increasingly employed their own version. Posing their own struggle as the one for independence, democracy, equal rights, freedom, and liberty—against owners they described as aristocrats, tyrants, despots, monarchists, parasites, and idlers—workers and organized labor placed themselves within the republican tradition.[7]

By the time the Civil War ended, republican precepts permeated labor's ranks. The years 1865 to 1895 regularly witnessed workers assailing capitalists as aristocrats opposed to freedom, liberty, equality, and justice. Workers added their distinctive cant by labeling the new capitalists—"proud capital" and "the moneyed power"—one more antirepublican force trying to steer the nation from its proper course. Capital, they argued, must be subdued or else its unchecked power would result in monarchy and aristocracy, and the disappearance of those rights that citizen-workers had died for in 1776. American workers must step to the fore to guard the revolutionary inheritance and to ensure their own and the nation's future.[8]

To argue that republicanism belonged only to Americans—workers or no—would be incorrect, however. Republicanism ought to be judged an international phenomenon—perhaps the key ingredient of working-class struggles throughout the nineteenth-century Western world.[9] During the years surrounding the American and French revolutions, republicanism gained credence among European workers. As lower and middling orders fought the aristocracy and monarchy in the name of freedom and forged the tenets of republicanism in conflict with the ancien régime, republicanism gained ascendency among the rising middle class and their underlings. For half a century workers and their masters united behind liberal democracy and workers achieved an education in the lessons of republicanism. However, in the wake of the failures of 1848, and even earlier in some cases, the bourgeoisie and the working class charted increasingly disparate republican courses. For their part, the bourgeoisie balked at the potentially subversive social implications of republicanism while remaining committed to its less threatening political program. Workers, by contrast, favored a broader interpretation—a republicanism that could be applied to their changing material world of workplace and community, as well as to the political arena. Never entirely separate from its trans-class past—a past characterized by a degree of ambivalence toward the state and a class-specific agenda—working-class republicanism increasingly sounded like the language of workers with a different view toward the future. English, Irish, German, and French workers thus expanded republicanism's horizon. Those who left for the United States did not forget the lessons they had learned. From Massachusetts to Washington ethnically diverse bodies of workers found republicanism the binding agent for cooperation and a useful counter to industrial capitalists' circumscribed republicanism and egoistic individualism.

One essential complement to republicanism—and one with an equally international following—was the mechanic ideology.[10] A commonsensical notion served as its central premise: only those who work and labor create wealth; therefore, only those who work deserve a share of the wealth and all who do work deserve a fair share of the wealth they create. Such thinking enjoyed a welcome audience in colonial America. In the North, where the majority of people had ties to small-scale agriculture or manufacturing, the mechanic ideology reflected the reality of their world. Some also knew of the biblical injunction that all must labor. A few may have been influenced by natural law doctrine that held that workers possessed an inherent right to the product of their labor. More likely, most Americans fell sway to the logic of the mechanic ideology simply by looking around them and continued to subscribe to some variant of it until well into the nineteenth century. As Paul Faler discovered among Lynn's master and journeymen shoemakers in the early nineteenth century, "the primacy of labor seemed self-evident" and the notion that labor created all wealth beyond dispute.[11]

If labor created all wealth, then those who did not labor did not create wealth. Society could therefore be said to comprise two groups: those who labored, created wealth, and advanced society; and those who neither labored, created wealth, nor advanced society. Accordingly, farmers, artisans, miners, seamen, shopkeepers, and even small manufacturers qualified as workers, while bankers, bureaucrats, financiers, larger manufacturers, and ne'er-do-wells lived on the wealth others created and should therefore be judged parasites, leeches, vampires, and aristocrats. What's more, the combination of the mechanic ideology and republicanism led some to reason that workers constituted the backbone of the Republic— the citizen workers who acted as the Republic's protectors. Idlers, by contrast, endangered the Republic in their greed for unearthed wealth and power. Workers pumped blood into the veins of body-republic and must safeguard the nation from the bloodsuckers who would leech it dry.

In the colonial or early national period, this sort of thinking did not belong exclusively to labor. So long as the distinction between employer and employee, master and journeymen seemed cloudy, the ideology served as much to cement as to divide the two parties. Together they employed it against speculators, investors, and financiers, who clearly did not labor. Jeffersonians and Jacksonians combined the mechanic ideology with republicanism to yield vicious harangues against Federalists and Whigs, both of whom they judged parasites and money-aristocrats who harbored monarchical designs. In time broad application of the mechanic ideology became less common. Class lines never became clearly demarcated until the end of the century, but workers brought the ideology more into line with their environment and experiences. They argued that the wage system violated the basic tenets of the mechanic ideology, taking too much from those who created wealth while allowing nonproducers to reap inordinate rewards. The same people who sought to destroy the republic and to impose tyranny also sought to steal workers' wealth in order to live in idle luxury. Such thinking became an important characteristic of the labor movement, from which would proceed a body of anticapitalist critique. Moreover, the very ambiguity that some found a weakness in the mechanic ideology—the issue of defining who was, and who was not, a worker—allowed labor to garner broad support among Americans, including some whom we would describe as lower middle class today.

Support did not come only from native workers.[12] Like republicanism, the mechanic ideology had a strong international flavor. In fact, its European history paralleled that of its New World counterpart. Those same decades that witnessed a wave of revolutions for liberal democracy saw European artisans embracing the central tenet of the mechanic ideology—that workers create all wealth and that they have a natural right to the products of their labor. Initially such thinking would be used against the ancien régime, since its existence depended upon practices antithetical to the mechanic ideology. For that reason, the ideology generated criticism against the political apparatus and served as an ancillary to republicanism. The revolutions of 1848 permanently altered workers' thinking on the matter, however. Changing political and economic circumstances left workers as the primary standard bearers of the mechanic ideology and their use of it increasingly led to social criticism with anticapitalist overtones. Disgusted with the limited meaning of democracy and the individualist ethic promulgated by the bourgeoisie, workers found in the mechanic ideology the emotional and intellectual justification for collective associational activities and for the repudiation of liberal individualism. When German forty-eighters, Irish Fenians, English trade unionists, and

Welsh miners came to the United States, they discovered common ground with native-born workers. Despite their undeniable differences, the workers in this period were bound by strong links. As the material reality of capitalism prodded them toward cooperative effort, foreign- and native-born workers found in republicanism and the mechanic ideology a basis for dialogue and even united effort.

Labor's republicanism and mechanic ideology became a recognizable characteristic of song-poetry and helped lend it a sort of ideological continuity similar to those musical-literary devices described above. Song-poets remind us of the power of both traditions to pull the heartstrings of workers and of a significant portion of other Americans too, and the reasons both served labor well. They provided a practical standard for social judgment and a means for justifying the labor movement. They also established the labor movement as heir to the nation's most celebrated principles and yielded a much different vision for the nation's future. For their part, song-poets reflected this development while simultaneously making their own contribution to it. To song-poets the rising order represented an antirepublican, anti-American force that threatened the rights of workers and the nation as a whole. The only hope for deliverance lay in the awakening of workers and dedication to the principles embodied in the labor movement.

Workers' republicanism surfaced even while the Civil War raged. Boston printers found intolerable irony in the fact that workers died in disproportionate numbers to end slavery only to be deprived of their rights by their employers.[13] A determined group of owners, unwilling to accede to the printers' scale, aroused the latter's worst fears about the kind of dependency generated by capitalism. With defiance and trepidation printers struck in 1863, seeking to assert their rights and independence and to gain a fair share of wealth. An anonymous song-poet, impassioned by republicanism, exhorted workers not to tolerate their oppression:

> Rouse, Workingmen, will ye crouch down,
> Beneath employers' threatening frown?
>   Are ye not men?
> Will ye submissive bow the neck
> To yoke oppressive at their beck,
>   Like goaded beasts?
>
> Have ye not rights as well as they?
> Are they to rule and ye obey,
>   Like abject slaves?

No! justice, honor, manhood, all
That man ennobles, sternly call
  For union firm.

Yield but the right they now contest,
Ye to the winds may fling the rest,
  Nor hope to rise.
But lower, deeper, baser sink,
Till robbed of e'en the right to think
  As well as act.

Despite the threats and scorns, the author used the remaining verses to repeat the charge that labor must stand firm in its resolve and not shirk its duty. Their fight, he said, was a fight for independence and for workers' just reward. Only if the owners accepted scale could printers feel assured of their fair share.

The author's references to slavery could not have been lost on his audience. However, the most effective feature of the song-poem derives from linking the printers' fight with the struggle for rights going back to American independence. Workers had a duty, counseled the author, to carry forth the revolutionary mantle. As citizen workers guarding the Republic they possessed certain rights —including a decent wage—that had to be protected or all would be lost. To yield but a single right would lead to the loss of other rights, followed by dependency, and eventually the yoke of beasts and abject slaves would adorn the workers' necks. Simply stated, the power of the song-poem came from comingling the voices of Tom Paine, Abe Lincoln, and molders' union president William Sylvis.

That voice surfaced elsewhere as well. In 1889 H. C. Dodge summoned republicanism for his work "The Future America," producing what might be the most powerful song-poem of the era.[14] Dodge astutely chose to parody "My Country 'Tis of Thee," a decision that neatly juxtaposed the original against the author's own futuristic-prophetic scenario of national degeneration. Dodge portrayed a land controlled by an aristocracy of wealth where workers lost the rights their forebears fought to achieve. Nevertheless, a message of faint hope emanates from Dodge's song-poem as he tacitly summoned workers to their task before his predictions materialized. The author spoke as prophet patriot, cajoling his audience:

My country, 'tis of thee
Land of lost liberty,
  Of thee we sing.

Land which the millionaires,
Who govern our affairs,
    Own for themselves and heirs—
        Hail to thy king.

Land once of noble braves
But now of wretched slaves—
        Alas! too late
We saw sweet Freedom die,
From letting bribers nigh,
Our unprized suffrage buy;
        And mourn thy fate.

Land where the wealthy few
Can make the many do
        Their royal will,
And tax for selfish greed
The toilers till they bleed,
And those not yet weak-kneed
        Crash down and kill.

Land where a rogue is raised
On high and loudly praised
        For worst of crimes
Of which the end, must be
A hell of cruelty,
As proved by history
        Of ancient times.

My country, 'tis of thee,
Betrayed by bribery,
        Of thee we sing.
We might have saved thee long
Had we, when proud and strong,
Put down the cursed wrong
        That makes a king.

Dodge's song-poem sharply reveals the meaning of republicanism for workers. His terminology—liberally sprinkled with words
and phrases such as "liberty," "freedom," "noble braves," "toilers,"
as well as "millionaires," "heirs," "wealthy few," "rogue," and
"king"—echoed the revolutionary and Jacksonian era. Here, however, tradition provided a tool for criticizing social injustice while
simultaneously buttressing workers' spirits. Few workers, even the
foreign born, could have missed a parody of so sacrosanct a text as
"My Country 'Tis of Thee." They would have understood the author's intent when he compared millionaires to royalty and spoke
of the wealthy's power to install their king on an American throne,

to exercise their royal will, and to impose a tax on servile toilers. The author played upon native workers' worst fears, knowing they loathed comparison of the United States to countries with monarchy, aristocracy, and royalty. Any worker, and a goodly number of shopkeepers and farmers as well, would have bristled to hear that the grand republican experiment had been dashed on the rock by a cabal of the wealthy few. The emigré could easily relate to a work overflowing with antiaristocratic, antinoble, and antimonarchical sentiments aimed at a rising industrial and financial elite. Workers involved in a host of movements in the U.S., Canada, and Europe would have winced to be described as wretched slaves unwilling to rebel in support of their ancestral, if not natural, rights. Beyond its particular patriotic challenge for citizen workers, "The Future America" dared workers to step forward for liberty before it disappeared.

Seventeen years prior to Dodge's treatment, West Virginia union member and cooper J. E. L. delivered a similar message and challenge.[15] In a work addressed to fellow coopers, the author relied heavily on republicanism, chiding his mates for not attending to their republican duties and advising them to join their union to secure justice. He informed native workers of their obligation to safeguard freedom and reminded them of their ancestors' struggle for liberty and independence:

> So strange it seems, so strange to me,
> While in this land of liberty,
> That men, whose noble sires
> Bravely faced proud Britain's fires,
> Risking life, and all in their possession,
> Before they would bow or kneel to oppression,
> Are you content to have it said
> That you have betrayed the noble dead!

Obviously J. E. L. knew that no citizen worker would have been "content to have it said." The stanza left no doubt that workers counted as the legitimate heirs to the revolutionary torch and the author drew on every cliché to make it so. The description of the U.S. as the land of liberty, of workers' forebears as the noble sires who fought the British rather than bow or kneel to oppression, of the worker as the "you" who might have betrayed the noble dead explicitly linked workers with the revolution and its achievements. The line now ran from Jefferson to the labor movement.

J. E. L. took the song-poem beyond a narrow patriotic plea by broadening his argument. According to the author, foreign-born workers shared a stake in the defense of republican principles and should join the workers' struggle:

> Perchance from a foreign shore
> You have fled, a serf to be no more,
> To a land where, if you do but aspire,
> You can carve a name higher, higher;
> Then, why, oh why, do you your life enslave,
> Become a willing tool to a Capital knave!
> Within your reach is a noble band
> Who only wait to take you by the hand.

In their defense, then, native- and foreign-born workers might cooperate against the new enemy, "a Capital knave." The rewards of the struggle extended beyond the political arena of earlier plebeian struggles and freedom fighters no longer marched only for democracy. Economic rewards and social justice awaited, and the labor movement composed the unit of struggle. The author's closing stanza went to the heart of the matter:

> The object of this brave, united band,
> Is to proclaim throughout the land,
> That coopers will, in every sense,
> For their labor require just recompense.
> No more will they work day and night,
> For that purpose God gave us light;
> Tyrants and capitalists tremble at our stride,
> For they know no longer can they o'er us ride.

The effort to explain the labor movement in relation to earlier battles for republican principles involved more than rhetorical flourish. Clearly, since much of the working class had been born or raised in the United States, republicanism could be called a birthright. In the sense that song-poets and workers served as the bearers of musical-literary traditions that influenced song-poetry, so too did they carry republicanism. Song-poets' and workers' republicanism, like the musical-literary elements of song-poetry, however, became more than the sum total of traditions. Factors more immediate to Gilded-Age workers and song-poets also shaped their republicanism.

At times the link between antebellum reform and workers' republicanism could be more direct than cultural inheritance.

For example, J. O. Barrett, a song-poet whose works surfaced at Knights of Labor meetings, had been directly involved in movements for social change prior to the advent of the Knights of Labor.[16] From his home in Sycamore, Illinois, he worked for abolition and actively promoted the spiritualist movement throughout the 1860s. Barrett offered his song-poetry skills regularly to the latter cause, contributing works to its newspaper, the *Banner of Light*, and to the popular songster *The Spiritual Harp*. In 1869 he also edited and contributed compositions to the second edition of the songster. When the labor movement moved into the forefront, he went to work on labor song-poems. By Barrett's mode of reckoning, the republic, a millennium, and the labor movement had close ties, and he judged labor the logical choice as both the republican and millennial standard bearer. The final stanza of his song-poem "The Labor Battle Song" evoked his sense of the movement's universal importance:

> Lift up then the starry banner,
> let it float o'er land and sea,
> As the sign of human justice
> and of righteousness to be,
> For the labor of the people
> shall be guards of liberty,
> As we go marching on.[17]

Barrett's experience in republican-based antebellum reform linked labor to earlier American reform and also injected republicanism with the spirit and substance of immediate events. In the same way that his song-poetry included traditional elements of form and style—but also reflected the music of antislavery, spiritualism, and Stephen Foster's sentimental parlor ballads—so, too, his republicanism reflected not only a republican intellectual inheritance, but a republicanism that had served in the fight to end slavery and to bring about a truly humane world.

Barrett's pattern may not have been common among song-poets or the labor movement. After all, the labor movement had its own agenda, and its character became increasingly class-specific as the social relations of production changed. However, individuals like Barrett were not atypical. The labor movement still found room for such people, so long as republicanism still counted for a great deal. Labor song-poet and activist B. M. Lawrence followed a pattern much like Barrett's. Likewise, A. J. H. Duganne enlisted in a host of antebellum reforms before allying with the Knights of Labor.[18]

For four decades his song-poems would be favorites among workers, no doubt in large part because republicanism served as their ideological core.

Duganne's republicanism ultimately degenerated into a spread-eagle patriotism and virulent xenophobia, an indication of the potentially ugly underside of American republicanism. Nonetheless, Duganne's antebellum work recalls the international character that republicanism possessed. In his *Poetical Works*, for example, Duganne mixed romanticism, religion, and prolabor sentiment with heavy doses of an international republicanism. He paid homage to workers and the American republican experiment, but also invoked the spirit of 1848. In a thirty-page section titled "Year of the People"—written for "The Heroes of '48 and the Martyrs of '49 These Lyrics of Liberty, In Memoriam"—Duganne praised workers for their role in the revolutions of 1848, lent his support to the battle for liberty, and called upon the Irish to rise in arms against their English oppressors.[19]

This international perspective moved directly from various sources into Gilded-Age labor. Almost forty years after Duganne's paean to 1848, Knights of Labor members James and Emily Tallmadge would include J. O. Barrett's song-poem "Home Rule for Ireland" in their labor songster.[20] For Barrett the Irish struggle for independence could be viewed as one more in a long history of struggles for republican principles and one that paralleled workers' struggle in America. Barrett's third verse and chorus outlined the thinking that led him and thousands of others to this conclusion:

> Johnny Bull now better cease his game of gambling cards,
> For the exiled, patriot sons are solid-breasted guards—
> "Death to tyranny is just!" said ancient Irish bards,
>   While we are marching to freedom,
>
> Hurrah, hurrah, we'll bring the jubilee,
> Hurrah, hurrah, for the flag that makes us free;
> So we'll bless our brothers who are pleading o'er the sea,
>   While we are marching to freedom.

Barrett's song-poem illustrates the international context within which labor's republicanism took shape. Individuals did not have to be born in the United States to find intellectual kinship with working-class republicanism and to find in republicanism what David Montgomery has referred to as "the mental links between material condition and action."[21] Workers participating in the Irish Land League in the United States moved into the Knights of

Labor with relative ease in the 1880s and even prior to that discovered in republicanism the basis for cooperation with German, English, and American workers.[22] Similarly, German-born workers involved in the battles of 1848 and forced into exile found themselves involved in the antislavery fight and then in working-class struggles, as the international meaning of their "plebeian radicalism" became apparent and what John Jentz and Richard Schneirov termed "social republicanism" followed thereafter.[23] In 1879 Gustav Lyser, song-poet and editor of *Fackel*, turned his song-poem written on the dedication of a flag for a German workers' organization into a plea for workers to uphold the legacy of 1776.[24] Lyser called on workers to defend the gains of the American Revolution against the new foe, those "parasites" and "wealthy tyrants" stealing workers' wealth and destroying the republic. Lyser was anything but a patriotic American. He simply believed that the fight for the working class represented the extension of those same principles fought for in 1776 and 1848.

No one saw this more clearly than John James, miner, Scottish immigrant, labor leader, and song-poet. James needed no lessons in American history to defend workers by invoking republicanism. Perhaps he had learned his republicanism from fellow song-poets in the British Isles. In the wake of the American and French revolutions and Jacobinism, miners and dockworkers had churned out hundreds of song-poems in the name of "Reason, Truth, Virtue, Justice, Equality, Liberty, and Knowledge," "ringing with the temperament of Paine" while offering workers as true patriots.[25] For whatever reason, like Irish immigrant-socialist J. P. McDonnell's work, James's "rhetoric was bathed in working-class republican ideology. Saturated by it. He believed in 'America' and also believed it was being ruined."[26] Such convictions lent James's 4 July 1868 song-poem "Invocation to Workingmen" a sense of immediacy and purpose.[27] He summoned workers:

> Hark! the call has now resounded
> To the nation's utmost end;
> Hark! the trumpet now has sounded,
> Workingmen: Attend, attend
> It is justice that invokes you,
> It is duty calls aloud;
> Freedom only sits and mocks you
> From her pedestal so proud.

James then chastised workers for the passivity that left their rights deteriorating and prodded them to arrest the degeneration:

> She is everywhere surrounded
> By proud capital. And why?
> You her pride hath deeply wounded,
> Sitting doubting, idly by.
> Energy alone can gain her,
> Purity of purpose, too,—
> Upon them, workmen all obtain her,
> Win her smile and heart so true.

In the five stanzas that followed James sought to bolster work-ers' spirit, assuring them of the nobility of their struggle against "proud capital," "the money'd power." Unity he deemed essential. He concluded by reiterating his summons and underscoring the significance of the task:

> Let us onward, hoping, trusting—
> O'er the nation's greatest length;
> Be our firmness free from rusting,
> Unity's our staff and strength.
> Liberty is now before us,
> If we only forward press.
> Tarrying does ever gore us,
> Now's the day to have redress.

Everywhere song-poets agreed that a plague had settled on the land and threatened to destroy the Republic. Song-poet J. F. saw treason in the making, "traitors" and "thieves" among the "corpo-ration" who stripped labor of its rights.[28] These thieves, however, violated both the tenets of republicanism and the mechanic ideol-ogy, as J. F.'s song-poem demonstrates. Workers lost not only their rights but a fair share of the wealth they created as well. Song-poets' anger over workers' loss of rights was thus compounded by an equal degree of anger over what they considered nothing more than the outright stealth on which capitalism based itself. Only concerted effort promised to right such wrongs and put capital in its place.

In the opening stanzas of his "Verses for the Toiler," J. F. pre-sented a version of the mechanic ideology long popular with work-ers. The mainstream press might offer glowing tributes to industrial magnates, but for J. F., workers deserved the greater praise:

> Where'er the son of toil may go
> And lift his horny hand,
> These riches in abundance grow
> And plenty fills the land.

> All priceless stores of wisdom, too,
>   Are found in labor's realm,
> And wealth that's not discovered yet
>   Remains for time to tell.
>
> By labor we promote the health
>   Of body and of mind,
> While rogues that feed on ill-gained wealth
>   Disease and trouble find.
>
> Labor is noble in its place
>   And holy in its end;
> It honors all the human race
>   And makes us honest men.

If one agreed with such thinking, the debasement of labor could be seen only as a violation of basic economic and moral principles. Labor stood at the center of civilization's advancement and the act of laboring possessed an inherently noble, holy, honorable, and honest quality. Yet nonworkers held the upper hand and, according to J. F., "steal our daily bread away / And crush us to the ground." J. F.'s hope lay in the Knights of Labor, an organization that promised to right the wrongs against labor and to put civilization back on course. Like many song-poets and hundreds of thousands of workers, J. F. felt strong ties to that organization because its goals really did count for something as grandiose as the title the Noble and Holy Order of the Knights of Labor.

One need not have been a member of that organization, however, to hear strains of the mechanic ideology mingled with republicanism. Boston printers who struck in 1863 did not hear just that owners had violated their rights as citizen workers. In the final stanza of the song-poem on the strike, they also heard the author proclaim:

> For labor is the world's true wealth,
> The poor man's capital in health,
>   Which who employs
> Must pay the usury that is just—
> Not what he would, but what he must—
>   Its market worth.[29]

In the decades that followed, song-poets would continue to make similar arguments and pleas. When B. M. Lawrence compiled his songster in 1878, for example, the mechanic ideology— along with republicanism and evangelical Protestantism—formed the work's ideological foundation. Lawrence found in the mechanic ideology the basis for glorification of workers and denigration of nonworkers. He alternately assailed banks, railroads, bondholders, politicians, merchants, doctors, lawyers, landlords, speculators, and employers and branded them "idle drones," "robbers," "money thieves," "shylocks," "knaves," and "money kings." Few other than workers and farmers escaped criticism. Lawrence's concern with issues less than directly related to workers reminds us of the heterogeneous character of the labor movement. Lawrence's faith in organized labor never faltered, however, and his belief that labor created all wealth never changed. His thinking was simple and direct:

> Whatsoever men sow they must reap,
>     Since the rich to the whirlwinds have sown,
> More just laws they must now learn to keep,
>     Then what workingmen earn they will own.[30]

Nonproducers' disregard for such principles led Lawrence to believe his society was in grave danger. Throughout his song-poems he lashed out at those "wealthy drones" and "money thieves" who lived in luxury at the expense of "honest men," "the hungry poor."[31] In "When Workingmen Combine" he enumerated the injustices to labor and offered a rendering of the mechanic ideology that became almost a cliché in the labor movement.[32] He posed a series of rhetorical questions to incite his audience:

> Shall those who raise the fruits and grains,
>     Who feed and clothe the race,
> Tramp through the land and for their pains,
>     Starve, branded with disgrace?
>
> Shall banks and railroad kings unite
>     For base and selfish ends,
> And those who labor for the right,
>     Prove false and not true friends?
>
> Shall idle drones still live like kings
>     On labor not their own?
> While true men starve, shall thieves, and rings
>     Reap what they have not sown?

As readers guessed, Lawrence resoundingly answered *no*. He advised workers to enlist in the labor movement and, as in so many of his song-poems, lent support to greenbacks.

The mechanic ideology provided workers with more than a means of self-congratulation or even simple economic and ethical analysis. In workers' hands, its logic yielded acerbic social criticism, as good and evil and virtue and wickedness became identifiable. Lawrence could pique the emotions of readers as he argued that workingmen, honest men, and true men—"those who raise the fruits and grains, / Who feed and clothe the race"—stood hungry, starving, and "branded with disgrace." Workers born in the United States or Europe understood when Lawrence restated the charges that the rich, the "idle drones," the "wealthy drones," the "thieves and rings,"—those who "reap where they have not sown"—traveled "proudly in Paris and Rome" and "live like kings."

Such depictions became formulaic. Mrs. S. M. Smith's ever-popular "Labor's Ninety and Nine," for example, presented a more carefully constructed description that nonetheless resembled the format and message of Lawrence's song-poems.[33] Smith waxed indignant over the theft of workers' wealth by a greedy upper class as she explained how 99 percent of the population lived in hunger and cold to support the 1 percent who reveled in luxury:

> They toil in the fields,—the ninety-and-nine—
>   For the fruits of the mother earth;
> They dig and delve in the dusky mine,
>   And bring its treasures forth;
> But the wealth released by their sturdy blows
> To the hands of the one forever flows.
>
> From the sweat of their brows the desert blooms,
>   And the forest before them falls;
> Their labor has builded humble homes,
>   And cities with lofty halls;
> But the one owns cities and homes and lands,
> While the ninety-and-nine have empty hands.

Despite her critical tone, Smith retained her optimism. Her concluding stanza admonished workers to prepare for the coming dawn, when labor would be victorious and humanity could "Rejoice, for Labor shall have its own."

Not surprisingly the Knights of Labor gave a warm welcome to song-poets such as Smith. Their work confirmed beliefs already prevalent among members of that organization and also served as a method for promulgation elsewhere. So popular did the combination of republicanism and the mechanic ideology become that one could hardly open a Knights of Labor newspaper, attend a lecture, read a pamphlet, or be involved in a labor dispute without hearing words and phrases like Smith's and Lawrence's. Nothing seemed to tap workers' emotions like a speech peppered with references from these cultural traditions. In an era when capitalism had not yet completely transformed labor, and when a managerial middle class had yet to develop, diverse types of American workers could be swayed by these traditions, find some credibility in the analysis which they promoted, and might join the Knights of Labor as they strove for the cooperative commonwealth based on anti-individualist strains of the republican and mechanic ideologies. Even those who found the Knights sorely lacking in substance, as many socialists would, or who disagreed with the author's faith in the ballot, would still have been stirred by the first three verses and the refrain of Thomas Leahy's song-poem, "Come Join the Knights of Labor Boys."[34] Leahy employed a well-worn formula:

> We build gilded carriages, fine mansions and halls,
> But not for the brave sons of labor,
> And we go to work when the bell or whistle calls,
> But where are the fruits of our labor?

> While the law has the banker and broker for pets,
> Who fatten on the fruits of labor,
> The brawny wealth producer, a thought never gets,
> Though working day and night at labor.

> The bite of the usurer, the landlord and rent,
> And the trader who lives on labor,
> Swallow up between them, the wealth by nature sent,
> To cheer the hearts and homes of labor.

> Labor forever, hurrah! boys, hurrah!
> 'Tis the life of the nation, the prop of the law
> And we'll raise it to that station, where no man can draw,
> Millions from our labor, hurrah! boys, hurrah!

More than repetition of stock phrases, however, took place when Leahy wrote this song-poem. Undoubtedly, some of what Leahy, other song-poets, and countless other prolabor people from the era used could be described as a kind of unconscious cultural baggage bequeathed to anyone who grew up in the United States. On the other hand, events gave song-poets' mechanic ideology a contemporary tenor. In the first place, within the struggles between workers and employers in the antebellum period, the mechanic ideology had served both parties. By the Civil War, however, increasing economic differences would lead to different interpretations of the mechanic ideology. Although antebellum labor reform generally conformed to a standard mold, workers gradually came to articulate their interests separately from employers. Secondly, in the northern campaign against slavery, workers and nonworkers alike could rally around the mechanic ideology as they sought to specify the differences between free labor and slave labor societies. The budding Republican party made significant headway by incorporating some variant of the mechanic ideology into the larger free soil–free labor ideology.[35] Here too class differences would eventually surface, as David Montgomery has demonstrated.[36] Nonetheless, the spirit of the antislavery struggle and antebellum reform would carry into Gilded-Age labor, either directly in the form of individuals—including song-poets such as Lawrence, Barrett, and Duganne—or indirectly in countless song-poems, speeches, articles, letters, picnics, pamphlets, and parades. Gilded-Age workers who sought collective redress could thus adopt the pose of guardians of the republic and protectors of the wealth of workers, and legitimately believe they represented the American reform tradition as well.

At the same time, the mechanic ideology in labor's hands was not unique to the United States. Gustav Lyser brought to the U.S. both the lessons of 1848 and the mechanic ideology.[37] An Irish immigrant, however, provides the most convincing evidence for the international parameters of the mechanic ideology. "Puddler poet" Michael McGovern repeatedly ventured to make sense of the world through the lens of the mechanic ideology. In "The Puddler's View of Present Systems," McGovern stated most workers' understanding of the way society operated:

> The plutocrats, the goldbugs, and the tariff lords who rule us all;
> The press and politicians that will tell us lies to fool us all;
> The ministers and bishops who e'er preach on Christ and pray for all;
> The warriors who'd kill the foes that would invade and slay us all;
> The hoboes and the millionaires who never work at all, at all;
> Would one and all be starving did the workingman not toil for all.[38]

Even before entering the United States McGovern knew the mechanic ideology's meaning well enough. In the hands of workers, the mechanic ideology disregarded national boundaries.

McGovern's experience as a puddler also had an impact on his thinking. His workmates, after all, did refer to him as the Puddler Poet and he needed no prompting to recall his place in the nation's class structure. Like so many song-poets and workers, McGovern's thinking about labor and capital mingled the ideological traditions of republicanism and the mechanic ideology with notions shaped by wage labor. This mixture of ideological tradition and class permeates his *Labor Lyrics and Other Poems* and provides the major line of continuity in the work. McGovern lambasted iron mill bosses, lawyers, politicians, judges, presidents, millionaires, plutocrats, "railroad kings," "monarchs of the mines," Congress, clerics, and anyone else who threatened the Republic and robbed workers of the wealth they created. At the same time he remained adamant in support of his union and the nation's toilers. Scabs and nonunion workers rated just above those bosses who refused union scale and tyrants like Carnegie and Frick who sought to destroy unions. Union members and the labor movement stood for, at the very least, liberty, justice, equality, freedom, and a wage that provided for workers' independence and, at the very most, a society that bordered on utopia. In "The Workingman's Song" McGovern showed the results of social analysis proceeding from ideological traditions:

> They tell me I'm a "Sovereign,"
>     That I am truly free;
> And yet no wealthy, idle men,
>     Have e'er hobnobbed with me.
> The only time they bow to me
>     Is when they seek my vote
> To place them where their hands may be
>     E'er clutching Labor's throat.
>
> The wealth I toil for goes away
>     To plutocrat and lord,
> While I but get starvation pay,
>     Below a slave's reward.
> Of mansions capped with spire and dome
>     By Hudson, Thames, and Rhine.
> The poorhouse is the only home
>     Which I may claim as mine.[39]

This same mixture of tradition and class also left McGovern with a positive vision of the future. Not only could the labor movement wrest better wages, working conditions, and hours for workers, and insure their pride and independence, but as McGovern explained in " 'Tis Coming," they could bring a better world in general:

The era of equality 'mongst men will soon be here,
And no one should with coming evolutions interfere.
No! Ev'ry one should hurry on the climax—sure to come—
When men will not pay tribute to a plutocrat or bum.

The time is surely coming when the automatic man
Will do the work for all on the co-operative plan.
The country's tables then will not be set but for the few—
We'll all sit 'round the board and say, "We'll dine as well as you."[40]

Such song-poems and the thinking they represented enjoyed tremendous popularity among workers. Caustic criticism of the new order, praise for workers' role in the Republic and the economy, acclaim for the labor movement, and a grand vision of social purpose flowed directly from republicanism and the mechanic ideology. The spirit of the revolutionary generation, antebellum reform, European movements for liberal democracy and social reform, and a burgeoning working class bent on making a better world all melded together in a fashion that appealed to hundreds of thousands, perhaps millions, of people in the United States. Particular material conditions may have prompted workers to action, but their rendering of republicanism and the mechanic ideology in light of those conditions and the subsequent application to society at large would give workers a way to try to understand their world.

This mainstream version of what some call American labor radicalism never sat well with some workers and activists. They found in it muddled thinking that led to inadequate social and economic analysis and an ideologically weakened labor movement. Some historians agree, considering the thinking of German socialists and anarchists a more convincing view of the world and a better guide for the nation's working class.[41] Activists proffered this latter guide throughout the United States, making significant inroads in some regions, influencing labor radicals, but never supplanting the hold of those in the mainstream in the 1870s and 1880s. As often as they fought their ideological opponents, the radicals had to give ground and work in cooperation. A greenback-labor party or something similar was often better than no worker party at all. The Knights of Labor admittedly seemed to command the attention of most American workers despite efforts to wean them from an incorrect line of thought about capital and labor.

Certainly song-poets' republicanism and mechanic ideology demonstrate weaknesses within the mainstream of the labor movement. First, inordinate faith in the Republic and the principles it stood for—including the notion that it ought to operate in the interest of all its citizens—led song-poets and like-thinking individuals to shy from class politics.[42] Much as their experience prodded many toward class-specific politics, they could never completely assent to a working-class party any more than they could to a capitalist one. Although most workers perceived that the captains of industry now dominated both political parties and had their interests protected by office-holding lackeys, workers never believed the political arena a suitable area in which to rectify class wrongs. Indeed, the government of the Republic ought to act neutrally to ensure independence, liberty, freedom, justice, and equality for everyone, without regard for class. Followers of republicanism frequently concluded that workers should use their right to vote to oust the parasites' political lieutenants and to revitalize an impartial government. Perhaps the only true believers in republican principles left in the country, they withheld endorsing a working-class party even though both major parties seemed to have become the parties of capital, and the government an organ of the capitalist class.

This brand of republicanism and the mechanic ideology may have also been what made so many workers so susceptible to patriotic pleas that offered precious little for workers. Faith in the Republic made workers its defenders against the plutocrats and aristocrats of industry, but that same faith could degenerate into spread-eagle patriotism. In his popular compilation, Michael McGovern devoted fourteen pages to "Anent Our Trouble with Spain," in which he elevated workers' patriotism to the loftiest plane.[43] True, McGovern's was a class-conscious patriotism that deserves careful scrutiny by historians. McGovern really believed the war would advance the agenda of republicanism begun in 1776, and he made it clear that he suffered few delusions about the way the wealthy manipulated war for class-specific gain. Still, his republicanism could degenerate into self-defeating muscular sloganeering about workers being the best soldiers:

> You wealthy ones, who fear to fight,
> Make room for those who dare;—
> Consign the flag—now threatened—to
> The fighting workmen's care.
> For 'mongst the first who aye respond
> To Liberty's commands,
> Are those from labor's channels with
> The hoofs upon their hands.[44]

Throughout the Gilded Age, however, labor's republicanism demonstrated a more serious shortcoming than patriotism. A more difficult question to wrestle with, and one the labor movement never resolved, was the issue of who qualified to be part of the movement to redeem the Republic. The battles of 1776 and 1848, after all, had said little about the freedom and rights of women, blacks, Chinese, and Catholic immigrants from Eastern and Southern Europe, and yet they comprised important segments of the Gilded-Age working class. If common ground between native-born workers and workers from England, Scotland, Wales, Ireland, and Germany could be found in republicanism and the mechanic ideology, the potential to broaden labor's base to include others would appear to have been technically possible. Certainly, the realities of capitalist exploitation convinced many in the Knights of Labor that skilled and unskilled, male and female, immigrant and non-immigrant shared equally in oppression and would benefit from joint collective action. Under the banner of "noble and holy" Knights and in the name of universal brotherhood, blacks and women did in fact become members.

Much as the Knights pressed the limits of the meaning of republicanism and the mechanic ideology, however, they could never entirely escape notions of racial inferiority or patriarchy. Blacks, women, and non-Western European immigrants remained second-class citizen workers even amongst the Knights. Chinese workers remained beyond the pale, and the most ardent supporters of labor sometimes become party to race baiting. Material forces may have pressed the labor movement toward an expansive view of "workers" to be counted among the citizen workers deserving a fair share of the Republic's wealth. Nonetheless, song-poets such as McGovern joined fellow workers who loudly proclaimed the virtues of the Republic and of labor while simultaneously making disparaging remarks about "Slavs and 'Tally Annes'/Hungarians and Chinamen with pigtail cues and fans."[45]

What the socialists and anarchists sought to discredit about mainstream labor radicalism was not its views on race, women, or nationalism, however. Both socialists and anarchists had abysmal records on such matters. Even on the question of how to view Eastern and Southern European workers, socialists often practiced their own form of chauvinism. For its more ideological opponents the most irksome aspect of mainstream labor's thinking was the fact that it provided no clear method for delineating the character of capitalism or class differences. In its place the Knights of Labor and other groups substituted a republicanism more suited for political than economic analysis and a mechanic ideology that belonged in a precapitalist world. People like Michael McGovern, B. M. Lawrence, James and Emily Tallmadge, Richard Trevellick, William Sylvis, and Terence Powderly relied on inadequate, outdated intellectual tools. With their tools no one could tell where the worker and the capitalist left off, who labor's friends and enemies ought to be, how the capitalist system operated, or what a "working-class" movement ought to do with itself. Song-poets' talk of "parasites," "tyrants," the "money power," "idle drones," "legalized monopolies," and the "usurer" destroying the Republic and stealing the wealth of those "who build gilded carriages, fine mansions and halls," and who "labor in the field, the shop, the mine, and store" sounded quaint—not to mention a strategic disaster for a labor movement. W. Wiley's chorus may have been rousing to workers but it seemed woefully inadequate guidance:

> Hurrah! Hurrah! labor free to all!
> Hurrah! Hurrah! hasten to the call!
> Shout the joyful tidings, King Capital must fall;
>   Now we are marching for Labor.[46]

However, opponents never supplanted this style of thinking or dislodged it from the labor movement. For all its faults song-poets' mode of reckoning with capitalism remained popular among the nation's workers. It seemed to speak to more workers in a way that ideological socialism never did—with a few important exceptions—and never would. Confused, vague, and fraught with shortcomings, song-poetry's brand of republicanism and the mechanic ideology captured the hearts of millions. For a brief moment in the 1880s that poorly outlined vision of a republic of and for toilers, of something other than a system of wage slavery, of a society based on cooperation rather than competition, seemed within reach. In what might justifiably be called the last serious challenge to the country's domination by industrial capitalism, citizens who called themselves workers and toilers moved forward under labor's banner. Their sense of engaging in not merely a labor movement, but a movement akin to a moral crusade of universal proportion, inspired them as they marched to "Our Battle Song" in the 1880s:

> Hark! the bugle note is sounding
>   Over all the land;
> See! the people forth are rushing,
>   Oh! the charge is grand!
>
> Storm the fort, ye Knights of Labor;
>   'Tis a glorious fight;
> Brawn and brain against injustice—
>   God defend the right![47]

## NOTES

1. On agrarian unrest at the end of the nineteenth century, see Good-wyn, *Democratic Promise.*

2. The historiography of republicanism is reviewed in Robert E. Shal-hope, "Republicanism and Early American Historiography," *William and Mary Quarterly* 39 (April 1982): 334–56. On republicanism's English ori-gins, see Caroline Robbins, *The Eighteenth-Century Commonwealthman* (Cambridge: Harvard University Press, 1961). On its colonial American background, see Bernard Bailyn, *The Ideological Origins of the American Revolution* (Cambridge: Belknap Press, 1967) and *The Origins of Ameri-can Politics* (New York: Vintage Books, 1967); and Foner, *Thomas Paine.* On antebellum labor and republicanism, see Dawley, *Class and Commu-nity;* Faler, *Mechanics and Manufacturers;* Bruce Laurie, *Working People of Philadelphia, 1800–1850* (Philadelphia: Temple University Press, 1980); Howard Rock, *Artisans of the New Republic: The Tradesmen of New York City in the Age of Jefferson* (New York: New York University Press, 1979); and Sean Wilentz, *Chants Democratic: New York City and the Rise of the American Working Class 1788–1850* (New York: Oxford University Press, 1984).

3. Robbins, *Commonwealthman,* 3–21; Bailyn, *American Politics,* 17–50, and *American Revolution,* 34–54, 55–92.

4. Bailyn, *American Politics,* 11–13, 52–57.

5. Foner, *Thomas Paine,* 72–78. On the role of nonelites in the Amer-ican Revolution, see the essays in Alfred Young, ed., *The American Revo-lution: Explorations in the History of American Radicalism* (DeKalb: Northern Illinois University Press, 1976).

6. On free soil ideology and its influence, see Eric Foner, *Free Soil, Free Labor, Free Men: The Ideology of the Republican Party before the Civil War* (London: Oxford University Press, 1970).

7. Wilentz, *Chants Democratic.*

8. On the relationship between the Republican party and workers dur-ing the Civil War era, see David Montgomery, *Beyond Equality.* See also Dawley, *Class and Community.*

9. The international dimensions of working-class republicanism in the United States have yet to generate considerable interest among histo-rians. The most useful sources are David Brundage, "Irish Land and Amer-ican Workers: Class and Ethnicity in Denver, Colorado," in *Struggle a Hard Battle: Essays on Working-Class Immigrants,* ed. Dirk Hoerder (De-Kalb: Northern Illinois University Press, 1986), 46–67; Jentz and Schneirov, "Social Republicanism"; and Bruce Levine, "In the Heat of Two Revolutions: The Forging of German-American Radicalism," in Hoer-der, *Struggle a Hard Battle,* 19–45. See also Colls, *Collier's Rant;* Cum-bler, "Transatlantic Working-Class Institutions"; Jones, "Rethinking Chartism"; Kealey and Palmer, *Dreaming of What Might Be;* Montgom-ery, "Labor and Republic"; Lidtke, *The Alternative Culture;* Oestreicher,

*Solidarity and Fragmentation;* Prothero, *Artisans and Politics;* and Sewell, *Work and Revolution.*

10. On the mechanic ideology, see Dawley, *Class and Community;* Faler, *Mechanics and Manufacturers;* Laurie, *Working People;* and Wilentz, *Chants Democratic.*

11. Faler, *Mechanics and Manufacturers,* 30–33.

12. See Jentz and Schneirov, "Social Republicanism"; Levine, "In the Heat of Two Revolutions"; Prothero, *Artisans and Politics;* and Sewell, *Work and Revolution.*

13. Anon., "Appeal to Workingmen," *Fincher's Trades Review,* 12 December 1863.

14. H. C. Dodge, "The Future America," *Bakers' Journal,* 23 February 1889. For similar parodies, see Ralph Hoyt, "America," *Journal of United Labor* 11 (July 1890): 1; and O. J. Graham, "American—1895," in Foner, *American Labor Songs,* 251–52.

15. J. E. L., "So Strange," *Cooper's Journal* 3 (July 1873): 405–6.

16. On J. O. Barrett, see *Banner of Light,* 13 March 1869 and 20 March 1869.

17. J. O. Barrett, "The Labor Battle Song," in Tallmadge, *Labor Songs,* 6–7.

18. On A. J. H. Duganne, see the *Dictionary of American Biography,* 492–93.

19. Augustine Duganne, "The Heroes of '48" in *Poetical Works,* 39–68.

20. J. O. Barrett, "Home Rule for Ireland," in Tallmadge, *Labor Songs,* 9.

21. David Montgomery, "To Study the People," 501.

22. Brundage, "Irish Land and American Workers."

23. Jentz and Schneirov, "Social Republicanism." See also Levine, "In the Heat of Two Revolutions."

24. Gustav Lyser, "Upon Dedicating the Colors of the Chicago Jagerverein on June 15, 1879," *Fackel,* 15 June 1879, reprinted in Keil and Jentz, *German Workers in Chicago,* 240–41.

25. Colls, *Collier's Rant,* 37.

26. "Interview with Herbert Gutman," *Radical History* 27 (May 1983): 208.

27. John James, "Invocation to Workingmen," *Workingman's Advocate,* 4 July 1868.

28. J. F., "Verses for the Toiler," *Journal of United Labor* 6 (February 1886): 2575. For similar works, see James Cairn, "Answer to Gowen's Letter," *National Labor Tribune,* 29 March 1879; D. H. Edwards, "Because a Man's Poor," *National Labor Tribune,* 8 May 1880; Eugene Geary, "A Rally for Labor," *Journal of United Labor* 7 (August 1886): 2138; Michael Heaney, "Unite, Men, Unite," *Carpenter,* June 1886; Mrs. Jacief, "The Land of Our Fathers," *Truth,* 25 October 1882; Joseph Lee, "The Warning," *Cleveland Citizen,* 20 May 1893; J. J. M., "Awake, Oh, Awake," *Cooper's Journal* 3 (June 1872): 344; James Jeffrey Roche, "For the People," in Swinton, *Striking for Life,* 428–29; Thomas Selby, "Knights of Labor," *Journal of United Labor* 6 (November 1885): 1122; John Thompson, "Gideon Is

Coming," *Knights of Labor*, 30 October 1886; and W. Wiley, "Labor Free to All," in Tallmadge, *Labor Songs*, 20. See also John Thompson "America," *Knights of Labor*, 18 December 1886. Thompson modeled his song-poem after a poem by Thomas Paine.

29. Anon., "Appeal to Workingmen," *Fincher's Trades Review*, 12 December 1863.

30. B. M. Lawrence, "The Right Will Prevail," in Lawrence, *Greenback Songster*, 3.

31. B. M. Lawrence, "Hope for the Toiling," in Lawrence, *Greenback Songster*, 4.

32. B. M. Lawrence, "When Workingmen Combine," in Lawrence, *Greenback Songster*, 19. For later variants, see James Tallmadge, "When Workingmen Combine," in Tallmadge, *Labor Songs,*" 22; and Anon., "When Workingmen Combine," *Carpenter*, August 1889.

33. Mrs. S. M. Smith, "Labor's Ninety and Nine," in Tallmadge, *Labor Songs*, 25. On its history see Foner, *American Labor Songs*, 142–44.

34. Thomas Leahy, "Come Join the Knights of Labor Boys," in letter to Terence Powderly, 19 May 1886, *Powderly Papers*, Reel 16. See also Anon., "Storm the Fort," *Labor Leaf*, 30 September 1885; Eugene Geary, "A Rally for Labor," *Journal of United Labor* 8 (August 1886): 2138; and William Stockman, "Our Rights," *Labor Leaf*, 29 September 1886.

35. See Foner, *Free Soil, Free Labor, Free Men*. See also George Clark's songster, *The Free Soil Minstrel* (New York: Martyn and Ely, 1848).

36. See Montgomery, *Beyond Equality*.

37. Lyser, "Upon Dedicating the Colors." See also "Our Dear Police," *Vorbote*, 4 May 1878, reprinted in Keil and Jentz, *German Workers in Chicago*, 240.

38. Michael McGovern, "The Puddler's View of Present Systems," in McGovern, *Labor Lyrics*, 20.

39. Michael McGovern, "The Workingman's Song," in McGovern, *Labor Lyrics*, 38–39.

40. Michael McGovern, " 'Tis Coming," in McGovern, *Labor Lyrics*, 50.

41. Dawley, *Class and Community*. For somewhat critical comments on such thinking, see "Interview with Herbert Gutman." See also Montgomery, "Labor and Republic," 206–8.

42. On politics and the Knights of Labor, see Fink, *Workingmen's Democracy*.

43. Michael McGovern, "Anent Our Trouble with Spain," in McGovern, *Labor Lyrics*, 114–28.

44. Michael McGovern, "The Men Who Guard the Flag," in McGovern, *Labor Lyrics*, 116–17.

45. Michael McGovern, "The Puddlers' Jubilee, August 1896," in McGovern, *Labor Lyrics*, 27–28. See also " 'Poor Jack,' The Dago He's the Hero," *Coast Seamen's Journal*, 27 July 1898.

46. W. Wiley, "Labor Free to All," in Tallmadge, *Labor Songs*, 20.

47. James Tallmadge, "Our Battle Song," in Tallmadge, *Labor Songs*, 15.

# 5

# Labor Song-Poems and True Religion

Sonng-poets, activists, journalists, union officials, lecturers, and rank-and-file workers writing letters to the editor all contributed to a more class-specific understanding of the world. Still, those attached to the mainstream of the labor movement insisted that their own and the movement's interests should be equated with all humanity's interest. The labor movement may have stood on the shoulders of the working class, but its crusade still could be considered a crusade in the name of universal brotherhood and the betterment of humanity.

This dimension of broad and lofty moral purpose for the labor movement—what Gregory Kealey and Bryan Palmer termed "moral universality" in the Knights of Labor—had deep roots among workers in this period.[1] Those roots had their origins, however, in more than simply the "tree of liberty." Something besides this stood behind the ennobling sentiments expressed by Karl Reuber in a song-poem he composed for organized labor:

> Events with prophecies conspire
> To rise for the Right, our zeal to fire;
> Behold the expected time draw near
> Where Labor reigns, the dawn appears
>
> The untaught workman waits to know
> What Labor-gospel will bestow
> Men, women, children, to receive
> The freedom Labor has to give.
>
> Come, let us with a grateful heart
> In blessed labor share a part

> Our Labor Unions' offerings bring,
> Come, Brothers, Sisters, aid and sing:
>
> Auspicious dawn! Thy rising ray
> With joy we view, and hail the day.
> Justice, arise! supremely bright,
> All fill the world with purest light.[2]

Reuber's religious allusions and millennialist overtones, coupled with his decision to title one of his songsters *Hymns of Labor*, indicate that religion, or more specifically Christianity, imbued his song-poems with a keen sense of moral purpose. For Reuber, the labor movement fought not only for workers' improvement but also for a better world based on New Testament principles of morality.

Some members of the labor movement judged Reuber's kind of thinking anathema. Commenting on a similar tendency among British song-poems from the Chartist period, Karl Marx said he found them disagreeable because they contained so much "religious nonsense."[3] Nonetheless, Reuber remained more the rule than the exception in the labor movement in the United States. He and thousands of others found religion as invaluable as republicanism and the mechanic ideology in making sense of their world. Infused with a character that only their more immediate encounter with contemporary capitalism provided, religion became transformed from an inert cultural inheritance into a crucial part of the labor movement and the crusade for humanity.

That religion had an important bearing on labor protest, the labor movement, and workers generally has traditionally been disregarded by labor historians. Religious historians examined topics related to religion and labor.[4] But only after the seminal work of E. P. Thompson, Eric Hobsbawm, and Herbert Gutman did labor historians consider the special role of religion in working-class history.[5] Their scholarship demonstrated that religion profoundly shaped workers' views of industry and their attempts to protest its abuses. According to Gutman, evangelical Protestantism exercised tremendous influence on American workers' understanding of society and permeated the Gilded-Age labor movement. In contrast, Paul Johnson recently argued that evangelical Protestantism rendered Americans more conservative.[6] In his study of the Second Great Awakening in Rochester, New York, between 1815 and 1837, Johnson explains revivals as middle-class events whereby middle-class residents discovered the means to understand, legitimize, and organize a society increasingly characterized by factory production and wage labor. Evangelical Protestantism provided "the moral imperative around which the northern middle class became a class" and would be used by "convert" owners who sought to impose their religious standards on workers.[7]

Certainly organized Protestantism's history suggests a conservative interpretation. Protestantism never proffered a prolabor stance at any time from the sixteenth to the twentieth century.[8] Not that it remained static. Evangelical revivals in the years 1725 to 1750 broke the hold of narrow legalistic Calvinism and boded more drastic changes for the future. George Whitefield unleashed an evangelical impulse that mixed conversion efforts with moderate anticlericalism, less strident intellectualism, an initial foray against conservative Calvinism, and mild emotionalism at gatherings.[9] Followers sometimes felt moved to criticize British authorities and support the movement for American independence as well.[10] These trends were carried to completion during the second "awakening" from 1795 to 1830. Under the leadership of Charles Finney revivalism became institutionalized and a vaguely defined free will doctrine gained ascendancy over Calvinistic determinism. Finney's critics fell into retreat, and most eventually jumped on the revival bandwagon themselves.[11]

Calvin's Protestantism had thus changed significantly by 1830. Revivals, and all their accompanying techniques, became standard fare; clergy more skilled in technique than in the fine points of theology proliferated. A belief in a benevolent God, in a religion of the heart, and in the human ability to overcome sin and to become saved with God's help also found general acceptance, with important consequences. Large numbers of Protestants sharing an optimistic view of God and human ability became convinced that as they worked to overcome their shortcomings they gradually reached perfection and holiness. What's more, as more individuals reached that state, society would be reformed as well. Promulgation of Christianity seemed to promise perfection for the individual, the nation, and the world—a perfection that heralded the millennium and the kingdom of God. Finney remained cautious, devoting himself to saving souls. His followers, however, combined soul saving with improving the world. By 1850 the millennialist impulse and perfectionism had become the central theme of Protestantism and a key ingredient in antebellum social reform. Perfectionism became the backbone of an effort to reform society and make it holy.[12]

Protestants thus sought to administer to the nation's spiritual and social needs, founding a maze of organizations and institutions, including tract societies, reading rooms, temperance groups, orphanages, missions, urban ministries, and homes for unwed mothers.[13] Antislavery and abolitionism also drew considerable support from the perfectionist-millennialist ranks.[14] Nevertheless, except for the most militant abolitionists, these religiously oriented reformers remained socially conservative. The majority emerged from the ranks of the middle and upper class and thought and acted accordingly.[15] They rarely attacked business. Their aid to the poor was patronizing and even coercive, fraught with anti-immigrant, anti-Catholic, and anti-working-class attitudes. Opposed to unions, reformers argued that social reform began with individual, not social, change.[16]

Workers noticed Protestantism's social conservativism in these decades. Still, this fact did not dissuade them from absorbing the basic message of Protestantism. The belief in a benevolent God, in human ability and perfection, and in the millennium and the kingdom of God percolated into the ranks of the working class and profoundly influenced its view of itself and its perception of society. Without any theological coaching and long before social-gospel types courted them, however, many workers, including song-poets, began to question the religious establishment, while offering their own ideas about Christianity's proper course. Workers sympathetic to the labor movement moved to strong criticism, arguing that both Protestant and Catholic churches had strayed from their divine course and that the word of God and Jesus had been disregarded. A far cry from the clergy's religion and from the conservative Christianity Paul Johnson located among Rochester's elite, workers' theology combined elements of traditional evangelical Protestantism—and to a lesser degree of popular religious traditions—with a perspective gained from their own experience. Workers articulated and advocated a religion they labeled "true religion," one that they claimed more closely followed the teachings of God and Christ.

Song-poems demonstrate that the theological tenets of true religion were generally based in evangelical Protestantism. Song-poets, for example, took free will for granted, assuming that neither one's spiritual nor social station had been predetermined by God. In fact, they had even less use for the notion of preordination than revival preachers had. What's more, writers insisted that God could not possibly be Calvin's wrathful deity but was instead a deity of love, friendship, and benevolence. In addition, song-poets joined their mentors in discarding a stern intellectual religion in favor of a religion of the heart. Finally, the spirit of perfectionism and millennialism proved as important to labor writers as it had been to revivalists. For song-poets the Kingdom of God promised more than other-worldly reward. With such an optimistic view of the human potential, the possibilities for a better world seemed fully realizable.

The social implications of these religious tenets emerged as song-poets modified them in labor's image. First, free will came to mean not only that individuals controlled their spiritual destiny but also that their position in society had not been predetermined. The fact that people faced poverty, unemployment, and low wages could not be viewed as divine plan but rather as the result of actions taken by groups who ran society for their own narrow interests. Therefore, should enough people decide they wanted to alter society, an individual's or group's position could be improved. Second, writers believed that God's benevolence extended beyond individual spiritual affairs to material welfare. Since God would never countenance oppression and domination, the exploitation of workers stemmed from the sinful behavior of a ruling class aided and abetted by the clergy. Third, religion of the heart—a tenet typically understood to mean that salvation must include a heartfelt religious state and not just an intellectual one—was projected unto the social sphere. Song-poets argued that if people had religion of the heart their condition would manifest itself in brotherly, cooperative behavior toward others. In short, Christ-like actions would accompany the Christ-like spirit.

This social emphasis carried into other tenets of Protestantism. Individual spiritual concerns had relatively little significance for advocates of true religion. For them an individualistic emphasis violated the word of God and the teaching of Jesus since Christianity by definition must include good works. True religion must be an active, socially directed religion. Correspondingly, song-poets modified the individualist slant that evangelicals gave to perfectionism and millennialism. Great numbers of song-poets argued that perfection of society and the kingdom of God came not through change in the individual but only through change in society.

Labor song-poets did not simply absorb and redefine certain tenets of Protestantism; they also added their own. God, for example, extended special benevolence toward workers. All persons had an equal place in God's eyes, but those subjected to oppression enjoyed particular favor. God considered them his chosen people, among those with a reserved place in the heavenly kingdom. In addition, God looked upon their struggles as part of the deity's own struggle for a better world. God stood on the side of the exploited as they fought for justice. Christ, moreover, complemented this effort. Indeed, the most original characteristic of true religion was its focus on Christ and elevation of Christ as role model. In part, this tendency reflected a general postbellum shift in Christianity toward greater emphasis on Christ. Song-poets and the labor movement also found themselves heir to a centuries-old tradition that identified Christ as a man of humble origins—a poor man, a man of lower station, a carpenter. Song-poets and others labeled Christ a worker and embraced him as one of their own, celebrating his involvement among the poor, the downtrodden, and the oppressed. His noteworthy mixture of humble origins and social actions rendered him a model of ethics. Song-poets pointed out that Christ campaigned for both the spiritual and material welfare of those in need. Those seeking to emulate Christ, song-poets counseled, must also preach a message of justice and fight for the oppressed. Anyone who professed belief in real, or true, religion could not act otherwise.

The true religion that found steady service among song-poets and that figured so prominently in movement culture owed its most obvious debt to evangelical Protestantism. To say that true religion manifested a Protestant sensibility, however, deserves qualification. First, while the roots might be traced to Protestantism, this religion also derived from antebellum reform. Labor inherited from earlier reform movements a certain Christian character, if not zeal. Virtually every reform effort before the Civil War exhibited a degree of religious fervor spawned by the Second Great Awakening. That the labor movement absorbed this spirit cannot be surprising, for its ties to antebellum reform have been documented elsewhere. Spiritualists, for example, had even broached the issue of true religion as early as 1860. Some spiritualists with no ties to the working class nevertheless shared with workers a contempt for the established church and its dogma and the need for an active, socially conscious religion.[17] Song-poets such as B. M. Lawrence and the anarchist Dyer Lum had first shown religious impulses with millennialist and perfectionist overtones as spiritualists, not as labor song-poets or activists; Lum never rid himself of his perfectionist past. Even the anarchist camp's atheism, agnosticism, and antireligion did not exempt them from the impact of the religious milieu in which so many had been raised. They hated capitalism and the clergy, but many could never completely discount New Testament teachings.[18] Other labor groups would claim more direct ties to religion, and justifiably so, but a spiritualist thinker and song-poet named Cora Richmond would head the clemency movement for the Haymarket defendents,[19] and anarchist Dyer Lum's song-poems would overflow with a religious fervor equal to that of any writer.[20]

Second, while many immigrants would have shied from explicit Protestantism in the mainstream labor movement, not all would have been offended by it. Important religious differences did exist between native workers and immigrants, and these cannot be disregarded. Nevertheless, Protestant workers from the British Isles shared a considerable body of religious beliefs with those calling for true religion. British Protestantism shared with its American counterpart a distinctly conservative, anti-working-class bias. But as many historians have noted, workers often fashioned their own religious beliefs as they sought to hold their own in the spiritual and material world. The "religious nonsense" that Marx observed among Chartists derived in part from this process, as would the religious impulse frequently noted among Methodist miners. British Protestantism bequeathed an accommodationist strain to workers, but its rebellious working-class personality could also emerge. As a result, when English, Scottish, and Welsh workers emigrated to the United States, they found themselves quite at ease with the standard tenets of mainstream Protestantism and sympathetic with labor's true religion.[21]

Other immigrant groups present a more problematic relationship to true religion. Catholic church officials noticed Protestant influence in the labor movement, and their caution toward the Knights of Labor and other unions stemmed from this observation. Yet Catholics also constituted an important element in the movement and song-poetry. Michael McGovern and Patrick Fennell remained devoutly Catholic but also wrote song-poems with a strong religious component and with certain beliefs similar to those of their Protestant comrades. In addition, despite embracing religious beliefs as diverse as Lutheranism, Catholicism, and free thought, German workers also contributed song-poems advocating everything from trade unionism to socialism to anarchy. While they may not have found true religion to their liking, song-poets from these backgrounds still found points of agreement in particular tenets of it.

Two factors help explain this apparent paradox. First, while movement culture recalls Protestantism, sectarianism and dogma declined under the weight of a working-class influence. Song-poets would have had an interest in aiding workers, not in advancing Protestantism. More often, Catholic workers would have been sympathetic when other workers argued that society did not measure up to the standards of Christianity, that workers enjoyed God's favor, that the movement embodied Christian principles. Conflicts between working-class Protestants and Catholics rarely developed over doctrinal differences. They would not have argued over notions of a benevolent God, of religious social concern and good works, of Christ as role model, and of the need for heartfelt religion. True religion retained a Protestant temper, but in labor's hand it was stripped of sectarian garb.

Second, significant elements of the immigrant population harbored strong anticlericalism. Irish Land League supporters, German socialists and anarchists, and Czech socialists and free thinkers, from Catholic and Lutheran backgrounds, expressed general displeasure, if not disgust, for clergy and church establishment. Some embraced one of varying brands of irreligion, as happened among a fairly large number of those allied with labor in Chicago.[22] The millennialism and perfectionism pervasive in the mainstream of the labor movement found no welcome with such individuals, but the anticlericalism and New Testament morality would have. Anticlericalism and hostility to religion could often be traced to simple disgust with churches in relation to workers and not in some clearly defined ideology of antireligion. Therefore, Irish and German song-poets could espouse anticlericalism as well as sympathy with what they also believed to be the true religion.

Workers who felt affinity for the labor movement and the values embodied in true religion frequently targeted clergy and established churches for criticism. Their censure could be simple but effective. During a speech by a local clergyman, New York workers hissed at every mention of the word "church." By contrast, they demonstrated their commitment to basic Christian values by cheering each reference to Jesus.[23] The motivation for such behavior was clear among those attached to labor. In 1867 a contributor to one publication summarized labor's conception of the relationship between capital, labor, and the clergy: "The Church has too frequently ranged itself on the side of the oppressor. In all reforms, in which labor and capital have been directly interested, the Church has thrown its influence in behalf of the money changers."[24] From then until the end of the century this view found repeated support.

Song-poet N.E.M. evolved a more elaborate religious view that prompted more hostile feelings toward clergy and churches. In his "Modern Christianity" in 1890 the author vented his dissatisfaction with a fervor that mounted with each verse:

> Trusts and tramps are multiplying,
>   God have mercy on this land;
> Some are starving, freezing, dying,
>   While around on every hand
> Food and fuel is abounding;
>   But so 'cornered' that the poor
> With salvation's cymbals sounding,
>   Must these horrors all endure.
>
> Gorgeous temples, where the lowly
>   Son of God is oft envoked
> To incline His Spirit Holy,
>   And forgive them that provoked
> God to anger, are erected,
>   Costly mines of treasured gold,
> While His loved ones, crushed, neglected,
>   Suffer miseries untold.
>
> He was poor, despised, and lowly
>   Minded, without house or home,
> While His followers are slowly,
>   Surely, aiming to become
> Lords and owners of creation,
>   Grinding down the lowly poor,
> Who in want and desolation
>   Must all misery endure.
>
> Are they Christians who thus corral
>   What we eat, and drink, and wear,
> With the one hand, and point a moral
>   With the other; while our share
> Of production is unequal
>   To sustain our mode of life?
> Troubles follow—and the sequel—
>   Anarchy, and strikes, and strife.
>
> God have mercy on the toilers!
>   Old and bent before their time.
> God rebuke them, heartless spoilers,
>   Who have not a thought sublime,
> Or a Christian fellow-feeling

For their neighbor's wants and woes;
Who put on their stock-religion
With their Sunday-meeting clothes.

What are Christ's apostles doing
To cast out this devil, GREED
That's today his hands imbruing
In the poor's life-blood; that feed
On the hearts of widows, orphans,
That have struggled to be free?
Oh for some good Christ to drown them
With the swine beneath the sea.[25]

Such anticlericalism had some precedent among oppressed groups in Western civilization. For all their domination by both Catholic and Protestant officialdom and the aristocracy, rural and urban lower classes had long harbored anticlerical views. Occasionally these views became public, threatening the status quo while simultaneously passing along a subversive message to sympathizers. In 1716 a small village in Gloustershire, England, for example, spawned a charivari, replete with an anti-aristocratic and anticlerical message, according to one elite observer. Authorities quickly put a lid on the insurrectionary blasphemy, but anticlericalism remained a strong, if submerged, plebeian belief.[26] A less rebellious anticlericalism also had some precedent in the United States. Evangelicals and religious novelists remained socially conservative, but their work also included a strong current of anticlericalism.[27]

Whatever the origins of workers' anticlericalism, clergy's behavior would only have strengthened it. Prior to the Civil War, Protestantism ardently defended capitalism and the interests of the ruling elite. As religious historian Henry May described it: "Support for the moral, political, and economic status quo was ingrained in American Protestantism by habit and history."[28] Following the war, clergy offered greater solace. An array of services for the downtrodden became available—Sunday schools, employment programs, industrial training, family counseling, aid for young women, social activities, libraries, lectures, temperance campaigns, Americanization courses, and homes for the homeless. Nonetheless, organized labor would still be judged anathema by all but a few maverick ministers. Many clergy used their pulpits to issue venomous edicts against the labor movement and labor's collective efforts. Well into the 1880s clergy regularly charged unions with destruction and violence, called strikes the harmful work of agitators, branded the eight-hour movement a shameful attempt to increase vice, and deemed socialists a lot of criminals, alcoholics, and foreigners. Even in 1894, when many clergy openly acknowledged the role of unions, they still dismissed Eugene Debs and the American Railway Union as a social menace.

Labor leaders and rank and file knew they had few friends in the clergy. Samuel Gompers, Terence Powderly, John Jarrett, Eugene Debs, and Richard Trevellick, subjected clergy to varying degrees of opprobrium.[29] Comments from church leaders on workers' attitudes suggest workers felt similarly.[30] Officials noted that workers had become convinced that churches allied with big business against labor and that workers responded by going to church less frequently.[31] Still, workers generally remained unsympathetic to infidelity, symbolized by National Labor Union delegates' cool reception to a moderate antiprayer proposal at their 1870 convention.[32]

Song-poets, however, delivered large quantities of anticlericalism. William Camack of Jellico, Tennessee, took his religious convictions seriously, and his earnestness estranged him from the religious establishment. In unassuming style, he explained his position to fellow workers in "The Church and the Workingman."[33] Asked by a minister to account for his absence from Sabbath service, Camack's "Brother Jones" responded:

> Well, Parson Jones, I'll answer you
> In language plain and fair:
> The church is not what it ought to be,
> And I cannot visit there.

Brother Jones further explained that he loved to go to church when he learned the lessons of Christ. Unfortunately, Jones informed his pastor, the teachings of Christ had been discarded:

> And the reason I've quit is this:
> The church has lost the way;
> She follows not the path of old;
> And the cross has lost its sway.
>
> They follow not the laws of Christ,
> That lowly Nazarene;
> The Bible on the shelf is laid;
> And gold is king supreme.
>
> You've got a church without a Christ,
> Like a ship without a tiller;
> And wreck you will upon the shores of sin,
> With your load of gold and silver.

Fill up your pews by following Christ,
If the pathway is fraught with labor;
Tell the people if they love God;
  They must also love their neighbor!

Preach the truth that rents and profits,
And interest (or usury), is thievery,
And try to hold to gold and God
  Is sacreligious knavery.

And if you'll do this, I'll promise that
The time will not be long
Till you'll have a crowded house of workingmen,
  With their humble prayer and song.

Camack's criticism of the church was informed by convictions paralleling the tenets of true religion. Free will, for example, exists as an assumption, as implied by Camack. Similarly, while the author never mentioned perfection or the millennium, his work was suffused with their spirit. Camack had no doubt that humans could make the world better for everyone and do so on the basis of Christian principles. A world of injustice existed because some chose mammon over God and received no clerical stricture. Above all, Christ stood at the center of Camack's religion. The author discovered in Christ, "that lowly Nazarene" of humble origins, the role model for Christians to emulate. Christ, as Camack saw it, did not countenance a church of "gold and silver" or a society where capital and clergy tried "to hold to gold and God" and business practiced usury and thievery. The clergy refused to heed God and Christ, choosing to follow the exploiters in worshipping mammon and in not opposing capital's immoral practices. The church had simply put the "Bible on the shelf" and for that reason deserved workers' contempt.

Other song-poets agreed with this assessment. Like Camack they harbored a belief in some kind of real or true religion sharply at odds with clerical practice. John Digham told readers of the *Baker's Journal* in 1888 that any preacher who dared to tell workers to be happy, patient, and content with their lot deserved workers' reproof.[34] Digham pointed out that the notion of contentment was contrary to true religion, and he advised workers to turn a deaf ear to sinful clergy:

So vacillating poets write and well-fed parsons preach.
Oh, heed them not, deluded man, they're blasphemies they teach;
Those fawning slaves, to serve the rich, the wrath of God defy,
And boldly vow men's evil deeds are blessings from on High.

> List not those slimy pandering knaves arraign the King of Heaven,
> And thus profane the noble gifts gen'rous God had given—
> The Great Creator made the earth, proclaimed it good and fair,
> Gave it for man's inheritance for all alike to share.

Digham found the preaching of contentment incompatible with true Christianity because it implied an immutable world. By his reckoning God was "a gen'rous God" who made the earth "good and fair." This world did not operate by unchanging fixed laws; by acts of free will individuals and groups made themselves, society, and the world more perfect.

St. Louis song-poet Joseph Fairfield took the clergy to task in "The Holy Will of God."[35] Fairfield reminded workers that clerics commonly referred to labor's plight as "the will of God" and closed their eyes to evidence of men, women, and children suffering exploitation, unemployment, and substandard wages: "victims of despotic rule— / Of Mammon's iron rod." Those who declared such suffering to be the will of god the author called religious fools, if not knaves. The truly righteous believer could only agree with Fairfield that

> 'Tis time this foolish cry should cease,
>    'Tis time the people know;
> 'Tis time the despot be dethroned,
>    'Tis time the spoiler go,
> 'Tis time the workman should be freed
>    From bondage, wrong and fraud,
> 'Tis time he sees such things can't be
>    The holy will of God.

The somber tone employed by Fairfield, Digham, Camack, and N.E.M. contrasted sharply with that of Shandy Maguire. Maguire may have wearied of clerical decrees inviting passivity among workers, but he chose to treat the serious subject jocularly, if not flippantly, while still making his point. The opening lines of "Patience" humorously depicted the clergy advising ailing individuals to be patient.[36] The plea tortured the victim of "fever and chills," "gout," "rheumatics," "neuralgia," or "eyeballs" with "blood-colored sockets." Maguire then proceeded unexpectedly to a mocking and pointed censure of clerical unctuousness:

> 'Be patient!' the preacher keeps telling
>    Poor souls without clothing or food,
> When rolling in richest of broadcloth,
>    And aping a sanctified mood.

> They'll feed you on texts from the Scriptures,
> And ask why you dare to complain,
> While at the same time they're regaling
> On porter-house steak and champagne.

Clerical indifference due to naiveté or misinformation might be grounds for mercifulness, according to song-poets, but those who took remunerative support from capital and, in turn, lavished intellectual support on capital practiced apostasy. They acted as partners in exploitation, apologetic tools and pawns of capital who abdicated Christianity for the sins of the flesh. Once more, song-poets laid siege to such spiritual betrayers.

Shandy Maguire again took the humorous route on this grave topic.[37] He told readers of the *Locomotive Engineer's Monthly Journal* that in fasting for Lent he had "masticated myriad bones / Of every kind of fish" and now longed for the taste of anything else:

> Oh! for a steak cut from a hog,
> Or off a cow, or yonder dog,
>   Ah, yes, or from a cat,
> A horse, a mule, a goat, an ass—
> I swear, this moment, by the mass
>   I'd masticate a rat!

But, like the Irish vaudevillian songster-comic, Maguire employed levity to make a social comment. He lightly but seriously gibed clergy again:

> The Bible says to fast and pray,
> 'Twas thus my pastor preached one day,
>   My pastor tells no fibs.
> Poor man! He looks as though he takes
> His penance out in sirloin steaks,
>   while I pick codfish ribs.

Other song-poets found slight humor in the topic and issued more truculent criticism. A. J. Jennings titled one song-poem "Mammon's Tools," a work the Denver *Labor Enquirer* prefaced with the remark: "Our Poet Tells of the Venal Preachers, Who are Hired by Money."[38] The author explained:

> Six-tenths of all that toilers earn
>   Is set aside as plunder,
> To it the rich men's preachers turn,
>   Kneel down, adorn, and wonder.

Jennings chastised the clergy as nothing more than comrades of the oppressors:

> They think the Master said in vain,
>   That love of money is the cause
> Of every great or little stain
>   Which mankind put on Heaven's laws.

Parodying the Lord's Prayer, Jennings contrasted clerical religion with true religion. He argued that when the clergy spoke "Our Father," they never bothered to consider "the disinherited" among God's children. Jennings believed otherwise, confident that God looked lovingly upon the outcast and downtrodden as the chosen few, guarded on earth and at his side at judgment. Moreover, he implied that as clergy prayed "thy will be done," they indulged in prevarication, since God would more surely will the destruction of the clergy rather than condone their behavior. Clerical concern for all people's "daily bread" Jennings found insincere, motivated by guilt, not conviction. The clergy never followed Christ's example, the example around which any true religion had to revolve, of ministering to the spiritual and material welfare of the downtrodden. Jennings considered the hypocrisy and pathetic irony of clerics asking for deliverance from evil since they had already given themselves up to a god of mammon: "Mammon's finger leads them / And 'love of money' steals the gold / That buys their clothes and feeds." Pessimistic about a change of heart among the clergy, Jennings followed prophetic tradition as he enjoined God's retribution:

> A few may hear; a few may heed;
>   And turn from darkness unto light,
> Renounce the villainy of greed,
>   And come out on the side of right.
> But most of them will sow the wind
>   Until, when clouds are feathered thick,
> The whirlwind's wrath shall strike them blind
>   And make their reeling hearts grow sick.
> The cup of trembling they've filled
>   From poverty to drink so fast,
> Shall through their pallid lips be spilled;
>   They'll taste its bitterness at last.

Coal miner Samuel Simon found clergy sorely wanting when measured against religious figures of the Old and New Testaments.[39] Jehovah had commanded: "In the sweat of thy face shall thou eat bread." Accordingly, the prophets had "preached the gospel without pay," working like commoners for their daily bread. Jesus did the same, ministering among the oppressed as he "labored hard too, at His trade, / And hence an honest living made." His apostles carried on this tradition, heeding the command: "Go hence and give with willing hand; / For, freely given has been my store / To you; then give unto the poor." Given these precedents, Simon believed that clergy ought to teach without regard to compensation, labor daily for their bread, and aid those in need. He waxed indignant as he recounted how clergy refused honest toil, indulged in a life of "ease and plenteousness," and never ventured a "willing hand" to succor the "humble poor." They impudently instructed the oppressed not to worry about their next meal, yet had the audacity to live in luxury themselves. Simon called clergy "hungry wolves" who "devour what was not theirs."

Repeated in conjunction with labor activities, such anticlericalism became standard litany for Gilded-Age workers and common ground for song-poets of every stripe. Simon himself wrote letters to the *United Mine Workers Journal* in 1892 and 1893, repeating his charges against the clergy.[40] Elsewhere, in 1886, "A Christian Woman" explained to readers of the Chicago *Knights of Labor* that clergy were "scheeming, hypocritical, praying Pharisees," false teachers who with "Judas-like kisses" took "blood-money" from the rich and violated the biblical injunction: "By their works ye shall know them."[41] God's kingdom went to the poor, according to the correspondent, while the clergy would receive well-deserved damnation. Letter writer B. Longrigg blurted a more stinging accusation: "You are Charged with Failing in Your Duty to the Children of God."[42] Longrigg argued that clergy profaned religion by allowing greed and exploitation to predominate and by siding with the vile rich who ground the poor for personal gain. Clergy were judged "false guides" who had rejected Christ. To these "hypocrites" and "blind guides" he issued a prophetic warning:

> Oh! ye ministers of the gospel! God will call you to account for your remissness of duty in allowing such evils to go unrebuked; the robbed widow and orphan will stand as menacing witnesses against you at the bar of Eternal Justice. And how many of God's poor men are there who were never invited to come to your church, because of their poverty? Robbed of his birthright, despised and dejected, and often made a criminal and a fugitive and a vagabond to wander over the face of the earth. I say in all earnestness and charity, let your voices be heard in thunder tones to warn your wealthy hypocrites of

the wrath to come, and make your calling and election sure—and if they will not turn let the blood be upon their own heads.

Song-poems, letters to the editors, essays, reprinted speeches, and editorials all fulminated against the nation's clergymen.[43] Writers even took individual clergy or clerical groups to task. Everyone from the early social gospel advocate Washington Gladden to an unknown Rahway, New Jersey, clergyman invited stricture.[44] None generated as much antipathy as Henry Ward Beecher, however; he quickly became a symbol of the clergy's seemingly flagrant disregard for Christianity. From 1871, when the *Workingman's Advocate* termed Beecher "the professional blather-skite of America," until his death in 1887, he drew regular fire.[45] In 1877 a song-poet blasted Beecher as "The Hireling Saint of Long Island" and alternately assailed him as a "hypocrite saint," "a bigot," and a "parrot" who sang the millionaire's tune. The author advised Beecher to follow the path of Judas: "Go hang yourself on some blasted tree."[46] No one challenged Arthur Cheesewright's tombstone-shaped epitaph written for Beecher upon his death:

> Here lie the bones of Henry Ward Beecher,
> A Foe to mankind and an overfed preacher;
> Good enough for the poor was water and bread;
> His life it is o'er—Thank God he is dead.[47]

Not all clergy fared as badly as Beecher. Those who fought for labor and the poor received labor's respect and blessing. Christian socialist and labor advocate Hugh Pentacost and Episcopalian bishop and pioneer social gospeler F. D. Huntington both counted friends among organized labor.[48] Less well known in religious circles, but among the most vociferous ministers for labor, the Reverend Jesse Jones and his partner E. H. Rogers—a carpenter, minister, song-poet—found even greater acceptance with labor.[49] Finally, those nearly anonymous clergy who fought with workers in their everyday battles also garnered praise.[50]

Such ministers remained exceptions. Writers summarily dismissed most clergy as "hypocrites," "knaves," "fools," "liars," "frauds," "imposters," "clackers," "Levites," "traitors," and "street fakirs." Appropriately, when B. M. Lawrence envisioned the millennial future in "What We Want," he included the following stanza:

> We want all men to know the Lord,
> When priests no more pervert the word,

> And love forever sheathes the sword,
> Then we'll have no CLERGY anymore.
> Free from creed-bound sect or school,
> We will bide the golden rule,
> Then we'll have no CLERGY anymore.[51]

Clergy were not alone as a subject for approbrium. Capitalists, as labor well understood, accounted for labor's exploitation and rampant social destruction. Much more than did the clergy, capitalists made a mockery of true Christianity. Unlike the clergy they did not employ religious argument to uphold the status quo. Indeed, Gilded-Age business argued that religion ought to be considered a spiritual matter with minimal relevancy to the world of industry.[52] Unlike antebellum elites Paul Johnson located in Rochester, New York, Gilded-Age businessmen kept religion out of the workplace.[53] Trying to use religion as a labor-management tool would have guaranteed open conflict with workers.

Still, the other-worldly bent of capitalists' Christianity did not leave workers satisfied either. Their bosses would claim to be Christians, donate money to church and religious organizations, and then argue that the laws of supply and demand determined wage levels while Christianity had no bearing on the issue. To many workers this sounded alarmingly unchristian, a religion of empty words and convenience. Owners might affirm their Christianity on Sunday, only to exploit workers during the remainder of the week. Writers accordingly judged owners the worst hypocrites and sinners, worshippers of the god of mammon.

As early as 1864 an anonymous song-poet summarized workers' feelings about the Christianity of the upper class. Writing to *Fincher's Trades Review,* the author of "Pharisees, Hypocrites"—one of many biblical allusions in the text—introduced the song-poem with a biblical quote that invoked the nonexploitative, cooperative spirit of true Christianity: "In as much as ye did unto one of them, ye did it unto me."[54] In contrast, religion wore the uniform of social class. Ruling elites who sat in church on Sunday would not even permit workers into their churches. According to the author, Christ's downtrodden followers rarely entered the palatial temples reserved for the wealthy:

> You sit in God's temples each Sabbath day—
> Beautiful spire-crowned temples they—
> Whose doors are open to those who pay,
> Where there's plenty of room for wealth to pray—
> But not a place for the poor.

The author disparaged this Sunday Christianity:

> You send money with lavish hands
> To clothe the heathen in distant lands,
> But you heed not the starving wretch who stands
> Ragged and weary, begging for alms
>     Right at your very door.

Such hypocrisy galled the author, since it permeated the lives of the elite. During the week wealthy churchgoers refused to heed the cries of the poor, those people Christ had called his own. The author reiterated capitalists' callous, unchristian behavior in successive fashion: "You heed not the cry of misery"; "You heed not the millions plodding along . . . the 'son of toil' "; "There's many a hovel may meet your eye . . . But like the priest and Levite you pass it by . . . "; and "You look not with pity on the woman of shame." Finally, the author specifically addressed the workplace and religion:

> You work the poor man day after day,
> You grudge him the beggarly pittance you pay
> And if he murmur you drive him away—
> And then 'thank God' when you kneel to pray—
>     That 'you are not like the other man.'

In concluding the author warned the practitioners of false religion that only the swiftest expiation would bring any hope for salvation:

> Oh, hypocrites, hypocrites, what will ye say,
> When you stand before God on that awful day
> When the earth like vapor shall pass away—
> And God's children shall call upon Him to repay
>     All the wrongs you have heaped upon them?
>
> You may call in vain for the mountains then,
> To hide you from God and your fellow-men,
> For man will accuse and he will condemn;
> For he has not said 'as ye do unto them
>     You do even so to him?'
> Go, dig your talent out of the ground
> And scatter your wealth to your brothers around,
> And God will cause your hearts to bound,
> And happy hearts your names shall sound,
>     And your souls will be free from sin.

A typical depiction and critique of upper-class, capitalist Christianity, "Pharisees, Hypocrites" reveals much about song-poets' conception of Christianity applied to capital and labor.[55] The song-poem included numerous—though not skillfully incorporated—biblical allusions to develop a message. The most obvious, and the one from which the others followed, was the title's allusion to pharisees and hypocrites. The New Testament contains countless passages in which Christ rebuked those who claimed to be follow-ers of God but acted to the contrary. Christ advised such people that their feigned commitment disgusted him. He exhorted such vile hypocrites to seek atonement or suffer damnation.

For example, in Matthew 23:14, Christ exclaimed: "Woe unto you Scribes and pharisees, hypocrites! for ye devour widows' houses, and for pretence make long prayers: therefore ye shall receive greater damnation."[56] Knowledgeable of this or similar pronounce-ments, the author employed them to discredit the capitalist brand of Christianity. The author of "Pharisees, Hypocrites" explained in the opening stanza that, like biblical pharisees and hypocrites, late nineteenth-century hypocrites also claimed sincerity and good faith in religion. Modern hypocrites sat "in the temples each sab-bath day" and made a "pretense of prayer." Meanwhile, the less fortunate starved at the temple gates. And, when the sabbath ob-servers left their sanctimonious surroundings, they turned a deaf ear to those "millions plodding along." Like their New Testament forebears, Gilded-Age elites made a "pretense" of prayer only to "devour widows' houses" and did nothing to help the poor or the "son of toil."

The author also referred to the poor and downtrodden in the New Testament, the people Christ befriended. Beggars, prostitutes, children, and workers found throughout the New Testament also populated "Pharisees, Hypocrites" and most other writings in this period. The author described the "ragged and weary, begging for alms" and crying out "for the crumbs that fall" from the tables of the rich; the millions living in starvation and "hovel"; and females forced into prostitution, the "woman of shame." Such ref-erences with an archaic ring became cliché among song-poets. Nonetheless, they had the effect of linking those victimized by in-dustry with those victimized in the New Testament. They thereby established capitalism's victims as the chosen people.

Indeed, the author of "Pharisees, Hypocrites" identified the down-trodden of both eras in interchangeable terms. Gilded-Age workers now belonged to Christ's flock and Christ was the standard-bearer of the working class. Capitalists who "did unto one of them" should know that "them" now denoted the working class. In addition, just as Christ warned hypocrites to seek atonement or face greater damnation, so, too, the author alerted capitalists of their impending fate. They must cease the sinful debasement of "God's children" and scatter their hoarded talent and wealth to all their "brothers."

Other song-poets echoed this message. Richard Lloyd's "Death and the Oppressor" recounted the arrival of Death with a divine summons for the "greedy, guilty soul" of the Oppressor, an individual who spent his life grinding the less fortunate.[57] Death informed the Oppressor that the Lord's judgment would be unmerciful:

> The widow's tear, the orphan's cry
>   Came up before the Lord,
> And thou this night shall surely die
>   And have thy due reward.
>
> Five minutes hence and thou wilt be
>   In hell's deep, dark recess,
> Prepared for every one else like thee
>   Who shall the poor oppress.

Terrified, the Oppressor begged for time to rectify his sinful injustices. Death, however, refused the request for supplication—more "time for mockery prayer"—as God's judgment stood resolute.

No victim of predestination, the Oppressor had determined his fate by his actions. The Oppressor may have professed Christianity, but from song-poets' vantage of true religion, this was no religion at all; the Oppressor had never known religion of the heart, never done good works, never considered Christ as a role model, never helped the downtrodden, and never tried to improve society or work for the kingdom of God. Lloyd repeated Christ's injunction against idle prayer, labeling it "mockery prayer." He also made allusions to widows, orphans, and the suffering poor of the New Testament, establishing their industrial progeny in the working class. Once more the message seemed obvious: if the working class bore kinship to the oppressed of the Bible, then exploitation of the working class amounted to no less than a sin in the eyes of God and one worthy of damnation.

Employing similar historical analogies in "The Megatherium and the Millionaire," F. Robinson also condemned the rich for hypocrisy and warned them of their unpleasant afterlife.[58] Robinson said an ancient monster known as the megatherium roamed the earth until extinct, only to be replaced by a modern "Saurian monster," "the pious millionaire." This millionaire, Robinson asserted, went about "Devouring widows' houses, while / Engaged in solemn prayer." God would treat such apostasy sternly, according to the author, and he reinforced his assessment with more biblical references:

> But though, they always pray to Christ,
> The millionaire must know,
> That Jesus told them plainly that
> To heaven they cannot go.

> That a camel could more easily
> Go through the needle's eye,
> Than for such selfish creatures
> To ascend to joys on high.

Robinson concluded that just as the megatherium had been banished from earth, so too would millionaires become extinct, out of place in a world of freedom and equality.

The most damning indictment of capitalists' religion may have been Samuel Simon's "The True Man, the Selfish Man, the Hypocrite."[59] Simon enumerated the differences between a true religion and a false religion by comparing the true man with the hypocrite. The former's religion proceeded from simple conviction—that Christians obey God's commands, succor the needy, and love neighbors as they would their brothers. The hypocrite "carries on his dark designs / Both in church and in the mines," affecting virtue while betraying Christ:

> Like Judas he will kiss his Savior
> As though he was his true believer,
> And then betray with a lie,
> And his great Savior crucify.

Capitalists would have rankled to be called "Judas," but their hypocrisy earned Simon's searing reproach.[60] Measured against the standard of true religion, elites fared as badly as the clergy. The true man, the believer in and practitioner of true religion, worked for social betterment and did so specifically by improving the condition of Christ's working-class children. Because the upper class separated Christianity from the wider social world, song-poets wondered whether owners could be considered Christians at all. Song-poets perceived that the only religion taken seriously by those running the country was a religion "based on Extortion and Greed / With Mammon its God and Plunder its Creed."[61]

No song-poet or other contributor to labor took issue with these or similar charges. Only the severity of the charge served to separate one song-poet from another or from journalists, correspondents, speakers, and lecturers who subscribed to true religion. None demonstrated greater sense of immediacy and purpose than St. Clair County, Illinois, miner and union member George Kinghorn.[62] Kinghorn wrote a letter to the *Workingman's Advocate* in 1870 to report "the death of a beloved brother of the Miners Union, of Lodge No. 9," and his anger could hardly be contained. His fellow miner, George Uttley, had died hopping a freight train while enroute to his wife, six children, and hometown. Miners' wages were always dismally low, and Uttley had gone on the tramp to ensure his family's survival. With his death, however, destitution now appeared unavoidable for the family. Enraged, Kinghorn assailed the hypocrites responsible for this situation, the wealthy class that lived "in sumptuous palaces, with every comfort and luxury that wealth can command" while refusing "the heartrendering agonizing cries of the millions of their downtrodden, oppressed fellow creatures." "The grinding, crushing, selfish actions of those favored ones" did not go unnoticed. Sounding the voice of working-class religious prophecy, Kinghorn cautioned the wealthy class: "A day of reckoning is fast approaching. The prayers of the widows and orphans are being heard. Then God helps those money kings. They may rest assured that the same mercy will be meted out to them that they have meted out to others."

Kinghorn's emotional letter employed both language and a message that proved the standard throughout the three decades after the Civil War. He and hundreds of others would relentlessly criticize the clergy and the leaders of the economic order for their refusal to put into practice the religion they claimed to follow.[63] Kinghorn could not see how people calling themselves Christian could pay a miner below subsistance wages, force him on the tramp, and literally allow his widow and orphans to face starvation. Businessmen might denounce Kinghorn and his comrades as "infidels," but Kinghorn, song-poets, and many other Americans believed otherwise.[64] They knew that Christ said "Whoever heareth these sayings of mine and doeth them" would be judged a true believer and that anyone who either did not believe or refused to obey such dictums would be judged an infidel. Therefore, capitalists were the real infidels, for they separated the spiritual and material world; they heard the word of God and professed belief but did not obey. They and their religious apologists, the clergy, would reap their appropriate rewards sooner or later.

Such a body of beliefs had taken workers a long way from the teachings of Charles Finney and from evangelical Protestantism. Indeed, Finney would have been horrified to learn of Christ's working-class children promulgating their own version of the true religion he once claimed to represent. Mingling Finneyite religious tenets, the antebellum reform spirit, anticlericalism, and the non-denominational lessons provided by industrial capitalism, song-poets fashioned an important tool for social evaluation and criticism. Neither clergy nor capitalists fared well in the evaluation process.

## NOTES

1. Kealey and Palmer, *Dreaming of What Might Be,* 394.

2. Karl Reuber, "Strive for Better Life," in Reuber, *Hymns of Labor,* 4–5.

3. Marx to Herman Schleuter, 15 May 1885, in Marx and Engels, *Literature and Art,* 113–14.

4. On nineteenth-century Protestantism, see Aaron I. Abell, *The Urban Impact on American Protestantism, 1865–1900* (Cambridge: Harvard University Press, 1943); James Bodo, *The Protestant Clergy and Public Issues, 1812–1848* (Princeton: Princeton University Press, 1954); Charles Cole, *The Social Ideas of Northern Evangelists, 1826–1860* (New York: Columbia University Press, 1954); Hopkins, *Rise of the Social Gospel;* Henry F. May, *Protestant Churches and Industrial America* (New York: Octagon Books, 1963); and Timothy Smith, *Revivalism and Social Reform in Mid-Nineteenth-Century America* (New York: Abingdon Press, 1957). See also Garth Rosell, "Charles Finney and the Rise of the Benevolence Empire" (Ph.D. diss., University of Minnesota, 1971); Milton David Speizman, "Attitudes toward Charity in American Thought, 1865–1901" (Ph.D. diss., Tulane University, 1962); and Joseph Howard Walsh, "Protestant Response to Materialism in American Life, 1865–1900" (Ph.D. diss., Columbia University, 1974).

On Protestantism's "institutional church," see Clifford Griffin, "Religious Benevolence as Social Control," *Mississippi Valley Historical Review* 44 (December 1957): 423–44, and *Their Brothers' Keepers: Moral Stewardship in the United States, 1800–1865* (New Brunswick: Rutgers University Press, 1960); Nathan Huggins, *Protestants against Poverty: Boston Charities, 1870–1900* (Westport, Conn.: Greenwood Publishing,

1971); Norris Magnuson, *Salvation in the Slums: Evangelical Social Work, 1865–1920* (Metuchen, N.J.: Scarecrow Press and the American Theological Library Association, 1977); and Carroll Smith Rosenberg, *Religion and the Rise of the American City: The New York City Mission Movement, 1812–1870* (Ithaca: Cornell University Press, 1971). For a critique of Griffin and the "social control" thesis, see Lois Banner, "Religious Benevolence as Social Control: A Critique," *Journal of American History* 60 (June 1973): 23–41.

On Protestantism's reaction to labor unrest, see Stephen George Cobb, "William H. Carwadine and the Pullman Strike" (Ph.D. diss., Northwestern University, 1970); Carl Warren Griffiths, "Some Protestant Attitudes on the Labor Question in 1886," *Church History* 11 (June 1942): 138–48; Carlos Schwantes, "Labor Unions and the Seventh-Day Adventists: The Formative Years, 1877–1903," *Adventist Heritage* 4 (Winter 1977): 11–19; and Lewis Frederick Wheelock, "Urban Protestant Reactions to the Chicago Haymarket Affair, 1886–1893," (Ph.D. diss., University of Iowa, 1956).

On Protestant religious leaders and organized labor, see James R. Aiken and James R. McDonnell, "Walter Rauschenbusch and Labor Reform: A Social Gospeller's Approach," *Labor History* 11 (Spring 1970): 131–50; and George H. Nash III, "Charles Stelzle: Apostle to Labor," *Labor History* 11 (Spring 1970): 151–74.

On Catholicism in the nineteenth century, see Aaron I. Abell, *American Catholicism and Social Action: A Search for Social Justice, 1865–1950* (Garden City, N.Y.: Hanover House, 1960); James D. Arnquist, "Images of Catholic Utopianism and Radicalism in Industrial America," (Ph.D. diss., University of Minnesota, 1968); Henry Browne, *The Catholic Church and the Knights of Labor* (Washington, D.C.: Catholic University Press, 1949). Robert D. Cross, *The Emergence of Liberal Catholicism in America* (Cambridge: Harvard University Press, 1958); William Barnaby Faherty, "The Clergyman and Labor Progress: Cornelius O'Leary and the Knights of Labor," *Labor History* 11 (Spring 1970): 175–89; Jay P. Dolan, *Catholic Revivalism: The American Experience, 1830–1900* (Notre Dame: University of Notre Dame Press, 1978); Robert C. Reinders, "T. Wharton Collens and the Christian Labor Union," *Labor History* 8 (Winter 1967: 53–70; Charles L. Sewrey, "The Alleged Un-Americanism of the Church as a Factor in Anti-Catholicism in the United States, 1860–1914," (Ph.D. diss., University of Minnesota, 1955); Willard Thorp, "Catholic Novelists in Defense of Their Faith, 1829–1854," *Proceedings: American Antiquarian Society* 78 (April 1968): 25–117; and Thomas E. Wrangler, "John Ireland and the Origins of Liberal Catholicism in the United States," *Catholic History Review* 56 (January 1971): 617–29.

On Samuel Gompers and religion, see Clyde Griffen, "Christian Socialism Instructed by Gompers," *Labor History* 12 (Spring 1971): 196–213. On Eugene Debs, see Harold W. Currie, "The Religious Views of Eugene V. Debs," *Mid-America* 54 (July 1972): 147–56.

5. See E. P. Thompson, *Making of the English Working Class*, particularly "The Transforming Power of the Cross," 350–400; Eric Hobsbawm, "Methodism and the Threat of Revolution in Britain," in *Labouring Men* (London: Weidenfeld and Nicolson, 1968), 23–33; *Primitive Rebels*; and "Religion and the Rise of Socialism," *Marxist Perspectives* 1 (Spring 1978): 14–33; Herbert Gutman, "Protestantism and the American Labor Movement," 79–117. Other historians who have recently devoted greater attention to the relation between religion and labor protest include Frederick A. Barkey, "The Socialist Party in West Virginia from 1898–1920," (Ph.D. diss., University of Pittsburgh, 1971); John Barkley Jentz, "Artisans, Evangelicals, and the City: A Social History of Abolition and Labor Reform in Jacksonian New York," (Ph.D. diss., City University of New York, 1977); and Charles George Steffen, "Between Revolutions: The Pre-Factory Urban Worker in Baltimore, 1780–1820," (Ph.D. diss., Northwestern University, 1977). The divisive influence of religion among workers is well known. See David Montgomery, "The Shuttle and the Cross: Weavers and Artisans in the Kensington Riots of 1844," *Journal of Social History* 5 (Summer 1972): 411–46. For a review of recent literature on religion and labor protest in England and America, see Bruce Tucker, "Class and Culture in Recent Anglo-American Religious Historiography: A Review Essay," *Labour/Le Travailleur* 6 (Autumn 1980): 159–69.

6. Paul E. Johnson, *A Shopkeepers' Millennium: Society and Revivals in Rochester, New York, 1815–1837* (New York: Hill and Wang, 1978).

7. Johnson, *Shopkeepers' Millennium*, 8.

8. On the divisions between official religion and popular religion in premodern European society, see the essays in James Obelkevich, ed., *Religion and the People, 800–1700* (Chapel Hill: University of North Carolina Press, 1979).

9. William G. McLoughlin, Jr., *Modern Revivalism* (New York: Ronald Press, 1959), 8–9.

10. On the role of evangelical Protestantism in the process leading to the American Revolution, see Rhys Isaac, "Preachers and Patriots: Popular Culture and the Revolution in Virginia," in Young, *American Revolution*, 125–56; Foner, *Thomas Paine*, 111–18; and William McLoughlin, "The American Revolution as a Religious Revival: The 'Millennium in One Country,' " *New England Quarterly* 40 (March 1967): 99–110.

11. McLoughlin, *Modern Revivalism*, 12–64.

12. Ibid., 67–121; Rosell, "Charles Finney," 47; and Smith, *Revivalism and Social Reform*, 114–24, 140–62.

13. On the history of these organizations, see Griffin, *Their Brothers' Keepers*; Rosenberg, *Religion and the Rise of the City*; and Smith, *Revivalism and Social Reform*, 163–77.

14. Ann Loveland, "Evangelicalism and 'Immediate Emancipation' in American Anti-Slavery Thought," *Journal of Southern History* 32 (May 1966): 172–88.

15. Johnson, *Shopkeepers' Millennium*, 102–15.

16. The question of motives among nineteenth-century reformers has been a topic of considerable debate. For a defense of the evangelicals, see Banner, "Religious Benevolence as Social Control"; Magnuson, *Salvation in the Slums*; and Smith, *Revivalism and Social Reform*. More critical are Bodo, *Protestant Clergy*, and Griffin, "Religious Benevolence as Social Control."

17. See the letter to the editor from 'A Lover of Truth,' under the title "True Religion," *Herald of Progress*, 15 September 1860.

18. On the anarchists and religion, see Joseph Jablonski, "The Haymarket Atheists," in Roediger and Rosemont, *Haymarket Scrapbook*, 107–10.

19. On Cora Richmond and spiritualists who frequently allied with, or sympathized with, anarchism, see Joseph Jablonski, "Spirit's Progress: Radical Mediums in the Haymarket Era," in Roediger and Rosemont, *Haymarket Scrapbook*, 145–48.

20. See, for example, Dyer Lum, "On the Way to Jericho," in Lum, *In Memoriam*, 28–30.

21. A number of historians have recently examined religion and labor in Great Britain. See Vic Gammon, "Babylonian Performances: The Rise and Suppression of Popular Church Music, 1660–1870," in Yeo, *Popular Culture and Class Conflict*, 62–88; Alan D. Gilbert, "Methodism, Dissent and Political Stability in Early Industrial England," *Journal of Religious History* 10 (December 1979): 381–99; J. F. C. Harrison, *The Second Coming: Popular Millenarianism, 1780–1850* (New Brunswick: Rutgers University Press, 1979); Peter d'A. Jones, *The Christian Socialist Revival, 1877–1914: Religion, Class, and Social Conscience in Late Victorian England* (Princeton: Princeton University Press, 1968); Thomas Walter Laqueur, *Religion and Respectability: Sunday Schools and Working-Class Culture, 1780–1850* (New Haven: Yale University Press, 1970); Robert Moore, *Pitmen, Preachers and Politics: The Effects of Methodism in a Durham Mining Community* (Cambridge: Cambridge University Press, 1974); and John Rule, "Methodism, Popular Beliefs, and Village Culture in Cornwall, 1800–1850," in Storch, *Popular Culture and Custom*, 48–70.

22. The anticlericalism of Irish Land League supporters among Denver's working-class Irish-Catholic population is touched upon in Brundage, "Irish Land and American Workers," in Hoerder, *Struggle a Hard Battle*, 46–67. On antireligion and anticlericalism among German socialists and anarchists, see Keil and Jentz, *German Workers in Chicago*, 221–346; Jablonski, "The Haymarket Atheists"; and Oestreicher, *Solidarity and Fragmentation*, 49–52. On free thought among Chicago's working-class Czech community, see Richard Schneirov, "Free Thought and Socialism in the Czech Community in Chicago, 1875–1887," in Hoerder, *Struggle a Hard Battle*, 121–42. On irreligion and the labor movement, see Bruce C. Nelson, "Freethinkers, Atheists, and Communists: Irreligion and Chicago's Social-Revolutionary Movement, 1870–1886" (Paper presented to the Annual Convention of the Organization of American Historians, 1989).

23. Alex M'Culloch, "The Church and the Labor Problem," *Iron Molders' Journal* (May 1896): 189.

24. Anon., "A Small Stream from a Large Fountain," *Workingman's Advocate*, 21 September 1867. Letters, articles, and song-poems of similar sentiment include Anon., "The Church and the People," *Coast Seamen's Journal*, 18 October 1893; Anon., "Religion of Mammon," *Alarm*, 1 November 1884; Wilfred Borland, "Wanted: A New Ethic," *Brotherhood of Locomotive Fireman's Magazine* 18 (June 1894): 549–54; Dhof, "Another Sermon," *Critic*, 16 January 1892; Nellie Mason, "Letter to the Editor," *Locomotive Engineer's Monthly Magazine* (July 1892): 613–14; John Mathewson, "Mammon's Toils," *Furniture Workers' Journal* 14 (February 1885): 7; and "The Old and the New God," *Furniture Workers' Journal* 14 (May 1885): 1.

25. N.E.M., "Modern Christianity," *Labor Leader*, 20 December 1890.

26. For an account of this incident, see David Rollison, "Property, Ideology, and Popular Culture in a Gloucestershire Village, 1660–1740," *Past and Present* 93 (November 1981): 70–97.

27. For a discussion of the clergy's portrayal in popular novels, see Grier Nicholl, "The Christian Social Novel in America, 1865–1918" (Ph.D. diss., University of Minnesota, 1964); and "The Image of the Protestant Minister in the Christian Social Novel," *Church History* 37 (September 1968): 319–34. See also Herbert Ross Brown, *The Sentimental Novel in America, 1789–1860* (Freeport, N.Y.: Books for Libraries Press, 1970); Louis Schneider and Sanford M. Dornbusch, *Popular Religion: Inspirational Books in America* (Chicago: University of Chicago Press, 1958); Elmer F. Suderman, "Criticisms of the Protestant Church in the American Novel, 1870–1900," *Midcontinent American Studies Journal* 5 (Spring 1964): 17–23; and Dana F. White, "A Summons for the Kingdom of God on Earth: The Early Social-Gospel Novel," *South Atlantic Quarterly* 47 (Summer 1968): 469–85. For a discussion of Catholic novelists, see Paul R. Messbarger, *Fiction with a Parochial Purpose: Social Uses of American Catholic Literature, 1884–1900* (Boston: Boston University Press, 1971); and Thorp, "Catholic Novelists," 25–117.

28. May, *Protestant Churches and Industrial America*, 6, 40–72, 91–111. See also Abell, *Urban Impact*; Bodo, *Protestant Clergy*; Cobb, "William H. Carwadine"; Cole, *Social Ideas*; Griffiths, "Some Protestant Attitudes on the Labor Question in 1886"; Huggins, *Protestants against Poverty*; and Magnuson, *Salvation in the Slums*.

29. On Gompers, see Bernard Mandel, *Samuel Gompers: A Biography* (Yellow Springs, Ohio: Antioch Press, 1963), 9–12. While Gompers rarely attended the synagogue, he was not antireligious. He stressed his humanitarian religion and the influence of Felix Adler and New Testament ethics. Nonetheless, his attacks on the clergy led Terence Powderly to brand Gompers a "Christ slugger." On Powderly, see Browne, *Catholic Church and the Knights of Labor*, and Griffiths, "Some Protestant Attitudes on the Labor Question in 1886." On Jarret, see George Gunton, ed., *Labor: Its*

*Rights and Wrongs* (Washington, D.C.: Labor Publishing Co., 1886), 251–58. On Debs, see Currie, "The Religious Views of Eugene V. Debs." On Trevellick, see Hicks, *Life of Richard F. Trevellick*, 44.

30. On working-class church attendance, see May, *Protestant Churches and Industrial America*, 61, 119–24; and Abell, *Urban Impact*, 61–68. See the comments of Washington Gladden, *Applied Christianity* (Boston: Houghton, Mifflin, 1886), 147–79, and John Coyle, "The Churches and Labor Unions," *FORUM* 13 (August 1892): 765–70.

31. "Workingmen and Churches," *Cleveland Citizen*, 21 January 1893, and Taral Frickstad, *From Behind the Scenes: The Churches and the Masses* (Oakland: Mail Print, 1894). For a different view, see William Hayes Ward, "Church Attendance," *North American Review* 137 (July 1883): 81–85.

32. Some German socialists had been critical of the National Labor Union for saying prayers at conventions. In 1870, F. A. Sorge introduced a resolution to ban prayer at such gatherings. The motion was tabled. See Montgomery, *Beyond Equality*, 201. See also Anon., "Liberal Christianity," *Workingman's Advocate*, 16 November 1867.

33. William Camack, "The Church and the Workingman," *Journal of United Labor* 13 (May 1894): 4. See also the anonymous "The Toilers and the Preachers," *Monthly Journal of the International Association of Machinists* 4 (January 1892): 24.

34. John Digham. "Blessings in Disguise," *Bakers' Journal*, 15 September 1888.

35. Joseph Fairfield, "The Holy Will of God," *St. Louis Labor*, 7 December 1895.

36. Shandy Maguire, "Patience," *Locomotive Engineer's Monthly Journal* 20 (July 1886): 470.

37. Shandy Maguire, "Church Musings," *Locomotive Engineer's Monthly Journal* 17 (May 1883): 245. See also Michael McGovern, "The Right Reverend Bishop, Soliloquizing," in McGovern, *Labor Lyrics*, 55–56.

38. A. J. Jennings, "Mammon's Tools," *Labor Enquirer* (Denver), 6 February 1886.

39. Samuel Simon, "Salaries Unwarranted," *United Mine Workers Journal* 2 (August 1892): 6.

40. Samuel Simon, "Traitors," *United Mine Workers Journal* 2 (August 1892): 3, and "Why So Few Attend Church," *United Mine Workers Journal* 3 (July 1893): 5.

41. "A Christian Woman," "Letter: Editor of the Knights of Labor," *Knights of Labor*, 27 November 1886. See also Dhof, "Another Sermon," *Critic*, 16 January 1892; and Vindex, "Labor and the Church," *Bakers' Journal*, 2 February 1889.

42. B. Longrigg, "To Preachers," *Labor Enquirer* (Denver), 14 February 1885.

43. Anarchist, "Church and State," *Alarm*, 13 June 1885; Anon., "Citizenisms: The Churches Are Dying," *Cleveland Citizen*, 10 February

1894; Anon., "The Old and the New God," *Furniture Workers' Journal*, 22 May 1885; Anon., "The Poor Man's Gospel," *Bakers' Journal*, 13 April 1889; Anon., "The Religion of Mammon," *Alarm*, 1 November 1884; Anon., "Shams and Humbugs," *Critic*, 24 May 1890; Hyams, "Clergymen Not Following the Savior," *Typographical Journal* 1 (January 1896): 106–7; Spokeshave, "Is Christianity Dying Out?" *Journal of United Labor* 9 (September 1888): 2697, and "Pretentious Benevolence," ibid. 3 (February 1883): 1; C. W. Wooldridge, "Wanted," *Cleveland Citizen*, 11 May 1892; and A. W. Wright, "Christ or Mammon," *Journal of United Labor* 11 (September 1890): 1.

44. See, for example, Anon., "A Clergyman from Rahway, N.J.," *Labor Leader*, 27 September 1890; Anon., "A Small Stream from a Large Fountain," *Workingman's Advocate*, 21 September 1866; William Holmes, "An Open Letter," *Alarm*, 15 November 1884; C. L. James, "An Open Letter," ibid., 20 March 1886; Samuel Shaw, "Society Has Been Warned," *Journal of United Labor* 10 (November 1889): 2; and William Whitworth, "To Rev. Mr. Spencer," *Cleveland Citizen*, 4 June 1892. See also "Rabbi Gries," ibid., 27 January 1894.

45. Anon., "Theory and Practice," *Workingman's Advocate*, 27 May 1871.

46. Old Quiz, "The Hireling Saint of Long Island," *Labor Standard* (Fall River), 11 August 1877.

47. Arthur Cheesewright, "An Epitaph: Henry Ward Beecher," *Labor Enquirer* (Denver), 2 April 1887. See also Anon., "Henry Ward Beecher," *Knights of Labor*, 4 December 1886; and E. H. Rogers, "The Death of Beecher," *Labor Leader*, 19 March 1887. In addition, see John Thompson, "Cookgustycuss," *Labor Enquirer* (Chicago), 16 April 1887. Thompson was probably criticizing well-known minister Joseph Cook.

48. Dyer Lum praised Pentecost in "O'Rossa and Pentecost," *Alarm*, 19 January 1889; and Joseph Buchanan praised Huntington in "Christian Worker," *Coast Seamen's Journal*, 13 November 1890.

49. On the effort of Jones and Rogers, see Hopkins, *Rise of the Social Gospel*, 42–49; and James Dombrowski, *The Early Days of Christian Socialism in America* (New York: Columbia University Press, 1936), 77–83. See also Foner, *American Labor Songs*, 224.

50. Praise for individual clergy appears in "A Clergyman's Views," *Knights of Labor*, 18 September 1886; "A Sermon to Workers," *Critic*, 4 September 1889; "A Voice from the Pulpit," *Knights of Labor*, 8 January 1887; "Church vs. Labor," *United Mine Workers Journal* 3 (February 1893): 2; "Preachers Not Needed," *St. Paul Labor* [*St. Louis Labor*], 5 January 1895; "The Pulpit Again," *Labor Enquirer* (Chicago), 28 August 1887; "Rev. E. M. Clark," *Knights of Labor*, 18 September 1886; "Rev. J. Coleman Adams: The Right to Strike," *Knights of Labor*, 20 November 1886; "Socialism without Dynamite," *Cleveland Citizen*, 20 January 1894; and "Workingmen and Socialism," *Critic*, 12 October 1889. Also see the ser-

mons in the *United Mine Workers Journal* 4 (June 1894): 2, and W. K. Ingersoll to Terence Powderly, 20 April 1886, *Powderly Papers*, Reel 15.

51. B. M. Lawrence, "What We Want—Part II," *Workingman's Advocate*, 25 April 1868.

52. On the financial support which business provided for religion, see Magnuson, *Salvation in the Slums*, 20–29; McLoughlin, *Modern Revivalism*, 217–81. See also Thomas C. Cochran, *Railroad Leaders 1845–1890: The Business Mind in Action* (Cambridge: Harvard University Press, 1953), 210.

53. Gutman, "Protestantism and the American Labor Movement," 80–81. See also Cochran, *Railroad Leaders*, 210.

54. Anon., "Pharisees, Hypocrites," *Fincher's Trades Review*, 2 April 1864.

55. For similar song-poems, see Mary Baird French, "The Weary Way," *Coast Seamen's Journal*, 7 September 1892; T. H. Mathias, "Labor Omnia Vincit," *Coast Seamen's Journal*, 5 September 1894; and Ednor Rossiter, "The Golden God," *Fincher's Trades Review*, 2 January 1864.

56. Two writers quoted this biblical passage: Anon., "Christmas," *Truth*, 27 December 1882; and N. H., "The Revolution Is Coming," *Granite Cutters' Journal* 7 (November 1883): 7.

57. Richard Lloyd, "Death and the Oppressor," *National Labor Tribune*, 12 August 1882.

58. F. Robinson, "The Megatherium and the Millionaire," *Journal of United Labor* 4 (September 1883): 553.

59. Samuel Simon, "The True Man, the Selfish Man, the Hypocrite," *National Labor Tribune*, 22 February 1890.

60. For song-poems similar to Simon's, see Francis D. Daly, "Labor," *Journal of United Labor* 7 (September 1886): 2174; D. R. Lewis, "A Song," *National Labor Tribune*, 27 August 1892; and Dyer Lum, "Modern Herods," *Labor Leaf*, 15 December 1886. See also Mrs. Henry B. Jones, "The Monopolist's Dream," *Locomotive Fireman's Monthly Magazine* 9 (September 1885): 546; James Laviers, "Mother Wealth, Daughter Poverty," *National Labor Tribune*, 22 March 1884; John Mathewson, "Mammon's Toil," ibid., 14 February 1885; and G.M.S., "The Miser's Wish," *Locomotive Fireman's Monthly Magazine* 11 (June 1887): 351.

61. Harry Flash, "The Gold Bugs," *Labor Leader*, 3 January 1891.

62. George Kinghorn, "From Illinois," *Workingman's Advocate*, 1 October 1870.

63. For examples of letters and articles criticizing the Christianity of the wealthy, and often that of the clergy as well, see Anon., "Heaven Is within You," *Advance*, 16 March 1889; Anon., "Sabbath Desecration," *Workingman's Advocate*, 14 November 1868; Anon., "Who Believes in Christ?" *St. Louis Labor*, 9 September 1894; Anon., "Who Is to Blame?" *Fincher's Trades Review*, 25 June 1864; T. V. Powderly, "Let the Truth Be Known," *Journal of United Labor* 13 (February 1893): 1; Scriptures,

"Christianity vs. Oppression," *Boston Daily Evening Voice*, 12 February 1866; Spokeshave, "The Fatherhood of God," *Journal of United Labor* 11 (December 1890): 1, and "A Talk with Christians," ibid. 9 (September 1888): 2701; and C. W. Wooldridge, "Some Teachings of Jesus No. 5," *Cleveland Citizen*, 18 March 1893.

64. See Chicago businessman J. V. Farwell's letters to the editor and the exchange that followed: "Our Letter Bag," *Knights of Labor*, 14 August 1886; Bert Stewart, "Our Letter Bag: A Reply to Mr. Farwell," *Knights of Labor*, 14 August 1886; "More from Wheelbarrow," *Knights of Labor*, 14 August 1886; and "Wheelbarrow to Farwell," *Knights of Labor*, 28 August 1886.

# 6

# Workers, the Labor Movement, and True Religion

R ELIGION'S impact on song-poets yielded more than social criticism. It also led song-poets toward a more inward-looking self-evaluation as they measured the status of workers and the labor movement against the standard of true religion. This calibration process produced an elevation of labor's own sense of self-worth and a suitable justification for the labor movement. When compared to their intellectual opponents—the clergy—and their economic opponents—the nation's economic elite—both workers and the labor movement fared extremely well. True religion promised redemption for those who suffered the inequities of industry and who felt the pangs of capitalism's intellectual apologists who relegated workers to moral inferiority and organized labor to social degeneracy. Song-poets may have said only what their audience already believed and wanted to hear. But they insisted that workers and the labor movement deserved tremendous praise because workers who followed a path designed by God enjoyed a close relation with Christ and because the labor movement embodied principles and ideals for which Christ had died.

More than strictly defined religious motivation generated this religiosity. Workers, after all, had few defenders in intellectual circles. Although politicians paid lip service to the notion that workers formed the backbone of society and clergy argued the virtues of labor, intellectuals more commonly celebrated the achievements of businessmen and industrial capitalism. They slighted labor's accomplishments and noticeable anti-working-class tenor permeated their books, lectures, sermons, and speeches. Clergy and theologians joined those who declaimed the merits of competition and individualism and attacked anyone who attempted to violate the immutable laws of the marketplace. Tampering with the status quo and joining the labor movement generated a hostile reception among clergy and most intellectuals. According to the clergy, the handiwork of God should be left alone.[1]

Workers, including song-poets, wasted little time responding to such pronouncements. They sought to understand the place of workers and the labor movement in society, and their examination was fraught with moral and religious overtones. However, they arrived at much different conclusions than did mainstream intellectuals. In the first place, as a logical outgrowth of their true religion—and ample doses of republicanism and the mechanic ideology—they portrayed workers as the moral equals, if not superiors, of the nation's elites. Workers, after all, created all wealth; the industrial order literally rested on their shoulders. Who could doubt labor's integral social function and inherent nobility? What's more, song-poets argued that the Bible decreed that all must labor to eat and that Christ had labored for his bread while teaching the gospel. Jesus worked as a carpenter, creating wealth in the same way that workers did. Lay and religious intellectuals did not deny Christ's divine character, did not argue that his working-class status resulted from character flaw, and did not equate his damnation of money changers with tampering with the status quo. Therefore, according to labor advocates, no one could deny that workers followed God and Christ as they pursued their livelihoods.

Whitebeard wrote from "Shoemaker Town," Pennsylvania, in 1869 to explain why workers stood closer to God as they labored for sustenance.[2] He used biblical references to prove that only labor earned its existence and that nonworkers deserved censure. Whitebeard reminded workers that the apostle Paul, a tentmaker by trade, castigated nonworkers, decreeing that "who will not work, ne'er let him eat." Moreover, said Whitebeard, "God gave the earth to men who toil; / Said 'he who builds the house, shall own.'" The author argued that according to biblical pronouncement capitalism's economic ascendance and domination had less to do with divine favor or moral rectitude than with outright theft from workers. Capitalists belonged among those "who will not work" and yet ate sumptuously and owned lavish homes. Whitebeard compared this reprobate behavior to Cain's, the biblical character who slew his toiling brother Abel to gain Abel's land. American capitalists would steal the wealth of labor so they might live in luxury. Intellectuals might try to disguise this exploitation, but Whitebeard believed the robbery was too obvious to go unrecognized for long.

The following year Whitebeard restated this line of reasoning in "The Toiler's Lot."[3] For nine stanzas he addressed labor's exploitation and referred to the mechanic ideology as he described how farmers, miners, blacksmiths, carpenters, cordwainers, and other workers received insufficient rewards for the wealth they created. Capitalists added salt to workers' wounds, the author added, by not only robbing them but transforming the nation into one "where toil is disgraced" as well. Repeating a common concern among workers, Whitebeard called for respect for workers' contribution, and he repudiated the economic and intellectual degradation of labor. To do so, he summoned Christ's example. For those workers who faltered under capital's scorn, Whitebeard pointed out that by laboring they fulfilled their Christian obligation and acted in accord with Christ's teachings. While other writers identified workers with the downtrodden of the New Testament, Whitebeard established direct ties between workers and Christ. He called Christ a "brother" who suffered all the indignities of his status when he labored as a carpenter. Workers need not tremble before capital or feel inferior, as they were Christ's noble heirs:

> The son of the Highest, the greatest e'er born
>   Once toiled with the compass, the hammer, and plane.
> He, too, was a brother and felt the proud scorn
> Of worldly professors, while men plucked the corn,
>   Who followed his footsteps through fields of rich grain,
>   Yet meekly they toiled mid their haughty disdain.

Whitebeard's reasoning found supplement in other song-poetry. Song-poets placed Christ at the center of their religion and proffered him as role model. Workers who followed Christ's path and God's commands by laboring to eat grew closer to God and Christ; their status became, at least in the eyes of song-poets, superior, rather than inferior, to that of their economic superiors. Following a logic similar to Whitebeard's, in "Dignity of Labor" Knights of Labor member F. Livingston proclaimed pride and dignity for workers:

> Those who toil to earn their bread
>   Need not blush to own their lot;
> They in noble footsteps tread,
>   And in a claim [?] to live have got.

> Toil is not the wage of sin;
>    For in Eden work was given.
> Man was made to work and win
>    Spoils of earth and bliss of heaven.[4]

More jubilantly, William H. Joice allayed workers' insecurities as he sang praise to the holiness of labor:

> Then lift your head, oh sons of toil,
>    Wherever you may be,
> Work is of God—'tis noble, and
>    Right noble—men are ye.[5]

The nation's ruling class had lived comfortably with Protestant arguments linking economic success with divine approbation. Now, however, song-poets came forth to challenge such thinking and to argue that individuals of working-class status commonly labeled economic, if not moral, flotsam enjoyed special favor with God. Workers stood for noble virtue in their labor and struggles and God counted them among the chosen few. To bolster such thinking, song-poets sometimes employed the setting of judgment. In "The Miser's Wish," for example, G. M. S. told the miser that heaven had no space for him because he refused to follow true religion, to redistribute his wealth, and to treat workers justly.[6] Humble workers who listened to God and Christ might assume salvation, but not the grinding employer:

> The miser had plenty of gold,
>    But none to the poor had given;
> Think you his dim eyes could read there his doom,
>    "No standing room even in Heaven?"
> All taken the seats that money can't buy,
>    Fill with those who from earth have been driven,
> And the angels will sing to welcome them in,
>    Not the rich—but the poor, into heaven.

Mrs. Henry B. Jones developed a variant of the judgment setting in "The Monopolist's Dream."[7] Using a dream format, Jones explained why capitalists found disfavor in God's eyes while workers stood at the deity's right hand. The monopolist, according to Jones, always counted himself among the blest. The world turned upside down, however, when he dreamed of his attempt to "ford the stream" leading "to the beautiful place." Here his wealth proved a liability. His sins against workers returned to haunt him. A child rowing across the stream declined to assist him and reminded him that when her dying mother requested money he curtly told her she must earn it. The monopolist also called to a woman floating the stream, but she rebuffed him as quickly as he had once dismissed her pleas for aid. Finally, he encountered an old man he knew "long, long ago." The man, a former employee, responded bitterly to the monopolist's pleas:

> "That," said the old man, "I will not do,
> For early and late long ago did I work
> And never a duty did I ever shirk,
> But to do what I did I was always behind,
> And to credit a dollar you were never inclined,
> But our Heavenly Father looked on all the while,
> And all your mean acts, He has here on file.
> 'Tis a terrible record your eyes will behold,
> Of what avail now is all your gold?—
> Twixt this world and the other there is a strong line,
> You then had your day, and now I have mine."

The monopolist "saved" himself when he woke from his dream and devoted the remainder of his life to "good acts" to atone for his sins. Mrs. Jones, G.M.S., and other writers, however, knew that God held capitalists in disfavor and excluded them from heaven for their sins.[8] The exploiters of the poor, the downtrodden, the oppressed, and the outcast made money at the expense of others, avoided labor and good works, and according to G.M.S. did nothing "To merit a Savior's love."[9]

Song-poets did not rest easy knowing that a ruling class that fattened on wealth created by workers might not pass through the needle's eye. To say that God counted workers among the chosen few was a more specifically working-class variation on the age-old notion that the poor reaped their rewards only in the afterlife. Not that workers would finally receive their reward; only they would receive the ultimate otherworldly reward. However, since true religion included a millennialist, perfectionist impulse and a bias toward socially active religion, song-poets never made otherworldliness a prominent element in their work. They devoted greater attention to this world and to the relation of the labor movement to true religion.

One might expect those who declared that workers stood at the right hand of God to view a movement for workers' rights in a favorable religious light. Song-poets asserted that the labor movement complemented true religion, embodied Christianity, and worked for the cause of Christ. Many song-poets portrayed the labor movement as heir to the movement established by Christ and his apostles. They claimed, moreover, that labor's struggles paral-

leled the struggle to establish the Kingdom of God on earth. In an
equation in which Christianity and the labor movement were
nearly tantamount, it followed that labor's triumph promised more
than a working-class victory; it would usher in the kingdom itself.

On the simplest level writers demonstrated the relationship of
Christianity to workers' struggles by pointing out that God actively sided with them in their earthly life. Robert Hume, a writer
whose song-poems frequently mingled religion and labor, described
God as workers' ally in "Labor Lyrics No. 9—Hymn":

> Courage, children!—He who loves you
> Won't desert you in the war;
> You, who know of life no morning,
> Early chained to Mammon's car.
> Listen, harken!
> You can hear Him from afar.[10]

A. Stewart told readers of the *National Labor Tribune* in 1878 not
to lose hope, for God's hand rested on labor's shoulder:

> Trust in your god above
>  Your father and your friend;
> The poor and needy's cause
>  He always will defend.
> Be upright, men; in truth stand fast,
> You'll get fair wages at the last.[11]

Stewart conceived God as an active agent of social change who
worked for truth with the working class. Together God and workers sought to defeat "all the powers of wealth" and tyranny, enemies who "combined with Satan's host, / In one ungodly throng."
Those employers who denied decent wages to workers followed the
path of the devil and represented nothing less than a malevolent
force of evil and antireligion.

Stewart's dark image of capitalism set his song-poetry apart
from most authors' work, but his general portrayal of a benevolent
God battling for the lowly and the working class found favor
among writers.[12] According to song-poets, God had offered Christianity as a religion of good works, social change, and justice as much
as of individual spiritual fulfillment. More than that, the deity's
benevolence extended beyond aid to the downtrodden and involved
the labor movement as well. God literally became the benefactor
of organized labor. Correspondingly, since labor's principles
equated with Christianity, labor's fight was Christianity's and true
religion's fight as well.

The Knights of Labor could therefore proclaim that they stood less for class-specific goals than for something as universally applicable as true religion. Victor Drury, a well-known Knights of Labor leader, Belgian immigrant, and Catholic with strong anticlerical predilections, summarized this view in a speech at the Minneapolis labor temple in 1887.[13] Drury's opening remarks struck a popular, though unoriginal, chord: "Labor is noble and holy, and to defend it and raise it up from degradation is a work worthy of the noblest and the best." Using religious imagery to describe the newly erected temple, Drury depicted the edifice as "an altar where all who want to be noble and holy themselves may come and worship labor." His rendering of the true religion that the temple would nurture offers evidence of workers' distinctive religious views:

> The fact that we call this edifice a temple indicates that we believe labor has a religious aspect. We recognize labor as worship and prayer. They who eat must work for their bread, that thereby they may be truly religious. He who refuses to work is the deepest of sinners, and for him there is no salvation from perdition. There is no paradize, no heaven for the drones. This means the true religion of the world, but does not mean that idle religion which drops from men's lips and falls idly as rotten apples to the ground. Labor is the noblest expression of human heart. It is duty, obedience, affection, love. I believe that the principles of our organization will finally prevail, and that the religion of selfishness will give place to the religion of altruism. And that will be the religion of the true spirit of Christ.

Song-poets agreed with Drury, arguing that the labor movement embodied true religion while pursuing the practical application of its principles.[14] They followed two different lines of reasoning to prove their point. First, some contrasted labor's religion with established religion. They argued that the latter practiced hypocritical, false religion in violation of true religion while the former aided the oppressed, received God's blessing, and fought for Christ as it fought for labor. Second, others employed historical reasoning—often in connection with the previous argument—to establish the movement as the legitimate heir to the cause of God and Christ. Song-poets offered historical evidence, comparisons, and analogies to prove the movement's ties with previous movements to advance true religion's agenda.

A "colored iron worker" and union member in Richmond, Virginia, employed the first method in his letter to the *National Labor Tribune* in 1882. He recounted a minister's failed attempt—"A

Fruitless Mission"—to convert Richmond workers to the cause of antiunionism: "A minister from Park's Church came to this city two weeks ago preaching anti-unionism; but the brother was too late, for he found that the true gospel of the A.A. of I.S.W. had been preached, and all the darkeys of any account, had been converted, baptized, and received the right hand of fellowship in the union."[15] This worker, like Drury, found that organized labor preached the "true gospel."

Charged with a millennialist, perfectionist spirit as vital as that of any antebellum reformer, Knights of Labor member Fitzpatrick from Cambridge, Massachusetts, presented a similar argument in a song-poem.[16] His opening stanza admonished capitalists that workers had put their army of crusaders into the field:

> Let the tyrants now tremble, and the gold-hoarding knaves
>> Who, 'neath religion's cloak, have secured the earth's yield
> To themselves, whilst the light shutting out from their slaves,
>> For the armies of God are encamped in the field.

Fitzpatrick reiterated his injunction in the remaining two stanzas. He informed those who forced workers to "toil for Hypocricy's false desires" that their reign neared termination; the labor movement now held "the light of God's truth" and fought as "the armies of God." Fitzpatrick's zeal found expression in an emotionally charged refrain that infused the capital-labor conflict with new meaning:

> We'll fight in this great holy war till we die;
> No longer in silence we'll whimper and sigh;
> No longer we'll cringe at the proud tyrant's nod,
> But defy him, and fight 'neath the banner of God.

Fellow Knights of Labor member Francis Daly considered the labor movement involved in a holy war as well.[17] Indeed, Daly decreed that those who pilfer the working class should prepare for the ascendance of God and worker partisans. Writing at the moment the Knights of Labor and organized labor seemed poised for triumph, Daly sounded the prophet's trumpet as he raised the spector of mammon's defeat:

> But beware of the future, the hand on the wall
>> As of old 'tis a story repeated,
> And mammon, the tyrant will once again fall
>> By the Lord and His people defeated.

> Yes, the God of the just and the great and the wise
> Once again will lead forward to glory,
> The cohorts of labor, whose shouts rend the skies
> As they ask to redress their sad story.

Song-poets and other writers sympathetic to socialism also saw the hands of God and labor advancing in tandem. Michael McGovern, a union supporter of moderate socialist leanings, even wrote a song-poem titled "The Socialist's Church."[18] McGovern portrayed the socialist church as the true religion manifested in a universe created by God. Everywhere he turned McGovern saw "true equality" in the natural order of things, despite the perversion of this revealed word by those preaching false religion. A somewhat mystical, spiritual work from a practical man, "The Socialist Church" nonetheless allowed McGovern to restate his belief:

> My church accepts the teachings of
> The "Nazarene" of old;
> It places social truths above
> Men's lusts and greed for gold.
> With heaven's glory beaming round
> It's one great earthly pew,
> Where God's theologies abound
> I grasp its truths anew.

A few followed a direct route, arguing as one essayist in *St. Louis Labor* did that "it is impossible for a person to be a Christian . . . and not be a Socialist."[19] The author found fault with so-called Christians less because they preached Christianity than because they did not "fearlessly practice it" to the point of working to alleviate those conditions that prohibited every man from loving his brother from the heart. The religion of the heart, so loudly proclaimed by evangelicals since the Second Great Awakening, had changed considerably in labor's hands. Rochester, New York's Jacksonian era elites would have gasped to know that a socialist supported heartfelt religion in 1894.

Other song-poets and allies of labor took a different tack, employing historical reasoning to demonstrate the labor movement's role as Christian standard-bearer. Such individuals saw a direct line of descent from Old Testament patriarchs to the labor movement, and they presented reams of evidence to prove the authenticity of their claims. One anonymous song-poet gave a somewhat light-hearted explication of this argument in the *Iron Molders' Journal*.[20] The author pointed out that even before King Solomon workers had formed unions and gained respect among the bulk of the populace. Not only that, but God—described as the greatest of skilled mechanics—conferred blessings on these unions at their moment of creation:

> The Mechanic who built all creation,
>   Who spanned earth and sea with His arch,
> Gave the plumb-line and square to "Trades Unions,"
>   And sent progress with them on the march;
> It was He made the craftsman noble
>   Before even the kingdoms were born;
> God gave to "Trades Unions" his warrant
>   This globe to enrich and adorn.

A more telling example of this line of reasoning existed in John Thompson's powerful song-poem "The Red Flag," a work that even the apologetic editors of the Chicago *Knights of Labor* admitted had "beauty and force."[21] The red flag symbolized more than the struggle to improve workers' conditions; it represented the centuries-old struggle to institute the kingdom of God on earth; and Thompson drew on a host of biblical references to prove his case. He effectively endowed the flag with animated character so it might speak for itself. In the opening stanza the flag described its divine parentage and working-class character:

> I come from my home in the sky
> Where the lightning strikes for right!
> In the voice of the Lord on High!
> Midst gloom of the hireling's might.

The stanzas and chorus that followed linked the flag of the labor movement to Moses, to the chosen people of the Old Testament, and to all who fought tyranny and oppression in the quest for justice and truth. The oriflamme, a "sign on the workman's fold," first appeared "at the birth of light," the creation, and had been "His sign in the 'burning bush.' " Now it spoke "as the 'prophets of old' / before the oppressor's door," as a sign of "my people and the blood of my Passover; binding workers and God." The red flag had guided the chosen people throughout history:

> From a darkness through the blood to the right
> Through Egypt's Red Sea to land,
> I'm waved by the Lord in might!
> And he leads his heroic band.

This same flag now stood at labor's helm, as the chosen people worked for the "coming morn." God's eternal struggle for truth over darkness bode well for workers, and Thompson's flag exuded optimism rather than doom:

> Oh! Red in his 'Let there be light!'
> First chosen at birth of day,
> His glory in liberty's fight
> In lightning the laborer's way.
> Oh! the earth cries out to the sky!
> And sky flashes back to the land
> Awake! for my promise is nigh,
> And 'thy kingdom is at hand.'

Thompson clearly felt at home in the Knights of Labor, where such sentiments abounded and formed part of the cornerstone of the organization from its inception. After his zenith as a labor leader, Knights of Labor founder Uriah Stephens still argued that his organization fought against "the great anti-Christ of civilization."[22] Stephens and thousands of members united in the belief that the labor movement had arrived as "messiahs ever come," with "God's seal of approval," and worked tirelessly for "God and Humanity." The Knights of Labor frowned on sectarianism, but the impression of the Knights as a Christian organization remained vital throughout the order's history.[23]

Other groups suggested a more temperate true religion–labor connection. In 1871 an anonymous cooper prodded his co-workers to join the Coopers' International Union—a union "ordained by God"—and reminded timid coopers that Christ himself had admonished workers to unionize, even dying on the cross for the "principles of union."[24] Anarchist and socialist song-poets and essayists repeatedly linked their cause with Christ's, pointing out that Christ had supported the downtrodden and faced harassment and ultimately execution from the authorities for doing so; now socialists and labor activists who fought for the downtrodden faced harassment, even execution, too. When Arthur Cheesewright protested the hanging of the Haymarket defendants in 1887, he suggested not only their status as martyrs but their divine purpose by comparing the victims to Christ.[25] Correspondingly, Dyer Lum's chapbook of poems—published just after the incident—castigated church and state as he simultaneously compared Albert Parsons and the others to Christian martyrs and drew on the Old Testament to paint a portrait of prophetic doom for capitalism.[26] Even the usually staid Chicago German socialists sometimes found in Old and New Testament justification for organized labor and a new social order.[27]

Coopers, socialists, anarchists, seamen, and locomotive engineers could agree on at least one thing—the labor movement's principles and goals found a clear complement in the tenets of the true religion of God and Christ. The hypocrites who populated and professed established Christianity did nothing to alleviate the hardships of workers, while the labor movement daily engaged the oppressors and false believers as it fought for the downtrodden, those chosen people of God. Heir to the legacy of both Old and New Testaments, the labor movement stood as the emissary of God, Christ, and true religion.

The content of song-poems, or any other kind of labor writings, was not the only indicator of true religion's influence on the labor movement. Many writers chose tunes from religious hymns as melodies for labor song-poems, demonstrating a clear, if sometimes unconscious, linking of the labor movement with Christianity. Moreover, the practice once more illustrates the manner in which workers reshaped their religious traditions to meet their own needs. Folk hymns, evangelical Protestant hymns, and the world of the Gilded-Age worker came together even in something so seemingly unimportant as the tunes and melodies for labor song-poems.

The prevalence of the hymn-tune technique—the borrowing of religious tunes for labor song-poems—can be illustrated by examining a number of song-poems employing the technique. Among the hundreds surveyed for this work, 145 provided information on melodies or tunes. Of them, 13 had original scores. The remaining 132 included melodies from 69 different songs. At least 30 of these 132 included tunes of documented religious hymns, representing 18 different religious hymn melodies or tunes. In sum, nearly 23 percent of song-poems with borrowed melodies employed tunes from religious hymns and almost 28 percent of all borrowed tunes came from religious hymns.

A variety of factors account for this practice. First, pragmatic considerations compelled writers to use tunes with simple melodies, a characteristic common to religious tunes. Second, for that same practical reason authors looked for familiar tunes, and audiences, long exposed to well-known hymns, often recalled them with minimal cueing. Even Catholic workers admitted knowing tunes to certain Protestant hymns, an underhanded compliment to Protestant missionaries and evangelicals who gained few converts but sang catchy tunes! Third, few workers interested in writing song-poetry had either the resources or time to pursue music training. Borrowing tunes, including hymn tunes, allowed them to overcome this obstacle.

Practical considerations alone, however, cannot explain the great number of song-poems with hymn tunes. The proportion of labor song-poems with hymn tunes and the proportion of all tunes derived from hymns goes well beyond the proportion of popular songs from the period that relied on hymn tunes. Had practicality been song-poets' primary motivation, popular songs would have been a more likely source for suitable tunes. Only a movement reliant upon religion could have employed so many hymn tunes. They borrowed hymn tunes just as they borrowed heavily from other musical-poetic devices, republicanism, the mechanic ideology, and assorted theological elements of Protestantism. Once more, Gilded-Age workers owed a recognizable debt to their cultural past.

To be sure, hymnody formed a tremendously popular (though sometimes disparaged) ingredient of Protestantism and Christianity. Congregational singing began with the Reformation, and thereafter church leaders encouraged singing in worship services of Protestant denominations.[28] Most Calvinists, nevertheless, restricted themselves to psalm singing until well into the 1700s. This practice, known as "psalmody," hindered the development of a dynamic Calvinist hymnody because hymns fashioned after biblical psalms had to conform to the original text and had to be sung to tunes from a small group of familiar songs. Many church and lay leaders considered psalms the inspired word of God. Lutherans, in contrast, displayed a more eclectic approach, ardently supporting psalmody while simultaneously using Catholic compositions, folk-song and broadside tunes, and writing new hymns. Lutheranism never made much headway in the British Isles or America, however, until the nineteenth century. Calvinist psalmody held the upper hand in American hymnody, a situation that may have contributed to the popularity of folk hymns and undoubtedly led to the decline of hymnody.[29]

Revitalization came largely as a result of the work of Methodist Isaac Watts. Watts's hymns gained favor during the nineteenth century, helping to break the hold of psalmody and revolutionize hymnody. His acceptance in the United States lagged behind Europe and only the tedious efforts of Watts's disciples John and Charles Wesley—as well as Timothy Dwight, Samuel Worcester, and Ashael Nettleton—ensured a wide audience for Watts's music. Viewing hymns as a tool for propagandizing and conversion, these composers strove for massive audience participation. Although opposed to the excesses of revivalism and its musical pandering, these writers contributed greatly to a simplified, more popular, singable style in hymns.[30] Indeed, they and Watts opened the door to even greater changes in hymnody, as secular and revival music realized tremendous gains by the Civil War.[31] Evangelicals expanded music's role, linking hymns directly to conversion and employing secular tunes, folk hymns, folk tunes, and, occasionally, original compositions to achieve maximum results.[32]

In postbellum America gospel hymns enjoyed an even greater audience. In fact, while the writing of standard hymns for denominational hymnals continued to flourish—and the line between gospel and nongospel hymns grew more problematic—gospel songs established a permanent place in society.[33] Under Dwight Moody and Ira Sankey, the preacher-songwriter team that enjoyed stardom in the Gilded Age, revival hymnody and the notion of the hymn as a "vital part of the communal aspect of public worship" reached its zenith (though some might describe it as the nadir!).[34] Their watered-down, stylized message and music reached millions, either directly at revivals or through their best-selling hymnals. Clergy and parishioner alike learned the hymn's power to tap the listeners' and singers' emotional roots and convey a theological, moral, or emotional message. The hymn as popular didactic had finally arrived.[35]

These developments could not have escaped the ears of workers. Even before the rise of Gilded-Age labor, antebellum reformers had relied heavily on Protestant hymns when they wrote music for their own cause. Popular Protestant chapbooks from the period, such as Waters's famous *Harp of Freedom* and *Golden Harp*, did double duty as evangelical and antislavery songsters. Spiritualist songsters may not have borne an obvious Protestant stamp, but their hymns bear a clear ideological and musical relationship to evangelical Protestantism. Therefore, when song-poets moved from antebellum reform to the Gilded-Age labor movement, they already had learned their musical lessons, including borrowing tunes from a wide assortment of hymns. The hymn-tune technique and the hymn's didactic temper did not arrive in the labor movement without clear ties to antebellum reformers any more than republicanism and the mechanic ideology did. Indeed, the tie could be direct in some cases. For example, when B. M. Lawrence sought a tune for a song-poem in his songster, he borrowed one he had learned during his antebellum reform days. He took the melody of

Waters's "Clear the Way"—a melody that did duty in a number of evangelical and antislavery hymns and appeared in *Harp of Freedom*—and employed it for his "Bound to Vote Down Wrong."[36]

Much more than a cultural trickling down or cross-fertilization process took place, however. The lower classes of North America and Europe had long generated religious music of their own outside the mainstream of established Protestantism, or even Catholicism for that matter.[37] Although church authorities may have frowned upon folk hymns as potentially blasphemous, their history antedated the advent of congregational singing. A substantial body of folk hymns appeared in England, for example, long before Watts. In addition, folk hymns and folk music in general exerted a sizable influence on Methodist composers in terms of tunes and general style. The interaction between Methodism and the music of Tyneside colliers and dockworkers, for example, moved in both directions—a process that unquestionably occurred throughout early nineteenth-century England, Ireland, Wales, Scotland, the United States, and Germany, if not elsewhere.[38]

Whatever the motives and influences, hymnody impressed itself on labor song-poets. They utilized the hymn-tune technique with particular adroitness, finding in the technique the practical means to singability, the necessary transferral of the emotion of the hymn to the labor song-poem, as well as an implied connection between labor and Christianity. Mingling the prolabor theme with a hymn tune, writers followed their mentors' lead in creating a tool of propaganda and a didactic.

When James Tallmadge and two other writers sought tunes for their song-poems, for example, they chose the tune from "The Wearing of the Green," one of America's best-known folk songs.[39] Originating in Ireland, "The Wearing of the Green" quickly entered oral tradition and spawned a host of variants. Sometime in the antebellum period it entered the United States as well. Its tune then made its way into numerous folk spirituals, some of which had themselves already been in oral tradition with different tunes![40]

In a similar vein, other song-poets took tunes from more recent Protestant hymns. M. A. Dalbey's Knights of Labor song-poem "Opening Ode" featured the tune of "O That Will Be Joyful," a work so popular among revivalists that a scholar recently located versions of its chorus in forty-seven antebellum religious songbooks.[41] James Tallmadge took the tune from "The Morning Light Is Breaking," a popular antebellum hymn, for a song-poem of the same name.[42] Appropriately, the hymn had also been a product of the hymn-tune technique: the music first appeared in an 1837 compilation of children's religious songs by the hymnologists Lowell Mason and George James Webb. Those authors set the tune to an anonymous text; then in 1842 the text of a Baptist minister's hymn replaced the original. Thereafter, the tune—referred to as "Webb," after the tune's author, or "The Morning Light Is Breaking," after its popular text—served as the tune for a number of hymns and songs, including George Duffield's famous "Stand Up for Jesus" and two other labor song-poems. Clearly, Tallmadge stood in good religious company in his choice of tunes.

No hymns had wider impact than those of Moody and Sankey. Although their religious messages appealed primarily to the middle class, their music was universally popular. Throughout the United States and the British Isles workers who shunned the Moody-Sankey revivals, with their anti–working-class, anti–labor movement themes, still sang their songs.[43] Singable, familiar, and accessible to the untrained, Moody-Sankey hymns proved ideal for the hymn-tune technique. More song-poems took the tunes of Moody-Sankey compositions, or works they popularized, than those of any other composer. The melody from one of their own compositions became the tune for six labor song-poems. "To the Work," one of Fanny Crosby's eight thousand compositions and one featured by Moody and Sankey in the 1870s, made its way into at least one labor song-poem.[44] Moreover, two songs by revivalist-composer Philip P. Bliss also served as tunes for later labor songs. Bliss's 1872 "Let the Lower Lights Be Burning" become a tune for Arthur Cheesewright's "The Red Flag Is Unfurled."[45] Bliss's "Pull for the Shore," a gospel song especially popular on the Moody-Sankey tours, surfaced in a B. M. Lawrence greenback-labor song-poem from 1878 and also in a nine-hour-day song-poem in 1890.[46]

Prominent among Moody-Sankey compositions, "Ninety and Nine," "Sweet Bye and Bye," and "Hold the Fort" served as tunes for at least eleven labor song-poems. In the mid-1870s, Mrs. S. M. Smith borrowed the tune of "Ninety and Nine"—arguably the most famous Moody-Sankey song—for "Labor's Bye and Bye," a work that circulated throughout labor circles for many years.[47] Labor historian Philip Foner has even argued that Smith's work, in its variant forms, "was probably the most widely reprinted song of the eighties and nineties."[48] Perhaps less popular in its original and labor formulation, "Sweet Bye and Bye" won over large working-class audiences long before Joe Hill and the Industrial Workers of the World sang their sarcastic parody of the work. Between 1878 and 1887 labor song-poets enlisted the tune for four song-poems.[49]

Fittingly, the tune from a hymn the Moody-Sankey team popularized, "Hold the Fort," served as the tune for more labor song-poems than any other tune, the most popular labor song-poem of the century and one of the most popular of all time.[50] Philip Bliss wrote the hymn to honor Union Army soldiers who heeded General Sherman's order to "Hold the fort." Moody and Sankey grew fond of the work and began featuring it at revivals. Almost immediately after they introduced it, labor picked it up and between 1872 and 1892 at least seven writers subjected it to the hymn-tune technique.[51] Of these the Knights of Labor version, "Storm the Fort, Ye Knights," captured the largest audience.[52] Much as Moody and Sankey would have abhorred the fact, thousands of members of the Knights, other organizations, and sympathizers sang the work as their anthem. Variants could be heard well into the twentieth century in the United States, Great Britain, and Australia.[53] Workers may have felt the hand of a different God from the anti-union, capitalist-apologetic God Moody and Sankey summoned, but for singing workers their cause and God's often marched hand in hand.

James Tallmadge's 1886 variant of the song-poem suggests the work's appeal.[54] In his opening stanza, Tallmadge literally issued the clarion call:

> Hark! the bugle note is sounding
> Over all the land;
> See! the people forth are rushing,
> Oh! the charge is grand!

In successive stanzas he sketched the outlines of the protagonists and a battle he viewed as more of a crusade than a social confrontation. Tallmadge skillfully combined religion with emotionally charged phrases from republicanism and the mechanic ideology:

> How the mighty host advances,
> Labor leads the van;
> The Knights of Labor are rallying by the thousands
> On the labor plan.
>
> Strong entrenched behind their minions,
> Sit the money kings;
> Slavery grabbers, thieves, and traitors
> Join them in their rings.

> Vile injustice fills their coffers
>   With their blood-bought gold;
> And the might of their oppression
>   Ruins young and old.
>
> Who will dare to shun the conflict?
>   Who would be a slave?
> Better die within the trenches.
>   Forward then, be brave!

But Tallmadge's resounding refrain undoubtedly generated the greatest enthusiasm. With its memorable Moody-Sankey melody and a strong sense of divine purpose, the song encapsulated the meaning of the labor movement for so many song-poets and workers. Few would forget the days when they sang:

> Storm the fort, ye Knights of Labor;
>   'Tis a glorious fight:
> Brawn and brain against injustice—
>   God defend the right.

Such words and tunes established the religious credentials for labor's cause, but they also gave added meaning to labor's potential triumph. If labor stormed the fort and the glorious fight ended in a victory for labor, then surely God would be victorious in some way. Implicitly Tallmadge's work joined labor and true religion as allies both in battle and in triumph. Labor victories ensured a world closer to perfection. Ultimately, for some writers at least, labor's final triumph would usher in the new age, the kingdom of God on earth.

Few writers found in religion the basis for a darker portrait of labor and religion's triumph. This was never an element in Gilded-Age labor as it would be in turn-of-the-century socialism.[55] Occasionally a song-poem evoked the bleak eschatology of premillennialism (or, more correctly, millenarianism), suggesting an apocalyptic finale as the prolegomenon to the kingdom's advent. However, even in "Armegeddon," song-poet Diabolicus retained a buoyant tone that belied his choice of titles.[56]

Most writers envisioned an optimistic future. Knights of Labor members in District Assembly 41 sang enthusiastically of labor's success: "See the Christ of Labor coming in the glory of the Lord / With the news of reformation that is heralded abroad."[57] The details of that commune and the reformation remained vague, but song-poets' vision of labor and true religion's triumph always involved the ascendance of workers. God's chosen people would reap the rewards, as would all humanity. Everyone would finally enjoy truth, right, justice, human rights, light, love, brotherhood, the golden rule, peace, equality, and freedom, and the victory would be especially sweet for outraged labor, who "Mammon / Long has ruled with iron hand."[58]

Some writers had more definite ideas about the meaning of mammon's defeat.[59] The most detailed scenario came from spiritualist-turned-greenbacker–labor supporter B. M. Lawrence. In eighty stanzas published over eight weeks in the *Workingman's Advocate*, Lawrence catalogued the benefits of a labor and true religion victory.[60] Lawrence argued that if labor broke the "tyrant's rule" workingmen "black and white" would achieve equal rights, pauperism would become extinct, land would be "free as air," and all wrongs against labor would be righted. Inequities in general would disappear—sexual inequality, intemperance, wars, elitist and non-universal education, "burlesque foreign fashion," along with contaminated foods and inadequate housing.

Lawrence pointed out that a better world necessitated loss for some groups in society. Reformation, liberation, and revolution meant laws of nature and love would replace man-made laws and lawyers. As truth replaced might as the standard of right, armies would disappear and men and women would pass just laws, making politicians obsolete. Further, no clergy would exist, as the true gospel and golden rule would prove adequate guides. Doctors would have no function since people would live simple, pure lives and practice "nature's cure." Finally, with labor united and society dedicated to true religion, bankers would become useless. All would live in a world of universal love, peace, brotherhood, the golden rule, and fair Eden's bloom." The world would be one

> With liberty for all, and wisdom from above—
> With liberty for all, truth, purity, and love,
> Evils all will disappear, and heaven will be here. . . .

An illustrative example of how far the melding of labor and religion might be taken, Lawrence's work nonetheless does not breathe the vitality of Michael Lynch's "In the Promised Land."[61] Lynch described a fictitious land "over stormy seas" that contrasted sharply with the United States: "Peace and happiness and plenty" ruled; creed and color meant nothing and "every man was a brother"; everyone did their part, "shouldered the burden," and made work "a pleasant thing." Those unable to work or care for themselves found others willing to aid them. What's more, women did not labor at difficult tasks or turn to prostitution for survival. The natural world provided a bountiful harvest and salubrious climate; machines became slaves of humanity rather than vice versa. Those who remained unconvinced of the possibilities of such a utopian world Lynch advised to take heart. He exclaimed that the promised land, the land of true religion practically applied, the kingdom of God, grew daily nearer:

> And joy was forever in that fair land, and no
> man envied his mate;
> And no man's treasures, where all were rich,
> were his brother's sleeping hate;
> and the kingdom that Christ had promised was
> now for all men to see,
> And the name of that happy kingdom was: The
> Land of the Soon To Be.

By the time Lynch's song-poem appeared in 1893, fewer song-poets could muster such optimism. Indeed, Lynch may well have been trying to bolster his own and workers' spirits in the wake of labor's increasing losses. Until the toll of those defeats mounted dramatically, however, song-poetry continued to display strong religious language, just as it had for three decades. Behind that language stood those Americans with strong religious and moral convictions—workers whose curious blend of religious elements of the past and their own more immediate experience inspired a different understanding of the world.[62] Who could blame Michael Lynch for trying to raise the crusader's banner one more time?

## NOTES

1. A complete discussion of the clergy's adoption and defense of laissez faire ideology can be found in Sidney Fine, *Laissez Faire and the General Welfare State: A Study of Conflict in American Thought, 1865–1901* (Ann Arbor: University of Michigan Press, 1956), 117–25; McLoughlin, *Modern Revivalism*, 217–81, 526; and May, *Protestant Churches and Industrial America*, 3–25, 44–55.

2. Whitebeard, "Trade and Spade," *Workingman's Advocate*, 3 April 1869.

3. Whitebeard, "The Toiler's Lot," *Workingman's Advocate*, 5 February 1870.

4. F. Livingston, "Dignity of Labor," *Journal of United Labor* 1 (November 1880): 70.

5. William H. Joice, "Labor Musings," *Cooper's Journal* 4 (April 1873): 167–68. See also Frances S. Osgood, "Labor," *Journal of United Labor* 1 (June 1880): 24. In addition, see National Labor Union president Richard

Trevellick's speech to coal miners in 1870, "Schuylkill County," *Working-man's Advocate*, 18 June 1870. Trevellick reminded miners that they bowed to God because "he is your creator," and, therefore, "as labor is the creator of capital, I say labor should not bow to capital."

6. G.M.S., "The Miser's Wish," *Locomotive Fireman's Monthly Magazine* 11 (June 1887): 351.

7. Mrs. Henry B. Jones, "The Monopolist's Dream," *Locomotive Fireman's Monthly Magazine* 9 (September 1885): 546. See also her song-poem "A Dream," *Railroad Brakemen's Journal* 4 (August 1887): 356–57.

8. See, for example, Anon., "Pharisees, Hypocrites," *Fincher's Trades Review,* 2 April 1864; Mrs. I. F., "The Brotherhood," *Locomotive Engineer's Monthly Journal* 4 (May 1870): 217; Richard Lloyd, "Death and the Christian," *National Labor Tribune,* 9 September 1882; and Edward Noonan, "An Incident of the Coal Strike," *Workingman's Advocate,* 17 June 1871. See also Michael McGovern, "When the Changing Whistle Blows," *National Labor Tribune,* 9 September 1882. McGovern used the factory whistle—a symbol of industrial capitalism and owners' efforts to impose factory order on its work force—as a metaphor for the day of judgment. See also Shandy Maguire, "An Hour with a Spook," in Maguire, *Random Rhymes,* 203–6. Maguire recounts a dream in which he visits hell. He discovers his former priest among the eternally damned. The priest admits that clerical religion had been a mockery of real Christianity. In addition, despite claims to the contrary, workers would go to heaven, but not the scoundrels who professed Christianity while practicing deception and oppression.

9. For another song-poet expressing sentiments similar to those of G.M.S. and Jones, see Robert Hume, "Labor Lyrics—No. 9 Hymn," *Boston Daily Evening Voice,* 7 February 1867. Hume wrote a series of similar "Labor Lyrics" for this publication in 1866–67. On Hume, see Foner, *American Labor Songs,* 110, 115–17, 122–24, 188–89, 219. For letters and articles in the labor press that argued that God favored the poor, see Anon., "The Dignity of Labor," *Workingman's Advocate,* 5 October 1867; Anon., "Is Labor Dignified?" *Workingman's Advocate,* 22 May 1869; Nathan an Essenau, "The Gospel," *Truth,* 2 June 1882, and "Jesus Christ," *Truth,* 28 April 1883; and C.W.W., "Some Teachings of Jesus," *Cleveland Citizen,* 18 February 1893.

10. Robert Hume, "Labor Lyrics—No. 9 Hymn," *Boston Daily Evening Voice,* 7 February 1867. See also A. H. Nunemacher, "Oh! Master of the Commonweal," *Locomotive Fireman's Monthly Magazine* 14 (June 3 1889): 525.

11. A Stewart, "Workingman's Doxology," *National Labor Tribune,* 30 November 1878.

12. See, for example, Richard Hinchcliffe, "The Light Streams In," *Workingman's Advocate,* 18 May 1872; and A. S. Farquaharson, "Acrostic," *Cooper's Journal* 3 (July 1872): 406.

13. Victor Drury, "Labor is Noble and Holy," *Journal of United Labor* 7 (June 1887): 2427.

14. See, for example, Gayoso Wheel, "My First Offer," *Monthly Journal of the International Association of Machinists* 2 (June 1890): 71. A union machinist from Memphis, Tennessee, Wheel admonished fellow machinists to join the labor crusade: "Come to the Savior, / Make no delay, / Join our Union, / And your dues always pay." See also M.W.S., "O.R.C.," *Railway Conductor's Monthly* 4 (July 1887): 365. Two other song-poems compared labor leaders to biblical religious leaders. See John James, "The Fallen Chieftain," in Sylvis, *Life, Speeches, Labors;* and Frank Foster, "To E.V.D.," *Labor Leader,* 5 January 1895. James compared Sylvis to a biblical patriarch and called for another Joshua or Elisha to step forth to lead labor. Foster compared Debs's incarceration during the Pullman strike to that of Saint Paul many centuries earlier. Other song-poems linking labor and Christianity include Francis M. Goodwin, "Knights of Labor Song," *Journal of United Labor* 7 (April 1887): 2359; Robert Hume, "Labor Lyrics— No. 4," *Boston Daily Evening Voice,* 4 January 1867; and C. L. Penhollow, "The New Era," *Journal of United Labor* 8 (December 1887): 2533. Finally, see the brief article by 'Old Honesty,' "True Knights of Labor," *Knights of Labor,* 14 August 1886. The author said: "Christ must have been a true Knight of Labor, being a carpenter's son; He was a master of His Father's trade. And this proves all Knights of Labor should be Christ-like."

15. 'A Colored Worker,' "A Fruitless Mission," *National Labor Tribune,* 25 March 1882.

16. Brother Fitzpatrick, "Odes," *Journal of United Labor* 5 (May 1884): 702.

17. Francis D. Daly, "Labor," *Journal of United Labor* 7 (September 1886): 2174. See also the song-poem by 'A Toiler,' "God Bless the Workingman," *National Labor Tribune,* 18 April 1874; and Nathan Ben Nathan, "A Parable," *Truth,* 25 October 1884. Nathan employed a host of references from the Old and New Testaments to defend communism as the only true religion. See also the articles that compared organized labor and socialism favorably with Christianity: Anon., "Christ vs. the Ministers," *Cleveland Citizen,* 25 November 1893; Anon., "Citizenisms: The Churchs are Dying," ibid., 10 February 1894; Anon., "Why Do the Heathens Rage?" *National Labor Tribune,* 2 May 1891; F.H.M., "Anti-Christ," *Labor Enquirer* (Denver), 14 April 1888; Pater, "A Sermon from a Brother," *Journal of United Labor* 8 (July 1887): 2455; and C. W. Wooldridge, "Some Teachings of Jesus," *Cleveland Citizen,* 2 February 1893, 4 March 1893, and 1 April 1893.

18. Michael McGovern, "The Socialist Church," in McGovern, *Labor Lyrics,* 67–69.

19. Ouvrier, "Who Believes in Christ?" *St. Louis Labor,* 9 September 1894.

20. Anon., "Trades Unions," *Iron Molders' Journal* (September 1884): 6.

21. John Thompson, "The Red Flag," *Knights of Labor,* 2 November 1886.

22. Uriah Stephens, "The Ideal Organization," *Journal of United Labor* 1 (June 1880): 34.

23. See, for example, Anon., "Nail It with Scripture," *John Swinton's Paper*, 23 May 1886.

24. Sixth Corps, "Union," *Coopers Journal* 2 (November 1871): 423–24. In a similar vein, see the articles and letters: 'A Unionist,' "Socialism and Christianity," *Labor Enquirer* (Denver), 24 April 1886; 'The Expositor,' "Death Sentence of the Savior," *Coast Seamen's Journal*, 12 December 1894; 'Old Salt,' "Is the Millennium Coming?" *Coast Seamen's Journal*, 20 August 1888; Robert Michael Siebert, "Christian Socialism," *Alarm*, 9 January 1886; Walter Vrooman, "The Boy Socialist," *Labor Enquirer* (Denver), 14 May 1886; George Ward, "The Ethical and Economic Basis of Socialism," *Locomotive Fireman's Monthly Magazine* 18 (June 1894): 562–65; and C. W. Wooldridge, "Some Teachings of Jesus, No. 6," *Cleveland Citizen*, 25 March 1893.

25. Arthur Cheesewright, "A Shout of Protest," *Labor Enquirer* (Chicago), 19 October 1887; reprinted in Roediger and Rosemont, *Haymarket Scrapbook*, 117.

26. See, for example, "Our Martyrs," "The Martyrdom," "Albert Richard Parsons," "The Coming Day," "Living Ghosts," and "On the Way to Jericho" in Lum, *In Memoriam*.

27. See Keil and Jentz, *German Workers in Chicago*, 312–18, 324–25.

28. On early Protestant hymnody, see Louis F. Benson, *The English Hymn: Its Development and Uses in Worship* (Richmond, Va.: John Knox Press, 1962), and Henry Wilder Foote, *Three Centuries of American Hymnody* (New York: Archon Books, 1968).

29. Foote, *Three Centuries*, 34–123, 143–86; and Benson, *The English Hymn*, 19–72.

30. Foote, *Three Centuries*, 143–91; 203–5; and Benson, *The English Hymn*, 108–314. See also R. Serge Denisoff, "The Religious Roots of the American Song of Persuasion," *Western Folklore* 29 (July 1970): 175–84.

31. The most useful discussion of the revival and its music is Dickson D. Bruce, Jr., *And They All Sang Hallelujah: Plain Folk Camp-Meetings Religion, 1800–1845* (Knoxville: University of Tennessee Press, 1974). See also James William Hall, Jr., "The Tune-Book in American Culture 1800–1820" (Ph.D. diss., University of Pennsylvania, 1967); Dorothy Horn, *Sing to Me of Heaven*; and Charles A. Johnson, "Camp Meeting Hymnody," *American Quarterly* 4 (Summer 1952): 110–26.

32. On the use of secular tunes in folk hymns, see George Pullen Jackson, *Spiritual Folk-Songs of Early America* (New York: J. J. Augustin, 1937). Jackson demonstrates that the line between sacred and secular music frequently blurred. See also his collection, *Another Sheaf*. Also useful for understanding the tunes of early nineteenth-century hymns is Hall, "The Tune-Book."

33. On hymnody in the Civil War era, see Foote, *Three Centuries*, 263–306. The most useful works on hymns of this period are Susan Tamke,

*Make a Joyful Noise unto the Lord: Hymns as a Reflection of Victorian Social Attitudes* (Athens: Ohio University Press, 1978); and Sandra S. Sizer, *Gospel Hymns and Social Religion: The Rhetoric of Nineteenth-Century Revivalism* (Philadelphia: Temple University Press, 1978).

34. Tamke, *Make a Joyful Noise,* 3. On Moody and Sankey, see McLoughlin, *Modern Revivalism,* 166–281. On their music, see Sizer, *Gospel Hymns,* and James Downey, "Revivalism, the Gospel Songs and Social Reform," *Ethnomusicology* 9 (1965): 115–25.

35. Sizer, *Gospel Hymns,* 4–8; and Tamke, *Make a Joyful Noise,* 3–8.

36. B. M. Lawrence, "Bound to Vote Down Wrong," in Lawrence, *Greenback Songster,* 45. For "Clear the Way" see Waters's *Harp of Freedom,* 30–31.

37. On the conflict in Anglicanism over "plebeian" choirs and bands in worship, see Gammon, " 'Babylonian Performances.' "

38. Colls, *Collier's Rant,* 117–62.

39. James Tallmadge, "Our Ship of State," in Tallmadge, *Labor Songs,* 28. See also Anon., "Thirty Cents a Day," *Workingman's Advocate,* 19 November 1872; and Anon., "The Shout for Liberty," *Trades,* 13 September 1879.

40. On "The Wearing of the Green," see Jackson, *Another Sheaf,* 75, 101.

41. M. A. Dalbey, "Opening Ode," *Journal of United Labor* 1 (March 1884): 102. On the tune "O That Will Be Joyful," see Lorenz, *Glory Hallelujah,* 88.

42. James Tallmadge, "The Morning Light Is Breaking," in Tallmadge, *Labor Songs,* 19. On the history of "Webb" and "The Morning Light Is Breaking," see McCutchan, *Hymn Tune Names,* 168–69; Julius Mattfield, *Variety,* 52–53; James Lightwood, *The Music of the Methodist Hymn-Book* (London: Epworth Press, 1955), 440; and John Julian, *A Dictionary of Hymnology* (London: John Murray, 1907), 1063–64. For other labor song-poems employing the tune "Webb," see Anon., "Progress," *Labor Leader,* 22 November 1890; and B. M. Lawrence, "The Greenback Boys Are Coming," in Lawrence, *Greenback Songster,* 47.

43. For a contemporary description of Moody and Sankey's music, see "Moody and Sankey," *The Nation* 22 (March 1876): 156–57. Not all their hymns were their own compositions. On the contribution of other composers, see Ira Sankey, James McGranahan, George Stebbins, and Philip P. Bliss, *Gospel Hymns Nos. 1 to 6 Complete,* rpt. ed. (New York: DaCapo, 1972); and Ira Sankey, *Sacred Songs and Solos* (London: Morgan and Scott, Ltd., 1895).

44. James Tallmadge, "To the Polls," in Tallmadge, *Labor Songs,* 17. On Fanny Crosby and the tune "To the Work," see Katherine Diehl, *Hymns and Tunes—An Index* (New York: Scarecrow Press, 1966); 397; and Brown, *Story of Hymns and Tunes,* 438–39.

45. Arthur Cheesewright, "The Red Flag Is Unfurled," *Labor Enquirer* (Denver), 10 March 1887. On Philip Bliss and the hymn "Let the Lower Lights Be Burning," see Diehl, *Hymns and Tunes,* 379; Brown, *Story of Hymns and Tunes,* 431–32; and Lightwood, *Methodist Hymn-Book,* 346.

46. B. M. Lawrence, "Down with the Bonds," in Lawrence, *Greenback Songster*, 45; and Anon., "Nine Hours A Day," *Granite Cutters' Journal* 13 (April 1890): 1. On the tune "Pull for the Shore," see Brown, *Story of Hymns and Tunes*, 372–73; and Sankey, *Sacred Songs and Solos*, 82–83.

47. Song-poems employing the tune "Ninety and Nine" include James Tallmadge, "Labor's Ninety and Nine," in Tallmadge, *Labor Songs*, 25; and Mrs. Holman, "Ninety and Nine," *Journal of United Labor* 5 (July 1884): 750. On Mrs. S. M. Smith and the history of labor's use of the tune, see Foner, *American Labor Songs*, 142. On the original tune, see Diehl, *Hymns and Tunes*, 926; Mattfield, *Variety*, 152; and Lightwood, *Methodist Hymn-Book*, 231–33. Sankey wrote the text of the hymn, but the composer is the subject of disagreement. Diehl lists John Frederick Bridge as the composer; Mattfield lists Sankey; and Lightwood argues that Sankey first wrote the poem and later composed the tune with direct intervention from God.

48. Foner, *American Labor Songs*, 142.

49. Song-poems employing the tune "Sweet Bye and Bye" include B. M. Lawrence, "The Right Will Prevail," in Lawrence, *Greenback Songster*, 3; James Tallmadge, "Labor's By and By," in Tallmadge, *Labor Songs*, 11; Anon., "Labor's By and By," *Labor Enquirer* (Denver), 2 July 1887; and Anon., "Coming By and By," *Trades*, 27 September 1879. The tune remained a favorite of labor well into the twentieth century. Joe Hill parodied "Sweet Bye and Bye" for his I.W.W. song "The Preacher and the Slave," *I.W.W. Songbook* (Chicago: Industrial Workers of the World, 1973), 64. On the original hymn, "Sweet Bye and Bye," see McLoughlin, *Modern Revivalism*, 237; Diehl, *Hymns and Tunes*, 1044; Mattfield, *Variety*, 128; and Lorenz, *Glory Hallelujah*, 99. Lorenz discovered that different religious groups employed a text similar to Sankey's but used a variety of tunes.

50. A complete discussion of the history of "Hold the Fort" appears in Paul Scheips' *Hold the Fort!* (Washington, D.C.: Smithsonian Press, 1971). For a text of the original, see Ira Sankey and Philip P. Bliss, *Gospel Hymns and Sacred Solos* (Cincinnati: John Church and Co., 1875), 16.

51. See Mrs. S. M. Smith, "Cooper Campaign Song," *Workingman's Advocate*, 14 October 1876; B. M. Lawrence, "Poll Your Vote," in Lawrence, *Greenback Songster*, 6; J. W. Jackson, "A Campaign Song," *Labor Enquirer* (Chicago), 17 September 1887; Anon., "A Battle Song," *Trades*, 10 May 1879; Anon., "Storm the Fort," *John Swinton's Paper*, 7 June 1885; Anon., "Storm the Fort," *Labor Leaf*, 30 September 1885; and Philips Thompson, "Spread the Light," *Journal of United Labor* 12 (June 1892): 1.

52. For a Knights of Labor version of the song, see Anon., "Storm the Fort," *Labor Leaf*, 30 September 1885.

53. On the popularity of "Storm the Fort" and its use in the twentieth century, see Scheips, *Hold the Fort!* 33–41. The I.W.W. version can be found in *I.W.W. Songbook*, 33. For a version sung by members of the Southern Tenant Farmers' Union in the 1930s, see *Songs for Southern*

*Workers* (Lexington: Kentucky Workers' Alliance, 1937), 12. See also Fowke and Glazer, *Songs of Work and Freedom*, 36–37.

54. James Tallmadge, "Our Battle Song," in Tallmadge, *Labor Songs*, 15.

55. See Barkey, "The Socialist Party in West Virginia," 74–76; and Garin Burbank, *When Farmers Voted Red: The Gospel of Socialism in the Oklahoma Countryside, 1910–1925* (Westport, Conn. Greenwood Press, 1976), 14–43.

56. Diabolicus, "Armegeddon," *Truth*, 22 March 1884. See also Dyer Lum, "On the Way To Jericho," in Lum, *In Memoriam*.

57. The district assembly's song-poem was reported in "Interesting Meeting," *Critic*, 4 August 1888.

58. For these and similar sentiments, see Francis Goodwin, "Knights of Labor Song," *Journal of United Labor* 7 (April 1887): 2359; Robert Hume, "Labor Lyrics—No. 9 Hymn," *Boston Daily Evening Voice*, 7 February 1867; Dy, "Labor Lay," *Journal of United Labor* 5 (September 1884): 786; Richard Hinchcliffe, "The Laborer's Prayer," *Workingman's Advocate*, 18 May 1872; and B. M. Lawrence, "What We Want—Number 5," *Workingman's Advocate*, 23 May 1868.

59. See the essays by C. W. Woolridge, "Some Teachings of Jesus, No. 6," *Cleveland Citizen*, 1 April 1893; and Anon., "Who Believes in Christ?" *St. Louis Labor*, 9 September 1894.

60. B. M. Lawrence, "What We Want," *Workingman's Advocate*, 18 April, 25 April, 16 May, 23 May, 30 May, 6 June, and 20 June 1868.

61. Michael Lynch, "In the Promised Land," *Journal of United Labor* 13 (April 1893): 3.

62. In the twentieth century Christianity has sometimes played an important function in the struggles of workers. See Liston Pope's classic account of the 1929 textile strike in Gastonia, North Carolina: *Millhands and Preachers* (New Haven: Yale University Press, 1942). See also Reuss, "American Folklore and Left-Wing Politics," 136–37; and Barkey, "The Socialist Party in West Virginia," 74–76. In a different vein, see John J. Bukowczyk, "The Transforming Power of the Machine: Popular Religion, Ideology, and Secularization among Polish Immigrant Workers in the United States, 1880–1940," and Kenneth Fones-Wolf, "Religion and Trade Union Politics in the United States, 1880–1920," *International Labor and Working-Class History* 34 (Fall 1988), 22–38, 39–55.

# Conclusion: The Decline of Labor Song-Poetry and Movement Culture

In 1894 the struggling American Federation of Labor bravely launched its official journal. Titled the *American Federationist*, the publication bore the appearance of its predecessors. Indeed, the first issue carried a song-poem on the seamen's union and the second contained Miriam Wheeler's "Labor Chant." The latter resembled countless works from the previous decades, echoing working-class fears of dependency with familiar strains of republican rhetoric. Wheeler compared the position of workers in the United States to that of workers in Europe—"the old and outworn country," "foul Europe," and "Squalid England"—hopeful that once united the working class would realize "a brighter day."[1]

If the song-poem and the *Federationist* were any indication, song-poetry had a future not unlike the thirty years that preceded. Between 1895 and 1899, however, the publication did not publish song-poetry and after 1899 only occasionally printed the works of nascent song-poets.[2] Nor was the journal alone in this regard. With the exception of short-lived populist papers and a few radical publications, both of which continued to feature song-poetry, labor publications operating after the depression printed fewer and fewer song-poems as the years went on.[3] Song-poetry declined measurably after 1900, never again to enjoy the level achieved in the Gilded Age.

Not that song-poetry vanished: George McNeill, Patrick Fennell, and Michael McGovern compiled collections of their song-poems after 1900.[4] Individuals and organizations unknown to an earlier generation also emerged to write and sing. The Industrial

Workers of the World and a host of Wobbly writers—Joe Hill, Ralph Chaplin, T-Bone Slim, and Harry McClintock—became fairly well known for their irreverent brand of musical and poetic merriment.[5] Similar, but less successful, attempts were made by members of the Socialist Party of America as well.[6] What's more, among isolated occupational groups, such as Kentucky coal miners, or among certain ethnic groups, particularly recent Jewish immigrant workers on the east coast, song-poetry remained vital.[7] Thereafter, activists representing diverse institutions and organizations stirred the masses with labor song-poems and musical activities. The Communist party, Brookwood Labor College, Commonwealth College, the Southern Tenant Farmers' Union, the Amalgamated Clothing Workers of America, the International Ladies Garment Workers Union, the United Auto Workers, the Jewish Workers' Musical Alliance, the Southern Workers' Alliance, and the A.F.L.–C.I.O., to name just a few, counted song-poets in their ranks.[8] Labor struggles generated new song-poems and singer-songwriters still build reputations as labor's troubadors.[9] Labor song-poetry can hardly be described as a dead letter after 1900. If it had declined during the 1890s, then a revival of sorts took place in the new century and in a reorganized labor movement.

That conclusion remains valid, however, only when sheer quantity of song-poems is considered. By other measures the song-poems of the twentieth century differed markedly from those of an earlier era, though the change took place gradually.[10] Despite quantitative revival after 1900, during no three decades in the twentieth century did the output of labor song-poems equal that of the years from 1865 to 1895. Furthermore, with the possible exception of the Industrial Workers of the World, at no time after 1900 did as many individuals contribute song-poems as in the previous decades. By the 1920s a small number of individuals wrote the majority of song-poems. As in many activities associated with the labor movement, professionalism crept into the song-poet's craft. Correspondingly, fewer labor papers and journals published after 1900 included song-poems in their pages; those that did rarely printed them as a regular feature. Socialist and populist papers kept their columns open for a brief time. Some ethnic labor papers also featured works by ethnic labor song-poets like those allied with Jewish workers in the needle trades. Some I.W.W. papers regularly included the work of budding proletarian writers. But the days had ended when unknown individuals wrote thousands of song-poems. Never again would a labor leader complain, as Terence Powderly did, that song-poems swamped his office.

Two other areas of comparison show an equally divergent pattern. Song-poems from 1865 to 1895 differed ideologically from those that followed. Republicanism, the mechanic ideology, and true religion had been central to Gilded-Age song-poems as well as to the mainstream of the labor movement, labor protest, and movement culture. After the turn of the century, however, these ideological elements of the labor movement waned, as different groups found different modes for expressing the interests of workers.

Equally important, in the twentieth century the use of song-poems was never so pervasive as it had been in the Gilded Age, when song-poems were firmly integrated into the network of activities that comprised the day-to-day operations of the labor movement. Changes in the labor movement and, perhaps more significant, changes in capitalism itself diminished song-poetry's role among labor. Picket lines might still give rise to singing a message of protest, and Yiddish workers' choruses might treat New York workers to uplifting concerts, but labor meetings in the hinterlands of Kansas no longer inspired a member like Maggie Linn to "declaim to perfection."

Explaining why song-poets like Linn and song-poems like Miriam Wheeler's "Labor Chant" no longer had a place in the workers' cause is more difficult than documenting their decline. Yet such an explanation is imperative, since it is the only way to begin to understand issues of larger concern to labor historians. For that reason, the remainder of this chapter attempts to explain the decline of song-poetry with an eye toward those broad concerns. Two questions emerge: first, why did song-poetry generally decline in the United States after 1900; second, why did the ideological content common to song-poetry—or, for that matter, labor protest, the labor movement, and movement culture—gradually disappear during the early part of the twentieth century?

In part, the answers to both questions may be traced to the repression and subsequent decline of organized labor in the 1890s.[11] Repression, of course, was nothing new to organized labor or the working class. Since the beginning of the nineteenth century capitalists had employed various antilabor measures: scabs, spies, private armies, unskilled labor, open shops, blacklists, and other weapons could be summoned. Also capital turned to government—local, state, federal—to constrain workers' collective initiatives. The courts, in particular, sometimes declared labor's weapons illegal. Finally, when business and courts proved inadequate for the task, government troops periodically intervened at capitalist behest.

The postbellum period offered labor only brief respite from such repression. Business counted its traditional arsenal of weapons. Moreover, the state's involvement increased as class unrest and general social unrest escalated and the time-worn measures of the past proved less effective and politically appropriate. Both the courts and the military played an increasingly integral role in halting labor's advance. The former brought the power of the law to bear on workers and charged organized labor with everything from murder or conspiracy to restraint of interstate trade. The latter crushed strikes with greater professionalism and increasing frequency as the century closed.

As historians have demonstrated, repression after 1885 differed from that of previous decades, largely in response to the crescendo of working-class protest from 1877 to 1886. Prior to 1885 the state frequently sided with business in labor disputes, but the process had remained haphazard and inefficient: local and state officials might show indifference to capital's directive; juries sometimes sympathized with labor; local and state militias often seemed ineffectual when facing working-class crowds; on some occasions law enforcement officers would not enforce probusiness edicts. The business community found this situation frustrating and wasteful, particularly as unrest increased and workers became more conscious of their self-identity in collective action. Capitalists began to request that government, especially on the federal level, pursue a more active role in labor relations. Cognizant of their potential, many federal officials had already begun to take the initiative in directing the nation's economic affairs. Business and government consequently moved into closer alliance, and capital received the signal it needed to check the power of labor. Henceforth, government became the critical party in capital-labor conflict, wielding the power necessary to force workers into submission, and the strength of the state was unleashed to an extent that left labor reeling.

Much of that strength became manifest in military actions against workers. State and federal troops with greater training, a higher degree of professionalism, and better equipment than their amateur predecessors regularly protected industry and the national interest from labor from the mid-1880s onward. Their deployment bode ill for workers: in a single year Tennessee coal miners; Idaho silver miners; Buffalo, New York, switchmen; and New Orleans dockworkers and their allies all fell victim to the federal military presence. Herbert Gutman suggested that 1892 might be the "really critical year" in the ruling-class counterattack and in shaping the labor movement of the future.[12] Clearly, these were critical years in labor's history. In 1894 workers battling the Pullman Company fell prey to a powerful armed force and the full legal powers of the federal government.

As might be expected, such repression—coupled with the economic depression after 1893—brought quantitative decline to the labor movement. Already facing a host of internal problems, the Knights of Labor rarely claimed a major victory after 1886. Membership plummeted. The American Federation of Labor, organized in 1886, enrolled skilled workers suspicious of the Knights and others hoping for a labor revival. In 1897, however, the A.F.L.'s membership barely reached 250,000. Eugene Debs's American Railway Union, and its 150,000 members, vanished in the wake of the Pullman defeat. By mid-decade independent unions of railroad workers and others included only 100,000 members. The United Mine Workers offered promise, but not until the end of the decade did it dare risk serious activity in the coal fields. By 1895 organized labor had no more members than it had had in 1865.

The movement's calamitous condition hardly created a productive environment for song-poetry or other movement culture activities. As membership dropped and the movement fell into disarray, labor song-poem writing ebbed. The number of potential writers and song-poems declined, as did the opportunities for presenting song-poetry. Fewer union members meant fewer local and national union bodies and thus fewer meetings, picnics, parades, conventions, and other gatherings suited for the presentation and singing of song-poems. Likewise, depleted membership resulted in fewer publications and decreasing circulation, limiting the outlets and audience for song-poets.

The movement's decline also reduced song-poetry in ways difficult—if not impossible—to measure. Labor's fighting spirit lapsed or broken, writers or potential writers had less reason to write than before. The precipitous decline in membership was compounded by organized labor's spiritual declension. Although workers with a vigorous fighting spirit might still produce song-poems in the face of adversity and stagnating membership, as the I.W.W. demonstrated repeatedly after 1905, a dearth of membership and *élan vital* left Gilded-Age labor with neither the reason nor the ability to generate song-poetry.

Had repression's impact been a question of numbers, the movement that remained after 1895 should have retained its basic approach to capital-labor relations and its characteristic language and ideology of protest. However, the overall effect of repression was as much qualitative as quantitative. The ideology that once pervaded labor on every level would disappear from both the labor movement and song-poetry after the turn of the century.

The reasons for this disappearance are complex. Partial explanation may lie in organized labor's mode of response to capital's counterattack. In the wake of the setbacks that followed, many leaders in the labor movement—for example, Samuel Gompers, Eugene Debs, Frank Foster, and Mother Jones—reevaluated their previous course, concluded that the old ways had become inadequate for workers' needs, and determined that labor must redefine the terms of battle. The battle of the previous decades had been waged in terms that had originated in an earlier period of American and international capitalism. Now, however, many workers concluded that the mode of thinking and goals engendered by these ideological traditions—namely, republicanism, the mechanic ideology, and true religion—were outmoded.

Some would follow the course charted by Samuel Gompers and the American Federation of Labor. Gompers made his peace with capitalism and now argued that labor had erred in trying to replace the wage system with some type of humane cooperative society or commonwealth. He urged workers to concentrate their energy on achieving basic economic goals. Gompers's opponents, by contrast, refused to accept the inevitable dominance of capitalism. Instead, they chose the radical path of socialism, a path that some argued would best be achieved through the ballot-box—a position advocated by Debs and the newly formed Socialist Party of America—and that others counseled would follow from direct economic action designed to capture the means of production—a position defended by the I.W.W.

This shift among leaders and organizations manifested itself in song-poems and no doubt contributed to the decline of an earlier genre of labor song-poetry. The A.F.L.'s policy of business unionism rendered it less and less receptive to writers who lambasted the wage system and called for a revived republic in which workers had liberty, equality, equal rights, and true democracy. The organization expressed little sympathy for writers who said the clergy were hypocrites, that capitalists found no place in heaven, that workers were the only chosen people of God, and that the labor movement embodied Christian principles.[13] Finally, the A.F.L. did not want to hear that capital robbed workers of wealth they created and that those who did not work for a living constituted social parasites, vampires, and leeches. The old language of protest found no home in the A.F.L.

Radicals in the Socialist party and the I.W.W. proved more tolerant of the old mode of thinking common among song-poets. Indeed, socialism made greatest headway among farmers in the plains states who welcomed and promulgated a brand of socialism akin to camp-meeting religion.[14] In that environment, republicanism, the mechanic ideology, and true religion—as well as song-poetry employing the constellation of ideas these represented—still enjoyed some favor. Even among the I.W.W. one could find lyrics that recalled the strains once heard at Knights of Labor meetings.[15] Generally, however, the older form and the vision of Gilded-Age song-poets would become an anachronism to radicals, who argued that socialism offered a more relevant and useful way to understand capitalism and to structure labor's advance. Appropriately, the Freiheit poets, who worked in the needle trades, spoke not only a different language in Yiddish but a different language in socialism as well.[16] Radicals after 1900 employed a song-poetry qualitatively different than that of Rees Lewis and Michael McGovern.

Although addressing the issue of song-poetry's demise in the context of the interaction between labor and capital allows a partial explanation of the decline, such a perspective assumes that only those factors directly related to the capital-labor conflict influenced song-poems and the belief system of workers. In reality, the song-poem was powerfully influenced by forces and events outside—though frequently parallel to—this narrow context. Considered in a wider context, song-poetry's decline directs us to the very meaning of capitalism and of the working class in the twentieth century.

One fundamentally significant event that had an impact on song-poetry and society was the rise of popular culture and the industry responsible for its production.[17] Entrepreneurs with nothing more than a keen sense of what Americans might purchase as entertainment established a massive popular culture industry that became integral to the social and cultural life of millions of Americans by the end of the first decade of the twentieth century. Nowhere did this popular culture have greater impact than among its most devoted audience, the working class. The rising popular culture borrowed heavily from older native and ethnic traditions but contributed to their demise as well. True, it frequently spoke a language working-class audiences understood. Yet it was a purchased form of entertainment that nonetheless left many previously vital traditions and practices—those that had shaped the ideas, values, institutions, and goals of workers for decades—by the wayside. Cultural activities previously carried on in a more specific working-class environment, and dependent upon that environment for creation and dissemination, were often replaced by products purchased as popular culture. An industry of no small size had stepped forth to meet cultural and social needs once the preserve of workers and their neighborhood and community institutions and organizations, including the labor union and a host of those inert activities that fed into the labor movement and movement culture.

Song-poems did not escape the influence of popular culture. Song-poetry developed in an environment in which musical, literary, and ideological traditions still performed an important role and the labor movement could fulfill economic, social, and cultural needs. As popular culture made inroads into that environment, and popular music and literature enjoyed a wider and wider working-class audience willing to purchase the industry's latest wares, traditions declined and the labor movement's noneconomic affairs receded in importance. The rise of popular culture did not signal the disappearance of worker traditions that nurtured and shaped song-poetry. But it did precipitate the devitalization of traditions and, as a result, song-poetry's as well.

To say this is not to denigrate popular culture. Rather, it is to remind us of the powerful role that popular culture played in workers' lives. Francis Couvares, for example, discovered that the rise of popular culture in Pittsburgh transformed the cultural habits of workers in the "plebeian city."[18] According to Couvares, the results could not have been more unexpected. Pittsburgh's elites had long found the leisure habits of the city's workers repugnant, but reform efforts failed because workers took slight interest in the respectable, nonlibertarian forms of leisure recommended by their social stewards. Eventually workers' behavior changed in ways not anticipated by these elites. With the rise of popular culture the city's plebeian character decayed. Workers turned to professional boxing and baseball, vaudeville, burlesque, nickelodeons, movies, and amusement parks for an entertainment that, however, rarely spoke a language of working-class protest. By the turn of the century, popular culture commanded the loyalty of a large portion of the city's working class, no matter what elites might think.

Pittsburgh's cultural metamorphosis reflected a general trend in society. In Chicago, the ethnically specific forms of culture that had fostered the movement culture of German workers declined as younger workers turned toward the nickelodeons, penny arcades, professional baseball teams, movie theaters, and other forms of entertainment established primarily by interloper businessmen after 1900.[19] Parallel developments throughout the city left few workers untouched, German or no. Likewise, Roy Rosenzweig found that in Worcester, Massachusetts, workers never mounted a serious challenge to capital but did create a massive network of class-specific cultural institutions and activities that placed them at odds with the city's ruling elite.[20] But he discovered as well that in the early twentieth century commercialized leisure replaced the older ethnic- and class-based cultures, a shift symbolized by the decline of the neighborhood rum shop and the rapid ascendence of the movie theater as the central institution of working-class social life. Throughout the nation workers turned their attention to products the popular culture industry offered as new forms of entertainment or as replacements for traditional indigenous forms.

This transformation engendered important changes in the song-poem, the labor movement, and the movement culture. In the late nineteenth century the labor movement derived its strength in part from its ability to integrate itself into the world of the worker by drawing on ideas and practices already familiar among workers. Moreover, it performed noneconomic functions in their lives. Few people in the labor movement needed to be prodded to involve themselves and their organizations in working-class social and cultural life if they hoped to garner support and develop alternatives to the system of wage capitalism. Although its character was more explicitly political and openly anticapital than most working-class cultural life, the movement became enmeshed in a complex network of institutions, practices, and activities in and out of the workplace. As the movement took on the trappings of an alternative movement culture, embodying a set of values and ideals attuned to the needs of workers, its credibility and legitimacy increased and its membership grew.

Myriad labor activities in this movement culture—parades, picnics, lectures, sporting events, athletic teams, dances, orchestras, and singing groups—provided labor with opportunities to publicize itself, to disseminate its message, and to promote solidarity in the ranks. In addition to regular business gatherings, union meetings and conventions became opportunities to present skits and recitations, to host a ball, to sing and perform music, as well as to visit with other members and their families.

Even labor song-poetry had a place. However, like the movement culture, the song-poem depended upon the continued vitality of certain indigenous cultural forms. As the cultural milieu of the working-class community began to change, movement culture and song-poetry suffered accordingly. With the rise of popular culture a significant portion of workers' indigenous cultural life became ennervated, at least among those who once comprised the labor movement.[21] Low-cost musical and literary products discovered a massive working-class audience, influenced workers' music and literature, and eventually displaced them altogether. As the musical, literary, and ideological structure on which labor song-poetry used to rest crumbled, song-poetry followed suit. Eventually labor song-poems like those written between 1865 and 1895 could be found only in isolated regions or occupations in which certain traditions remained less susceptible to immediate change.[22] When the organized Left finally rediscovered these styles and forms after 1929, they fought a rearguard effort to turn these "folk" traditions into proletarian tools. By then even the children of the most recent immigrants were dancing to the latest tunes heard on radios.[23]

The popular music industry's influence could not have been foretold in the early 1800s.[24] Before 1800 European firms dominated the publication and distribution of music in America. Most Americans, indifferent to or ignorant of recent continental trends, enjoyed the same music they had for decades. As the growing middle class began to assert its collective identity, music publishers gradually discovered the market necessary to support a domestic music industry. Nonetheless, the music industry, still the captive of traditional songs and broadsides, remained in transition until mid-century. Only in the 1840s did the middle class emerge as a major force: middle-class patrons who disassociated themselves from "old-fashioned music" established sentimental parlor songs of love and death as the predominant form in the music industry for decades to come.

This middle-class penchant for the sentimental had little immediate influence on the working class, which generally remained wedded to older musical fashions.[25] Nevertheless, by publishing minstrel and Civil War songs, music companies quickly capitalized on the purchasing power of the nation's work force. Long before they could afford the consumer durables associated with a consumer economy, workers became loyal consumers of varied forms of musical entertainment. Reflecting this trend, labor song-poets borrowed from the minstrelsy and war songs. No doubt workers found many of the musical and ideological conventions of this music attractive, as their British working-class counterparts found similar music-hall compositions to their liking. The favorable reception that workers gave to such music, however, also helped lay the foundation for a popular music industry. By the 1870s Tin Pan Alley had yet to arrive, but the industry stood on the verge of transformation.[26]

Since they quickly consumed popular music, workers undoubtedly helped usher in the new age at the end of the century. Gilbert and Sullivan, pioneers of popular music, would have been pleased to know that a song from their 1885 stage production *Mikado* furnished the tune for an 1891 labor song-poem.[27] Charles K. Harris, one of the first composers of Tin Pan Alley, would have been equally happy had he known his 1892 hit "After the Ball"—considered by many to be the first truly national hit song—two years later surfaced in Joseph Siemer's quite different "After the Strike."[28]

The influence of popular music and popular culture in general extended beyond the tunes of labor song-poems. During the 1880s, and particularly in the 1890s, the subject matter and style of hundreds of song-poems derived from sentimental songs and poems that had been the mainstay of the emerging popular culture industry. Although frequently written by workers and their spouses, these were not labor song-poems in the usual sense, but rather "sentimental" song-poems. Some writers had begun to take their musical and literary cues from the popular works of the day and produced sentimental song-poems that amounted to no more than imitation.[29]

Sentimental music and literature had similar histories. Initially written by middle-class authors and geared to a middle-class audience, they contained a strong anti-intellectual bias, avoided serious individual or social issues, covered a variety of topics typically related to love and affection, and relied on an affected style designed to provoke a particular emotional response.[30] During the late nineteenth century they reached wider and wider audiences, including the working class, or at least certain elements of it. Some labor song-poets who began to join their middle-class peers in the job of touching workers' emotions found rather quickly that by aping the formulaic portrayals of death in middle-class literature they might achieve their goal. Middle-class authors—male and female—had discovered some years earlier that dying children, wives, husbands, and lovers left readers teary-eyed and spiritually uplifted. Poets described death so frequently that historian Ann Douglas has described their production as little more than "exercises in necrophilia."[31]

Working-class writers seemed equally enthralled with the dying and the dead. Soldiers, sailors, engineers, brothers, husbands, friends, and children departed from life regularly and in copious detail as the century waned. Children, for example, captured the heart of Mrs. Henry B. Jones. Hardly a person to be included in the same category as a sentimental scribbler like Fanny Fern, Jones wrote an ode to "Little Odie" that rivaled Fern's or any other sentimental lamentation in the popular press.[32] The first stanza provides an adequate indication of Jones's subject and style:

> Gently close the waxen eyelids, fold his hands
> across his breast,
> Kiss the little marble forehead ere you lay him
> down to rest;
> Lovely bud so pure, so tender, naught on earth
> could seem more fair,
> Gone from all its pain and sorrow to the Savior's
> loving care.

A formulaic composition, it could be distinguished from those of the popular song and poem mill by a closing line informing readers that the child was "Brother Dedham's." Printed as it was in the brakemen's union journal, that reference meant that Dedham belonged to his trade's union. The most sentimental works of working-class writers might still bear the mark of their class.

Even writers depicting death within a working-class context and expressing mild protest often absorbed the spirit of sentimental poetry and song. As early as 1875, in "The Miner's Child," Jonathan Wickers left little doubt that owners deserved blame for the death of a child whose parents lived in poverty, but his recounting of the details read like other sentimental poems.[33] Wickers's stylized treatment trivialized death and reduced even the most pathetic victim of capitalist exploitation to another dying plantation-owner's daughter, a Little Eva.[34] In fact, labor song-poetry's growing sentimental strain may well owe much to the sentimentalism characteristic of antebellum reformers who entered the Gilded-Age labor movement with the baggage of earlier reform efforts.[35] Whatever the immediate source, such sentimentalism did much to denature the work of some labor song-poets. Song-poets like CATO, a relentless critic of capitalism, could write song-poems that bore a striking resemblance to the popular songs and poems of the day, complete with coquettish women, idealized visions of the middle-class home, stereotypical wives who upheld virtue and morality, and idyllic pastoral settings exclusive of industry.[36] One has to search hard to find any vestige of a working-class presence in such works. Increasingly, song-poets with a powerful working-class message found their models outside the traditions of music, literature, and ideology that formed the core of the Gilded-Age labor song-poem. They relied instead on parodies of popular songs and returned to traditions only after their rediscovery and revival by radical songwriters searching for ideological tools for proletarian struggle. Neither Joe Hill nor Pete Seeger could trace their cultural or musical lineage to Michael McGovern or Poet Mulhall.

While the rise of popular culture exerted its influence, a parallel event had a more profound impact on the nation's—and, perhaps, the Western world's—workers.[37] During those years, and until the time of World War I, economic transformation led to the restructuring of much of the economic base of the nation and therefore of the working class. If the working class had been "made" once, between the middle and closing decades of the nineteenth century—in an objective sense, as a class in itself—then it would now be remade in the years between the collapse of the Knights of Labor and the end of World War I. As this occurred the usefulness of the ideas and practices common to much of the labor movement in the Gilded Age diminished.

The postbellum movement had utilized an ideology built on the interplay of certain traditions and the experiences of workers within the workplace and capitalism as a whole at a certain stage of development. But this ideology—manifested so concretely in song-poems—eventually proved inadequate for attracting allies from the middle-class or recruiting new working-class members, because the structure of both groups had changed in ways that rendered the ideology increasingly irrelevant to their needs. As this happened, and as other events led labor down new paths, working-class consciousness changed and organized labor cast aside much of its former ideology. Song-poetry and the labor movement would revive in the new century, but the previous ideology would be found less prominently. Organized repression had its immediate impact on the thinking of labor, and popular culture hindered the kind of cultural network on which Gilded-Age labor flourished, but the restructuring of the social order and the remaking of the working class would change the rules of the game altogether!

Until the 1890s organized labor felt little necessity for discarding the republicanism, the mechanic ideology, and the true religion that permeated its words and actions. Many believed this ideological foundation had served labor well. Through the 1890s organized labor had made steady gains in membership and fighting strength. Labor candidates had been elected to offices from the local to national levels; even the old two-party system could no longer look askance at the working-class voting block and its interests. Workers in occupations formerly unorganized had a strong labor presence, and some of the most powerful titans of industry had yielded concessions to labor. Finally, labor had made legislative gains in both state and federal governments. Although wage capital had not been replaced by some more humane cooperative system, workers had made significant gains.

The ideological foundation of labor suggested more direct strengths as well. The ideology enjoyed wide and diverse appeal precisely because it spoke directly to many shopkeepers, farmers, artisans, and laborers, both natives and immigrants. These workers and producers could be deeply touched when the labor movement issued cries for liberty, equality, democracy; condemned capitalists as parasites, vampires, and leeches; and admonished workers to join the fight for a more Christian world. Individuals as diverse as Michael McGovern, an Irish-Catholic immigrant puddler; Patrick Maloney, a saloon keeper; James Tallmadge, a printer; Charles Haynes, a musician; and Mary Agnes Sheridan, a carpet-mill operative, could thus write song-poems supporting the labor movement. Insurance agent and alderman C. L. James could work diligently for labor in the backwoods of northern Wisconsin. Storekeeper Mrs. S. E. Lenfest could join a miners' local of the Knights of Labor in Aspen, Colorado. The kind of thinking represented in song-poems attracted such individuals, however, only as long as different groups in society perceived themselves as sharing similar identity and desire for common action. By the 1890s, as changes in the economy begat change in social structure, a shared identity became difficult.

From the early to late nineteenth century industrial capitalists busied themselves with building a solid base upon which to grow.

They had to locate new ways to generate capital and a labor force willing to work for wages under capital's direction; find raw materials and transport them efficiently to the point of production; and develop new methods of manufacturing and distributing products. By the 1870s and 1880s industrial capitalists had completed their initial phase of economic development, learned to expand their base, entrenched themselves in the nation's landscape, and established their ascendancy.

Despite regular growth, obstacles remained. Most of industry's growth occurred through the expansion of existing production processes. Americans had experienced an industrial revolution, but the technological and managerial expertise were slower to arrive:

> Capital accumulation was to be based on proletarianized but largely untransformed labor. Capitalists hired labor but relied on traditional techniques of production. They organized the production process in the social sense, gathering together labor, materials, tools, and other essential ingredients of production and disposing of the output. Yet, except where there was no preexisting organization of production to draw upon, they did not organize or transform the labor process in detail.[38]

This predicament unnerved employers who felt that it limited output and gave labor a degree of power and freedom. Business remained uncomfortably dependent on workers over whom control was more formal than real. Workers compounded the problem as they became more vocal in their protest and increasingly effective at collective organization. As protest escalated, capitalists encountered a depression that promised to place serious limits on their growth unless industry controlled its anarchic production and distribution methods.

Owners' response to this situation varied. To create a more favorable business environment and stabilize the marketplace, they pursued and received government assistance, cooperation, and direction. Internally, they took steps to ensure that knowledge and control of production became the domain of capital rather than labor. Business hired increased numbers of managers—lieutenants at the command of ownership—who had a minimal direct role in, but frequently guided, production and gradually came to command knowledge of the production process. Owners also became deeply engaged in the business of technological innovation, which they believed could yield more production by employees possessing fewer skills than their predecessors.

This varied response brought dramatic results in the twentieth century. As government assumed greater responsibility and business created a managerial sector, the size of the middle class mushroomed to meet industry's needs. Significantly, this was a new middle class—white-collar, professional, dependent on capital for its livelihood; employed to oversee, direct, and manage the nation's financial, natural, and human resources. A group without the traditional ties that could bind farmers, shopkeepers, artisans, and workers in an earlier era, the new middle class drew salaries from corporate institutions—private and public—and almost always thought and acted accordingly.

The search for stability and control brought still another change to society. As knowledge of production increasingly belonged to managers and technical innovations provided machines requiring fewer skills, unskilled or semiskilled labor could be recruited in areas where workers' knowledge of production processes had previously been essential. Therefore, the unskilled portion of the work force grew dramatically from the 1880s through the first two decades of the twentieth century. And since traditional labor markets proved insufficient in supplying workers, most of the new work force came from eastern and southern Europe. America quite literally had a new working class.

Already facing difficulties, organized labor had to confront a radically different economic and social structure. The shifting composition of the classes made labor's old ideology less and less relevant. The new middle class was not impressed by an ideology that indicted a system to which they owed their allegiance and existence. They could not be moved by the same words that a farmer in Kansas, a shopkeeper in Pittsburgh, a printer in Chicago, or a railroad worker in Oswego, New York, in 1865 or 1890 found so powerful.

Nor did the old ideology appeal to the new immigrant work force. These workers had not been raised in the shadow of 1776, 1789, and 1848. Recent arrivals had indigenous traditions that figured significantly in twentieth-century labor protest—as, for example, among groups as divergent as Yiddish-speaking garment workers on the East Coast and Serbian miners in Michigan or Utah—but generally these workers and their protest had little in common with an earlier generation of workers. Moreover, skilled workers still in the work force after 1900 grew reluctant to employ their old ideology, opting instead for a more narrow vision of their future and that of the nation. Suspicions between the new immigrants and older immigrant or native-born workers led the latter to ignore the collective grievances of new workers to a significant degree. Besides, as the years progressed the generation that had once defined the parameters of labor protest and done so much to imbue the labor movement with its basic character left the work force. Younger and newer workers found their predecessors' ideas outmoded. Who—trade unionist or socialist—cared to listen to the peculiar stanzas of a B. M. Lawrence or Shandy Maguire? What did workers in 1917 care to hear about the grand cause of guarding the Republic, crippling the vampires, or delivering true religion?

When Miriam Wheeler submitted her "Labor Chant" to the *American Federationist* in 1894, she was probably unaware of the complex process of which she was a part. Nonetheless, Wheeler's "Chant" embodied dying traditions and a particular kind of working-class consciousness that soon became extinct. Historians would be mistaken, however, to view the parallel rise of popular culture and creation of a new working class only as destructive.[39] To portray workers as victims of the popular culture and monopoly capital would be incorrect. In the first place, popular culture was more than some monolithic form imposed on workers: they profoundly shaped the new industry even as it shaped them. One need not subscribe to the notion that popular culture emerged only in response to consumer demand to believe that workers found some satisfaction in the new products offered by the industry. No doubt many people believed they purchased something of greater value when they watched the latest movies and heard the latest tunes than when they viewed worker-organized dramas or listened to working-class marching bands. And no doubt they still considered the store-bought entertainment as much theirs as they did the earlier forms. After all, they still didn't hobnob with factory owners and their progeny as they sat in the bleachers at professional baseball games or rode the roller coaster at the amusement park. A certain degree of egalitarian anti-elitism could be found in popular culture well into the twentieth century.

Second, and more importantly, when popular culture finally gained ascendence during the 1930s and 1940s, it bode well for labor. Perhaps popular culture really did act as a soporific, proferring an ostensibly flat, homogeneous, formulaic vision of the world. Yet it brought under control the babel of tongues that had divided workers and had been the bane of labor organizers and helped give workers a single language that allowed them to speak to each other across ethnic boundaries. In fact, as George Lipsitz recently argued, popular culture helped to "create a common frame of reference for diverse groups" and set the stage for the rise of the industrial unionism in the 1930s.[40]

From 1865 to 1895, however, workers had employed a different frame of reference and nowhere was that more obvious than among song-poets. The curious admixture that made up song-poetry proved a potent force in their hands. From song-poets' pens came ceaseless defense of labor's cause and caustic criticism of the rising order. The workers' cause was everyone's cause, for it stood for the Republic and democracy, for the right of workers to the wealth they created, for the true religion for which Christ had died. Labor's cause was to champion nothing less than all of humanity.

And yet, for all the song-poets' grand ideas, their works waned during the 1890s and never recovered. The song-poems written between 1865 and 1895 would become the curiosities and relics of a previous labor movement. Occasionally they might be recited or sung as reminders of an earlier generation's struggles to build a better America. Later workers, however, did not realize that these compositions represented a brand of class consciousness—of a "class for itself" in the actual sense as opposed to the ascribed variant some would have favored—once predominant among workers. Workers no longer understood that these song-poems stood for the highest ideals of a labor movement that for a brief moment under the aegis of the Knights of Labor stood face to face in challenge to the capitalist barons. Workers could no longer be moved by the words of H. C. Dodge's "America":

> My country 'tis of thee
> Land of lost liberty,
>     Of thee we sing.
> Land which the millionaires,
> Who govern our affairs,
> Own for themselves and heirs—
>     Hail to thy king.
>
> Land once of noble braves
> But now of wretched slaves—
>     Alas! too late
> We saw sweet Freedom die,
> From letting bribers nigh
> Our unprized suffrage buy;
>     And mourn thy fate.

Land where the wealthy few
Can make the many do
    Their royal will,
And tax for selfish greed
Thy toilers till they bleed,
And those not yet weak-kneed
    Crash down and kill.

Land where a rogue is raised
On high and loudly praised
    For worst of crimes
Of which the end, must be
A hell of cruelty,
As proved by history
    Of ancient times.

My country, 'tis of thee,
Betrayed by bribery,
    Of thee we sing.
We might have saved thee long
Had we, when proud and strong,
Put down the cursed wrong
    That makes a king.[41]

## NOTES

1. Miriam Wheeler, "Labor Chant." *American Federationist* 1 (February 1895): 281.

2. Thomas West, "Stick to Your Union," *American Federationist* 5 (February 1899): 230.

3. See, for example, *Age of Labor, Brotherhood of Locomotive Firemen's Monthly Magazine, Carpenter, Cigar Makers' Official Journal, Coast Seamen's Journal, Granite Cutters' Journal, Iron Molders' Journal, Railroad Brakemen's Journal, Socialist Alliance, Typographical Journal,* and *Western Laborer.*

4. McNeill and Maguire wrote most of their song-poems before 1900, but McGovern continued to write and publish until the 1930s. See McNeill, *Unfrequented Paths,* and Maguire, *Random Rhymes.*

5. The Industrial Workers of the World's song-poetry is treated in Kornbluh, *Rebel Voices.*

6. For examples of twentieth-century socialist song-poetry, see *Socialist Songs with Music* (Chicago: Charles H. Kerr, 1901), and *Socialist Songs with Music* (Chicago: Charles H. Kerr, 1902).

7. On Jewish labor song-poetry, see Aaron Kramer, "The Crest of a Great Wave: Seven More Yiddish Proletarian Poets," *Jewish Currents,* January 1986, 26–32; Solomon Liptzin, The *Flowering of Yiddish Literature*

(New York: Thomas Yoseloff, 1963) and *A History of Yiddish Literature* (New York: Jonathan David Publishers, 1972); and Robert Snyder, "The Paterson Jewish Folk Chorus: Politics, Ethnicity, and Musical Culture," *American Jewish Quarterly* 74 (September 1984): 27–44. See also Norma Fain Pratt, "Culture and Radical Politics: Yiddish Women Writers, 1890–1940," *American Jewish History* 70 (September 1980): 68–90.

8. On folk music and the American Left in the twentieth century, see Reuss, "American Folklore and Left-Wing Politics." See also Denisoff, *Great Day Coming* and *Sing a Song;* David King Dunaway, *How Can I Keep from Singing: Pete Seeger* (New York: McGraw-Hill, 1981); "Composers Collective of New York"; and Lieberman, "*My Song Is My Weapon.*"

For examples of Communist party music and poetry, see *Red Song Book* (New York: Workers Music League—Workers Library Publishers, 1932) and *Workers Song Book* (New York: Workers Music League, 1935). Particularly illuminating are reports of musical activities in the *Daily Worker* from 1932–48.

On Brookwood Labor College and Commonwealth College, see *Brookwood Chautauqua Songs* (Katonah, N.Y.: Brookwood Labor College, n.d.); *Brookwood Song Book* (Katonah, N.Y.: Brookwood Labor College, n.d.); and *Commonwealth Labor Songs* (Mena, Ark.: Commonwealth College, 1938).

On the Southern Tenant Farmers' Union, see *STFU Songbook* (Memphis: Southern Tenant Farmers' Union—Education Department, n.d.); on Amalgamated Clothing Workers of America, see *Amalgamated Songbook* (New York: Amalgamated Clothing Workers of America, 1948); on the International Ladies Garment Workers Union, see *Labor Sings* (New York: International Ladies Garment Workers Union, 1940) and *Let's Sing* (New York: Education Department—International Ladies Garment Workers Union, n.d.); on the United Auto Workers, see *UAW-CIO Sings* (Detroit: United Auto Workers of America, 1943); on the Jewish Workers' Musical Alliance, see *Song and Struggle* (New York: Jewish Workers' Musical Alliance, 1938); on the Southern Workers' Alliance, see *Songs for Southern Workers* (Lexington: Kentucky Workers' Alliance, 1937); on the AFL-CIO, see *AFL-CIO Songbook* (Washington, D.C.: Department of Education, AFL-CIO, 1958). In addition, see the songsters and compilations listed in the bibliography below.

A few useful bibliographies that include labor song-poems have been compiled, although none is complete. See David King Dunaway, "A Selected Bibliography: Protest Songs in the United States," *Folklore Forum* 10 (Fall 1977): 8–25; and R. Serge Denisoff, *Songs of Protest, War, and Peace* (Santa Barbara, Calif.: A.B.C.–Clio, 1973).

9. The most informative source on sound recordings related to labor is Reuss, *Songs of American Labor.*

10. The most useful works on twentieth-century labor song-poetry in the United States are Dunaway, "Composers Collective of New York"; Korn-

bluh, *Rebel Voices;* Korson, *Coal Dust on the Fiddle, Minstrels of the Mine Patch,* and *Songs and Ballads;* Lieberman, "My Song Is My Weapon"; Reuss, "Folk Music and Social Conscience" and "American Folklore and Left-Wing Politics"; and Snyder, "The Paterson Jewish Folk Chorus."

11. The impact of repression on organized labor after 1885 is described in James Holt, "Trade Unionism in the British and U.S. Steel Industries, 1888–1912: A Comparative Study," *Labor History* 18 (Winter 1977): 5–35. See also Herbert Gutman's comments in "Interview with Herbert Gutman."

12. Ibid., 208–9.

13. The argument that the A.F.L. had relatively less use for religion than Gilded-Age labor differs from that of Elizabeth and Kenneth Fones-Wolf, "Trade-Union Evangelism and the A.F.L. in the Labor Forward Movement, 1912–1916," in *Working Class America,* ed. Michael Frisch and Daniel Walkowitz (Urbana: University of Illinois Press, 1983), 153–84. See also Kenneth Fones-Wolf, "The Uses of Religion in the American Labor Movement: The Gompers Era" (Paper presented to the American Historical Association, 1988).

14. See Burbank, *When Farmers Voted Red;* and James R. Green, *Grass-Roots Socialism: Radical Movements in the Southwest, 1895–1943* (Baton Rouge: Louisiana State University, 1978).

15. See, for example, the lyrics in the *I.W.W. Songbook,* particularly Joe Hill's "Solidarity Forever," 4–5. The latter work is reminiscent of Knights of Labor works such as "Hold the Fort."

16. See Liptzin, *A History of Yiddish Literature,* and *The Flowering of Yiddish Literature.*

17. For a survey of popular culture in this period, see Russel Nye, *The Unembarrassed Muse: The Popular Arts in America* (New York: Dial Press, 1970). For a more critical analysis, see Stewart Ewen, *Captains of Consciousness: Advertising and the Social Roots of Consumer Culture* (New York: McGraw-Hill, 1976). In addition, see Couvares, *The Remaking of Pittsburgh;* Lewis A. Erenberg, *Steppin' Out: New York Nightlife and the Transformation of American Culture, 1890–1930* (Chicago: University of Chicago Press, 1984); George Lipsitz, *Class and Culture in Cold War America: A Rainbow at Midnight* (New York: Praeger Publishers, 1981); Rosenzweig, *Eight Hours for What We Will;* Warren Susman, " 'Personality' and the Making of Twentieth-Century Culture," in *New Directions in American Intellectual History,* ed. John Higham and Paul Conkin (Johns Hopkins University Press, 1979), 212–26. My understanding of American popular culture has benefited greatly from these works as well as that of historians of English popular culture. On the latter, see Asa Briggs, *Mass Entertainments: The Origins of a Modern Industry* (Adelaide, Australia: Griffin Press, 1960); Peter Bailey, *Leisure and Class in Victorian England: Rational Recreation and the Contest for Control* (London: Routledge and Kegan Paul, 1977); Hugh Cunningham, *Leisure in the Industrial Revolu-*

*tion* (London: Croom Helm, 1980); Storch, *Popular Culture and Custom*; and Yeo, *Popular Culture and Class Conflict*.

18. Couvares, *The Remaking of Pittsburgh*.

19. See Keil and Jentz, *German Workers in Chicago*.

20. Rosenzweig, *Eight Hours for What We Will*, 222–28.

21. Rosenzweig, *Eight Hours for What We Will*; and Lipsitz, *Class and Culture in Cold War America*.

22. In addition to the works on song-poetry among coal miners and Jewish workers already referred to, see Ruth Rubin, *Voices of a People: The Story of Yiddish Folksong* (Philadelphia: Jewish Publication Society, 1979). See also the essays devoted to the theme, "The Origins of Left Culture in the U.S.: 1880–1940," *Cultural Correspondence* 6/7 (Spring 1978).

23. On the organized Left's rediscovery of "folk music" in the 1930s, see Dunaway, "Composers Collective of New York"; and Reuss, "Roots of American Left-Wing Interest in Folksong."

24. The most useful surveys of American popular music are Hamm, *Yesterdays*, and Tawa, *Sweet Songs for Gentle Americans*.

25. See ibid., 5–10, 17–22, 32–40, 141–48. Tawa states that parlor songs were enjoyed by most antebellum Americans, including the working class. However, he offers little evidence to support his conclusion. Such songs did influence workers, but not until later. Only a handful of labor song-poems used the tunes of sentimental parlor songs. See "The People's Rallying Song," *Workingman's Advocate*, 8 June 1872. Its tune, "The Long Ago," first appeared in an 1843 composition by Thomas Bayly. On Bayly's song, see Mattfield, *Variety*, 84. See also B. M. Lawrence, "Sweet Rest at Home," in Lawrence, *Greenback Songster*, 26. The tune came from a sentimental religious piece composed by Marshall Pike and written in 1851. On Pike's song, see Mattfield, *Variety*, 84.

26. On the British music hall, see Peter Bailey, "Custom, Capital and Culture in the Victorian Music Hall," in Storch, *Popular Custom and Culture*, 180–208; Jones, "Working-Class Culture and Working-Class Politics," in Jones, *Languages of Class*, 179–238; and Summerfield, "Effingham Arms and the Empire" in Yeo, *Popular Culture and Class Conflict*, 209–40. On the origins of Tin Pan Alley, see Norm Cohen, "Tin Pan Alley's Contribution to Folk Music," *Western Folklore* 29 (1970): 9–20.

27. The tune came from Gilbert and Sullivan's "My Object All Sublime." On that tune, see Brunnings, *Folk Song Index*, 214. I. Matthysee used the tune for "A Blue Label Song," *Labor Leader*, 21 November 1891.

28. Charles K. Harris's career is described in Mattfield, *Variety*, 285–87, 297–302. For Joseph Siemer's song-poem, see "After the Strike," *United Mine Workers Journal* 7 (May 1894): 8.

29. Although some sentimental song-poems printed in the labor press were by popular middle-class authors, and the well-known sentimental works of the day regularly appeared, a significant portion of them were by working-class authors.

30. For a standard treatment of the rise of popular sentimental literature, see Carl Bode, *The Anatomy of Popular Culture* (Berkeley: Univer-

sity of California Press, 1960), 169–200. More useful is Ann Douglas, *The Feminization of American Culture* (New York: Avon, 1977).

31. Ibid., 240. See also her discussion, 240–72, and Tawa, *Sweet Songs for Gentle Americans*, 141–48.

32. Mrs. Henry B. Jones, "But Jesus Said," *Railroad Brakemen's Journal* 6 (June 1889): 262.

33. Jonathan Wickers, "The Miner's Child," *National Labor Tribune*, 3 July 1875. See also Anon., "Harry's Death," *Coast Seamen's Journal*, 23 November 1887; E. H. Belknap, "To a Mother," *Railway Conductor's Magazine* 6 (August 1889): 470; Thomas Curtis, "The Democracy of Death," *Journal of United Labor* 12 (August 1891): 1; Mary Baird French, "The Little Maid of Gettysburg," *Coast Seamen's Journal*, 2 March 1892; and Shandy Maguire, "Little Bessie Belisle," *Locomotive Engineer's Monthly Journal* 21 (July 1887): 511.

34. Wickers and a handful of other song-poets modeled some of their work after sentimental songs and poems earlier than the majority of song-poets. See, for example, Dugald Campbell, "Come Nearer Tae Me, Willie," *Fincher's Trades Review*, 21 November 1863, and "I Know Thou Art Changed," ibid., 26 September 1863; John James, "To the Dear Folk at Home," *Workingman's Advocate*, 8 August 1869; and Thomas Walter, "The Little Orphan's Song," ibid., 17 July 1869.

35. Spiritualist-reformer publications such as the *Banner of Light* and the *Herald of Progress* frequently published original song-poetry and fiction that bore the mark of the sentimental influence. In addition, Waters's *Golden Harp* featured sentimental compositions by Stephen Foster. This sentimental strain in antebellum reform is amply treated in Douglas, *Feminization of American Culture*.

36. Cato, "The Summer Girl," *Critic*, 16 July 1892. See also Anon., "Love's Promises," *Advance*, 11 May 1889; Thomas F. Canon, "A Roving in the Spring," *Typographical Journal* 6 (July 1895): 7; Mary Baird French, "Saint Christopher on the Mountain," *Coast Seamen's Journal*, 6 May 1891; Agnes Hempill, "Marguerite," *Journal of United Labor* 7 (May 1887): 2387; Alfred E. Hostelley, "The Shattered Idol," *Critic*, 21 May 1892; Xavier Leder, "Her Image," *Coast Seamen's Journal*, 31 October 1888; N.E.M., "Huckleberry Time," *Labor Leader*, 17 August 1889; Shandy Maguire, "To a Mother," in Maguire, *Random Rhymes*, 81–82; S. E. Olmstead, "Bells of the Year," *Laborer* (Haverhill), 20 February 1886; and Rhymer, "Thoughts of the Season and Beyond," *Critic*, 6 June 1891.

37. The discussion that follows in the remainder of this chapter has benefited from the work of numerous scholars, particularly David Gordon, Richard Edwards, and Michael Reich, *Segmented Work, Divided Workers: The Historical Transformation of Labor in the United States* (New York: Cambridge University Press, 1982); Montgomery, "Labor and Republic"; and Palmer, "Social Formation and Class Formation." Also valuable were Harry Braverman, *Labor and Monopoly Capital* (New York: Monthly Review Press, 1974); Alfred D. Chandler, Jr., *The Visible Hand: The Managerial Revolution in American Business* (Cambridge, Mass.:

Belknap Press, 1977); Gerd Korman, *Industrialization, Immigrants, and Americanizers: The View from Milwaukee, 1866–1921* (Madison: State Historical Society of Wisconsin, 1967); Levine, *Labor's True Woman;* David Montgomery, *Workers' Control in America* (New York: Cambridge University Press, 1979); Daniel Nelson, *Managers and Workers: Origins of the New Factory System in the United States, 1880–1920* (Madison: University of Wisconsin Press, 1975); David Noble, *America by Design* (New York: Knopf, 1977); and Steven J. Ross, *Workers on the Edge: Work, Leisure, and Politics in Industrializing Cincinnati, 1788–1890* (New York: Columbia University Press, 1985). More general in scope but also useful were Gabriel Kolko, *The Triumph of Conservatism* (New York: Free Press, 1963); James Weinstein, *The Corporate Ideal in the Liberal State, 1900–1918* (Boston: Beacon Press, 1968); and Robert Wiebe, *The Search for Order, 1877–1920* (New York: Hill and Wang, 1967).

38. Gordon, Edwards, and Reich, *Segmented Work, Divided Workers,* 79. See also 48–99.

39. Stewart Ewen's *Captains of Consciousness* argues for popular culture's destructive character.

40. Lipsitz, *Class and Culture in Cold War America,* 199, 221.

41. H. C. Dodge, "The Future America," *Bakers' Journal,* 23 March 1889.

# Selected Bibliography

## Manuscript Collections

Arnstein, Joseph. Labor Song Collection. Chicago: Northeastern Illinois University.

Powderly, Terence V. Papers [microfilm edition]. Madison: State Historical Society of Wisconsin.

Samuel, John. Papers. Madison: State Historical Society of Wisconsin.

Schilling, Robert. Papers. Madison: State Historical Society of Wisconsin.

## Labor Newspapers and Journals

*Age of Labor* (Oshkosh, Wis.), 1893–98.

*Alarm* (Chicago), 1884–89.

*Bakers' Journal* (Paterson, N.J./New York), 1888–95.

*Banner of Light* (Boston), 1857–71.

*Boston Daily Evening Voice* (Boston), 1864–67.

*Brotherhood of Locomotive Fireman's Monthly Magazine* (Dayton, Ohio), 1876–98.

*Carpenter* (Indianapolis, Ind.), 1881–96.

*Chicago Labor* (Chicago), 1893–94.

*Cigar Makers' Official Journal* (Suffield, Conn./New York), 1876–95.

*Cleveland Citizen* (Cleveland), 1891–95.

*Coast Seamen's Journal* (San Francisco), 1887–99.

*Cooper's Journal* (Cleveland), 1870–75.

*Critic* (Baltimore), 1888–93.

*Fincher's Trades Review* (Philadelphia), 1863–66.

*Furniture Workers' Journal* (New York), 1883–95.

*Garment Worker* (New York), 1893–95.

*Granite Cutters' Journal* (Rockland, Maine; Westbury, R.I.; Quincy, Mass.; Philadelphia; Barre, Vt.; Concord, N.H.; Baltimore), 1877–97.

*Herald of Progress* (New York), 1860–61.

*Iron Molders' International Journal* (Philadelphia/Cincinnati), 1864–1900.

*John Swinton's Paper* (New York), 1883–87.
*Journal of United Labor* (Marblehead, Mass.; Pittsburgh; Philadelphia), 1880–95.
*Knights of Labor* (Chicago), 1886–89.
*Labor Balance* (Boston), 1877–79.
*Labor Enquirer* (Chicago), 1887–88.
*Labor Enquirer* (Denver), 1882–88.
*Laborer* (Haverhill, Mass.), 1884–87.
*Labor Leader* (Boston), 1887–95.
*Labor Leaf–Advance* (Detroit), 1885–89.
*Labor Standard* (Boston/Fall River, Mass.), 1876–81. [Also published as *Socialist* (New York), 1876.]
*Labor Standard* (Paterson, N.J.), 1878–96.
*Locomotive Engineer's Monthly Journal* (Cleveland), 1867–95.
*Machine Woodworker* (Denver/Chicago), 1890–95.
*Miners' National Record* (Massilon, Ohio), 1874–75.
*Monthly Journal of International Association of Machinists* (Atlanta, Ga./ Richmond, Va.), 1891–95.
*National Labor Tribune* (Pittsburgh), 1873–95.
*Our Organette* (Indianapolis), 1882–83.
*Painter* (Baltimore), 1887–95.
*Progress* (New York), 1882–85.
*Railroad Brakemen's Journal* (Rock Island, Ill./Galesburg, Ill.), 1886–99.
*Railway Carmen's Journal* (Minneapolis; Chicago; Cedar Rapids, Iowa), 1893–95.
*Railway Conductor's Monthly* (Elmira, N.Y./Cedar Rapids, Iowa), 1884–85.
*Saddle and Harness Makers' Journal* (Boston/Itasca, Tex.), 1891–94.
*St. Louis Labor* (St. Louis), 1893–95.
*Socialist Alliance* (Chicago), 1896–99.
*Salt Workers' Journal* (Hutchinson, Kans.), 1894.
*Trades* (Philadelphia), 1879–80.
*Truth* (San Francisco), 1882–84.
*Typographical Journal* (Indianapolis), 1889–97.
*United Mine Workers Journal* (Columbus, Ohio), 1891–1900.
*Vulcan Record* (Pittsburgh), 1868–75.
*Welcome Workman* (Philadelphia), 1867–68.
*Western Laborer* (Omaha, Nebr.), 1893–95.
*Workingman's Advocate* (Chicago), 1864–76.
*Workman's Advocate* (New Haven, Conn.), 1883–91.

## Songsters, Chapbooks, and Compilations

*AFL-CIO Songbook.* Washington: AFL-CIO Department of Education, 1958.
Allan, Anne, ed. *Sing America.* New York: Workers Bookshop, n.d.

Almanac Singers. *Eight Union Songs of the Almanacs.* New York: New Theatre League, 1941.

*Amalgamated Songbook.* New York: Amalgamated Clothing Workers of America, 1948.

Auville, Ray, and Lida Auville, eds. *Songs of the American Workers.* New York: Workers' Library Publishers, 1934.

Bradbury, William, and Charles Sanders. *The Young Choir.* New York: Mark H. Newman, 1841.

*Brookwood Chautauqua Songs.* Katonah, N.Y.: Brookwood Labor College, n.d.

*Brookwood Song Book.* Katonah, N.Y.: Brookwood Labor College, n.d.

*The Campaign Scott and Graham Songster.* New York: D. E. Gavit, 1852.

Cebula, James, and James E. Wolfe. eds. *Rhyme and Reason: Molders Poetry from Sylvis to the Depression.* Cincinnati: Sylvis Society, 1984.

Chase, Murray. *Sing for Victory.* New York: Murray Chase-Industrial Worker Order, 1942.

*C.I.O. Songs.* Birmingham, Ala.: Birmingham Industrial Union Council, n.d.

Clark, George. *The Free Soil Minstrel.* New York: Martyn and Ely, 1848.

*The Clay Minstrel; or, National Songster.* New York: Greely and M'Elrath, 1844.

*The Comic Forget-Me-Not Songster.* New York: Philip Cozans, 1845.

*Commonwealth Labor Songs.* Mena, Ark.: Commonwealth College, 1938.

Dale, William P. *The Young Republican's Vocalist.* New York: A. Morris, 1860.

Duganne, Augustine. *The Poetical Works of Augustine Duganne.* Philadelphia: Parry and McMillan, 1855.

*Fattie Stewart's Comic Songster.* New York: Dick and Fitzgerald, 1863.

Fennell, Patrick [Shandy Maguire]. *Random Rhymes and Rhapsodies of the Rail.* Cleveland: Cleveland Printing Co., 1907.

———. *Recitations, Epics, Lyrics, and Poems Humorous and Pathetic.* Oswego, N.Y.: Patrick Fennell, 1886.

Friedman, Samuel H., ed. *Rebel Song Book.* New York: Rand School Press, 1935.

Gellert, Hugo. *Me and My Captain: Chain Gang Negro Songs of Protest.* New York: Hours Press, 1935.

———. *Negro Songs of Protest.* New York: American Music League, 1936.

Gibson, George Howard. *Songs of the People: The Voice of the Industrial Classes and People's Party of America.* Lincoln, Nebr.: Alliance Publishing Co., 1892.

Hille, Waldemar, ed. *The People's Songbook.* New York: Boni and Gaer, 1948.

Horton, Zilphia, ed. *Labor Songs.* Atlanta: Southern Regional Office of the Textile Workers Union of America, 1939.

*IWW Songbook.* Chicago: Industrial Workers of the World, 1973.

Kerr, Charles H., ed. *Socialist Songs with Music*. Chicago: Charles H. Kerr and Co., 1902.

*Labor Sings*. New York: International Ladies Garment Workers Union, 1940.

Lawrence, B. M. *The National Greenback Labor Songster*. New York: D. M. Bennett, 1878.

*Let's Sing*. New York: Educational Department of the International Ladies Garment Workers Union, n.d.

Lum, Dyer. *In Memoriam: Chicago, November 11, 1887*. Berkeley Heights, N.J.: Oriole Press, 1937.

McGovern, Michael. *Labor Lyrics and Other Poems*. Youngstown, Ohio: Vindicator Press, 1899.

McNeill, George E. *Unfrequented Paths: Songs of Nature, Labor, and Men*. Boston: James H. West, 1903.

People's Songs, Inc. *People's Songs Workbook No. 1*. New York: People's Songs, Inc., 1947.

Potter, R. K. *The Boston Temperance Songster*. Boston: White and Potter, 1846.

*Puts Golden Songster*. San Francisco: D. E. Appleton and Co., 1858.

Reuber, Karl. *Gedanken über die neue Zeit*. Pittsburgh: Urben and Bruder, 1872.

————. *Hymns of Labor: Remodeled from Old Songs*. Pittsburgh: Barrows and Osbourne, n.d.

————. *Poems and Songs*. Pittsburgh: Louis Holz, n.d.

Sankey, Ira D. *Sacred Songs and Solos*. London: Morgan and Scott, Ltd., 1895.

Shindler, Mary Dana. *United States Labor Greenback Songbook*. New Rochelle, N.Y.: George Lloyd, 1879.

*Sing Amalgamated!* New York: Amalgamated Clothing Workers of America, 1940.

*Sing While You Fight for a Fuller Life with Local 65*. New York: United Wholesale and Warehouse Employees Local 65, 1941.

*Song and Struggle*. New York: Jewish Workers' Musical Alliance, 1938.

*Songs for Southern Workers*. Lexington: Kentucky Workers' Alliance, 1937.

*Songs for the Union*. Philadelphia: A. Winch, 1861.

*Songs of the People*. New York: Workers' Library Publishers, 1937.

*Songs of the Southern School for Workers*. Asheville, N.C.: n.p., 1940.

*STFU Songbook*. Memphis: Southern Tenant Farmers' Union Education Department, n.d.

Tallmadge, James D., and Emily Tallmadge. *Labor Songs Dedicated to the Knights of Labor*. Chicago: J. D. Tallmadge, 1886.

*UAW-CIO Sings*. Detroit: Educational Department—United Auto Workers of America, 1943.

Vincent, Leopold, ed. *The Alliance and Labor Songster*. Winfield, Kans.: H. and L. Vincent, 1891.

Waters, Horace. *Harp of Freedom.* Part 1. New York: Horace Waters, n.d.
———. *Waters' Golden Harp.* New York: Horace Waters, 1863.
Workers Music League. *Workers Song Book.* New York: Workers Library Publishers, 1935.
———. *Red Song Book.* New York: Workers' Library Publishers, 1932.

## Books

Abell, Aaron I. *American Catholicism and Social Action: A Search for Social Justice, 1865–1950.* Garden City, N.Y.: Hanover House, 1960.
———. *The Urban Impact on American Protestantism, 1865–1900.* Cambridge: Harvard University Press, 1943.
Anderson, Perry. *Arguments within English Marxism.* London: New Left Books, 1980.
Ashton, John. *Chap-Books of the Eighteenth Century.* Welwyn Garden City, Hertfordshire, England: Seven Dials Press, 1969.
Bailey, Peter. *Leisure and Class in Victorian England: Rational Recreation and the Contest for Control.* London: Routledge and Kegan Paul, 1977.
Barry, Phillips. *The Maine Woods Songster.* Cambridge: Powell Printing Co., 1939.
———. *The New Green Mountain Songster.* New Haven: Yale University Press, 1939.
Beck, Earl Clifton. *Songs of the Michigan Lumberjacks.* Ann Arbor: University of Michigan Press, 1948.
Bensman, David. *The Practice of Solidarity: American Hat Finishers in the Nineteenth Century.* Urbana: University of Illinois Press, 1985.
Benson, Louis F. *The English Hymn: Its Development and Uses in Worship.* Richmond, Va.: John Knox Press, 1962.
Betten, Neil. *Catholic Activism and the Industrial Worker.* Gainesville: University of Florida Press, 1977.
Bodo, James R. *The Protestant Clergy and Public Issues, 1812–1848.* Princeton: Princeton University Press, 1954.
Briggs, Asa. *Mass Entertainment: The Origins of Modern Industry.* Adelaide, Australia: Griffin Press, 1960.
Browne, Henry. *The Catholic Church and the Knights of Labor.* Washington, D.C.: Catholic University Press, 1949.
Bruce, Dickson D., Jr. *And They All Sang Hallelujah: Plain Folk Camp-Meeting Religion, 1800–1845.* Knoxville: University of Tennessee Press, 1974.
Brunnings, Florence. *Folk Song Index: A Comprehensive Guide to the Florence E. Brunnings Collection.* New York: Garland Publishing Co., 1981.
Burbank, Garin. *When Farmers Voted Red: The Gospel of Socialism in the Oklahoma Countryside, 1910–1924.* Westport, Conn.: Greenwood Press, 1976.

Chase, Gilbert. *America's Music: From the Pilgrims to the Present.* New York: McGraw-Hill, 1966.

Child, James Francis. *The English and Scottish Popular Ballads.* 5 vols. Boston: Houghton Mifflin, 1882–96.

Clarke, John, Charles Critcher, and Richard Johnson, eds. *Working-Class Culture: Studies in History and Theory.* London: Hutchinson, 1979.

Cohen, Norm. *The Long Steel Rail: The Railroad in American Folksong.* Urbana: University of Illinois Press, 1981.

Colcord, Joanna. *Songs of American Sailormen.* New York: W. W. Norton, 1938.

Colls, Robert. *The Collier's Rant: Song and Culture in the Industrial Village.* London: Croom Helm, 1977.

Combs, Josiah H. *Folk-Songs of the Southern United States.* Austin: University of Texas Press, 1967.

Couvares, Francis. *The Remaking of Pittsburgh: Class and Culture in an Industrializing City, 1877–1919.* Albany: State University of New York Press, 1984.

Cross, Robert D. *The Emergence of Liberal Catholicism in America.* Cambridge: Harvard University Press, 1958.

Cunningham, Hugh. *Leisure in the Industrial Revolution.* London: Croom Helm, 1980.

Dawley, Alan. *Class and Community: The Industrial Revolution in Lynn.* Cambridge: Harvard University Press, 1976.

Denisoff, R. Serge. *Great Day Coming: Folk Music and the American Left.* Urbana: University of Illinois Press, 1971.

———. *Sing a Song of Social Significance.* Bowling Green, Ohio: Bowling Green University Press, 1972.

———. *Songs of Protest, War and Peace.* Santa Barbara: A.B.C.–CLIO, 1973.

Diehl, Katherine Smith. *Hymns and Tunes—An Index.* New York: Scarecrow Press, 1966.

Disher, Maurice Willson. *Victorian Song.* London: Phoenix House, 1955.

Doerflinger, William. *Shantymen and Shantyboys.* New York: Macmillan Co., 1951.

Dolan, Jay P. *Catholic Revivalism: The American Experience, 1830–1900.* Notre Dame: University of Notre Dame Press, 1978.

Erenberg, Lewis A. *Steppin' Out: New York Nightlife and the Transformation of American Culture, 1890–1930.* Chicago: University of Chicago Press, 1984.

Faler, Paul G. *Mechanics and Manufacturers in the Early Industrial Revolution: Lynn, Massachusetts, 1780–1860.* Albany: State University of New York, 1981.

*Farmers' Alliance Songs of the 1890s.* Nebraska Folklore Pamphlet no. 8. Lincoln, Nebr.: Federal Writers Project, 1938.

Fife, Austin, and Alta Fife. *Cowboy and Western Songs: A Comprehensive Anthology.* New York: Clarkson N. Potter, 1969.

Fink, Leon. *Workingmen's Democracy: The Knights of Labor and American Politics.* Urbana: University of Illinois Press, 1983.

Foner, Eric. *Free Soil, Free Labor, Free Men: The Ideology of the Republican Party before the Civil War.* London: Oxford University Press, 1970.

Foner, Philip. *American Labor Songs of the Nineteenth Century.* Urbana: University of Illinois Press, 1975.

Foote, Henry Wilder. *Three Centuries of American Hymnody.* New York: Archon Books, 1968.

Fowke, Edith, and Joe Glazer. *Songs of Work and Freedom.* Chicago: Roosevelt University Press, 1960.

Gillespie, Angus K. *Folklorist of the Coal Fields: George Korson's Life and Work.* University Park: Pennsylvania State University Press, 1980.

Goodwyn, Lawrence. *Democratic Promise: The Populist Moment in America.* New York: Oxford University Press, 1976.

Gordon, David, Richard Edwards, and Michael Reich. *Segmented Work, Divided Workers: The Historical Transformation of Labor in the United States.* Cambridge: Cambridge University Press, 1982.

Gray, Roland Palmer. *Songs and Ballads of the Maine Lumberjacks.* Cambridge: Harvard University Press, 1924.

Green, Archie. *Only a Miner.* Urbana: University of Illinois Press, 1972.

Green, James R. *Grass-Roots Socialism: Radical Movements in the Southwest, 1895–1943.* Baton Rouge: Louisiana State University Press, 1978.

Greenway, John. *American Folksongs of Protest.* New York: A. S. Barnes, 1953.

Grieg, Gavin. *Folk-Song in Buchan and Folk-Song of the North-East.* Hatboro, Penn.: Folklore Associates, 1963.

Griffin, Clifford. *Their Brothers' Keepers: Moral Stewardship in the U.S., 1800–1865.* New Brunswick: Rutgers University Press, 1960.

Grossman, John. *William Sylvis: Pioneer of American Labor.* New York: Columbia University Press, 1945.

Hamm, Charles. *Yesterdays: Popular Song in America.* New York: W. W. Norton, 1979.

Harrison, J. F. C. *The Second Coming: Popular Millenarianism, 1780–1850.* New Brunswick: Rutgers University Press, 1979.

Hicks, O. T. *The Life of Richard Trevellick.* Joliet, Ill.: J. E. Williams and Co., 1896.

Hobsbawm, Eric. *Primitive Rebels.* New York: W. W. Norton, 1965.

———. *Workers: Worlds of Labor.* New York: Pantheon Books, 1984.

Hoerder, Dirk, ed. *Struggle a Hard Battle: Essays on Working-Class Immigrants.* DeKalb: Northern Illinois University Press, 1986.

Hopkins, Charles H. *The Rise of the Social Gospel in American Protestantism, 1865–1915.* New Haven: Yale University Press, 1940.

Horn, Dorothy. *Sing to Me of Heaven: A Study of Folk and Early Ameri-*

can *Materials in Three Old Harp Books.* Gainesville: University of Florida Press, 1970.

Huggins, Nathan I. *Protestants against Poverty: Boston's Charities, 1870–1900.* Westport, Conn.: Greenwood Publishing, 1971.

Hugill, Stan. *Shanties from the Seven Seas.* New York: E. P. Dutton and Co., 1966.

Jackson, George Pullen. *Another Sheaf of White Spirituals.* Gainesville: University of Florida Press, 1952.

———. *Spiritual Folk-Songs of Early America.* New York: J. J. Augustin, 1937.

Johnson, Paul E. *A Shopkeeper's Millennium: Society and Revivals in Rochester, New York, 1815–1837.* New York: Hill and Wang, 1978.

Jones, Gareth Stedman. *Languages of Class: Studies in English Working Class History, 1832–1982.* Cambridge: Cambridge University Press, 1983.

Jones, Peter d'A. *The Christian Socialist Revival 1877–1914: Religion, Class and Social Conscience in Late Victorian England.* Princeton: Princeton University Press, 1968.

Julian, John. *A Dictionary of Hymnology.* London: John Murray, 1907.

Kaufman, Stuart B. *The Samuel Gompers Papers.* Vols. 1–3. Urbana: University of Illinois Press, 1986–88.

Kealey, Gregory. *Toronto Workers Respond to Industrial Capitalism, 1867–1892.* Toronto: University of Toronto Press, 1980.

Kealey, Gregory, and Bryan Palmer. *Dreaming of What Might Be: The Knights of Labor in Ontario, 1880–1900.* Cambridge: Cambridge University Press, 1982.

Kealey, Gregory, and Peter Warrian. *Essays in Canadian Working Class History.* Toronto: McClelland and Stewart, 1976.

Keil, Hartmut, and John B. Jentz. *German Workers in Chicago: A Documentary History of Working-Class Culture from 1850 to World War I.* Urbana: University of Illinois Press, 1988.

Kentucky Federal Music Project. *Kentucky Folk Songs.* Louisville: Kentucky Federal Music Project—Works Progress Administration, 1936.

Kornbluh, Joyce. *Rebel Voices: An I.W.W. Anthology.* Ann Arbor: University of Michigan Press, 1968.

Korson, George. *Black Rock: Mining Folklore of the Pennsylvania Dutch.* Baltimore: Johns Hopkins Press, 1960.

———. *Coal Dust on the Fiddle.* Philadelphia: University of Pennsylvania Press, 1943.

———. *Minstrels of the Mine Patch.* Philadelphia: University of Pennsylvania Press, 1938.

———. *Songs and Ballads of the Anthracite Miner.* New York: Grafton Press, 1927.

Laqueur, Thomas Walter. *Religion and Respectability: Sunday Schools and Working-Class Culture, 1780–1850.* New Haven: Yale University Press, 1970.

Laws, G. Malcolm, Jr. *American Balladry from British Broadsides*. Philadelphia: American Folklore Society, 1957.

Levine, Lawrence W. *Black Culture and Black Consciousness: Afro-American Folk Thought from Slavery to Freedom*. Oxford: Oxford University Press, 1977.

Lidtke, Vernon L. *The Alternative Culture: Socialist Labor in Imperial Germany*. New York: Oxford University Press, 1985.

Lieberman, Robbie. *"My Song Is My Weapon": People's Songs, American Communism, and the Politics of Culture 1930–50*. Urbana: University of Illinois Press, 1989.

Lipsitz, George. *Class and Culture in Cold War America: A Rainbow at Midnight*. New York: Praeger Publishers, 1981.

Liptzin, Solomon. *The Flowering of Yiddish Literature*. New York: Thomas Yoseloff, 1963.

———. *A History of Yiddish Literature*. New York: Jonathan David Publishers, 1972.

———. *Lyric Pioneers of Modern Germany: Studies in German Social Poetry*. New York: Columbia University Press, 1928.

Lloyd, A. L. *Come All Ye Bold Miners: Ballads and Songs of the Coalfields*. London: Lawrence and Wishart, 1952.

———. *Folk Song in England*. New York: International, 1967.

Lomax, John. *American Ballads and Folksongs*. New York: Macmillan, 1934.

———. *Songs of the Cattle Trail and Cow Camp*. New York: Macmillan, 1919.

Lorenz, Ellen Jane. *Glory Hallelujah: The Story of the Campmeeting Spiritual*. Nashville: Abingdon Press, 1978.

Lum, Dyer. *Social Problems of To-day; or, The Mormon Question*. Port Jervis, N.Y.: Lum, 1886.

———. *Economics of Anarchy: A Study of the Industrial Type*. New York: Twentieth Century Publishing Co., 1890.

Magnuson, Norris. *Salvation in the Slums: Evangelical Social Work, 1865–1920*. Metuchen, N.J.: Scarecrow Press and the American Theological Library Association, 1977.

Mattfield, Julius. *Variety Music Cavalcade, 1620–1969*. Englewood Cliffs, N.J.: Prentice-Hall, 1971.

May, Henry F. *Protestant Churches and Industrial America*. New York: Octagon Books, 1963.

McCutchan, Robert. *Hymn Tune Names, Their Sources and Significance*. New York: Abingdon Press, 1957.

McLoughlin, William G., Jr. *Modern Revivalism*. New York: Ronald Press, 1959.

McNeill, George E. *The Labor Movement: The Problem of Today*. New York: M. W. Hazin, 1887.

Moffat, Alfred. *The Minstrelsy of Scotland*. London: Augener, n.d.

Montgomery, David. *Beyond Equality*. New York: Alfred Knopf, 1967.

Moore, Robert. *Pitmen, Preachers and Politics: The Effects of Methodism in a Durham Mining Community.* Cambridge: Cambridge University Press, 1974.

Oestreicher, Richard J. *Solidarity and Fragmentation: Working People and Class Consciousness in Detroit, 1875–1900.* Urbana: University of Illinois Press, 1986.

Palmer, Bryan. *A Culture in Conflict: Skilled Workers and Industrial Capitalism in Hamilton, Ontario, 1860–1914.* Montreal: McGill-Queen's University Press, 1979.

Paredes, Americo, and Ellen J. Stekert. *The Urban Experience and Folk Tradition.* Austin: University of Texas Press, 1971.

Pope, Liston. *Millhands and Preachers.* New Haven: Yale University Press, 1942.

Prothero, I. J. *Artisans and Politics in Early Nineteenth-Century London: John Gast and His Times.* Baton Rouge: Louisiana State University Press, 1979.

Reuss, Richard, ed. *Songs of American Labor, Industrialization and the Urban Work Experience: A Discography.* Ann Arbor: Labor Studies Center, Institute of Labor and Industrial Relations, University of Michigan, 1983.

Rock, Howard. *Artisans of the New Republic: The Tradesmen of New York City in the Age of Jefferson.* New York: New York University Press, 1979.

Roediger, David, and Franklin Rosemont, eds. *Haymarket Scrapbook.* Chicago: Charles H. Kerr, 1986.

Rogers, Edward H. *An Essay: The Relations of Christianity to Labor and Capital.* Boston: Weekly American Workman, 1870.

Rosenzweig, Roy. *Eight Hours for What We Will: Workers and Leisure in an Industrial City, 1870–1920.* Cambridge: Cambridge University Press, 1983.

Ross, Steven J. *Workers on the Edge: Work, Leisure, and Politics in Industrializing Cincinnati, 1788–1890.* New York: Columbia University Press, 1985.

*A San Francisco Songster, 1849–1939.* History of Music Project. Vol. 2. San Francisco: Works Progress Administration, 1939.

Scheips, Paul J. *Hold the Fort!* Washington, D.C.: Smithsonian Institution Press, 1971.

Schneider, Louis, and Sanford M. Dornbusch. *Popular Religion: Inspirational Books in America.* Chicago: University of Chicago Press, 1958.

Sears, Minnie Earl. *Song Index and Supplement.* New York: Shoestring Press, 1966.

Sewell, William H., Jr. *Work and Revolution in France: The Language of Labor from the Old Regime to 1848.* Cambridge: Cambridge University Press, 1980.

Sharp, Cecil. *English Folk Songs from the Southern Appalachians.* New York: G. P. Putnam's Sons, 1917.

———. *English Folk Song: Some Conclusions*. London: Simpkin and Co., 1907.

Shepard, Leslie. *The Broadside Ballad: A Study in Origins and Meaning*. Hatboro, Penn.: Folklore Associates, 1962.

———. *The History of Street Literature*. Devon, England: David and Charles, 1973.

Simpson, Claude M. *The British Broadside Ballad and Its Music*. New Brunswick: Rutgers University Press, 1966.

Sizer, Sandra S. *Gospel Hymns and Social Religion: The Rhetoric of Nineteenth-Century Revivalism*. Philadelphia: Temple University Press, 1978.

Smith, Timothy. *Revivalism and Social Reform in Mid-Nineteenth-Century America*. New York: Abingdon Press, 1957.

Storch, Robert, ed. *Popular Culture and Custom in Nineteenth-Century England*. London: Croom Helm, 1982.

Swinton, John. *Striking for Life: Labor's Side of the Labor Question*. n.p.: American Manufacturing and Publishing, 1894.

Sylvis, James. *Life, Speeches, Labors, and Essays of William Sylvis*. New York: Clayton, Remsen, and Haffelfinger, 1872.

Tamke, Susan S. *Make a Joyful Noise unto the Lord: Hymns as a Reflection of Victorian Social Attitudes*. Athens: Ohio University Press, 1978.

Tawa, Nicholas E. *Sweet Songs for Gentle Americans—The Parlor Song in America, 1790–1860*. Bowling Green, Ohio: Bowling Green University Popular Press, 1980.

Thompson, Edward P. *The Making of the English Working Class*. New York: Vintage Books, 1966.

———. *The Poverty of Theory and Other Essays*. New York: Monthly Review Press, 1978.

Vicinus, Martha. *Broadsides of the Industrial North*. Newcastle upon Tyne, England: Frank Graham, n.d.

———. *The Industrial Muse: A Study of Nineteenth-Century British Working-Class Literature*. New York: Barnes and Noble, 1974.

Walkowitz, Daniel J. *Worker City, Company Town: Iron- and Cotton-Worker Protest in Troy and Cohoes, New York, 1855–84*. Urbana: University of Illinois Press, 1981.

Weiss, Harry B. *A Book about Chapbooks: The People's Literature of Bygone Times*. Hatboro, Penn., Folklore Associates, 1969.

Wilentz, Sean. *Chants Democratic: New York City and the Rise of the American Working Class 1788–1850*. New York: Oxford University Press, 1984.

Wilgus, D. K. *Anglo-American Folksong Scholarship since 1898*. New Brunswick: Rutgers University Press, 1959.

Wolf, Edwin, II. *American Song Sheets, Slip Ballads and Poetical Broadsides 1850–1870: A Catalogue of the Collection of the Library Company of Philadelphia*. Philadelphia: Library Company of Philadelphia, 1963.

Yearley, Clifton K., Jr. *Britons in American Labor: A History of the Influence of the United Kingdom on American Labor, 1820–1914.* Baltimore: Johns Hopkins University Press, 1957.

Yeo, Eileen, and Stephen Yeo, eds. *Popular Culture and Class Conflict 1590–1914: Explorations in the History of Labor and Leisure.* Sussex: Harvester Press, 1981.

Yerbury, Grace D. *Song in America: From Early Time to about 1850.* Metuchen, N.Y.: Scarecrow, 1971.


## Articles and Essays

Balch, Elizabeth. "Songs for Labor." *Survey,* January 1914, 408–28.

Bercuson, David. "Through the Looking Glass of Culture: An Essay on the New Labor History and Working-Class Culture in Recent Canadian Historical Writing." *Labour/Le Travailleur* 7 (Spring 1981): 95–112.

Botkin, B. A. "Folklore as a Neglected Source of Social History." In *The Cultural Approach to History,* edited by Caroline Ware, 308–15. New York: Columbia University Press, 1940.

Brazier, Richard. "The Story of the I.W.W.'s Little Red Songbook." *Labor History* 9 (Winter 1968): 91–105.

Brody, David. "The Old Labor History and the New: In Search of an American Working Class." *Labor History* 20 (Winter 1979): 111–26.

Coffin, Tristram P. "Folksongs of Social Protest: A Musical Mirage." *New York Folklore Quarterly* 14 (Spring 1958): 3–9.

Cohen, Norm. "The Persian's Crew: The Ballad, Its Author, and the Incident." *New York Folklore Quarterly* 25 (December 1969): 289–97.

———. "Tin Pan Alley's Contribution to Folk Music." *Western Folklore* 29 (January 1970): 9–20.

Cumbler, John T. "Labor, Capital, and Community: The Struggle for Power." *Labor History* 15 (Summer 1974): 395–415.

———. "Transatlantic Working-Class Institutions." *Journal of Historical Geography* 6 (July 1980): 275–90.

Currie, Harold W. "The Religious Views of Eugene V. Debs." *Mid-America* 54 (July 1972): 147–56.

Dawley, Alan. "E. P. Thompson and the Peculiarities of the Americans." *Radical History* 19 (Winter 1978–79): 33–60.

DeLottinville, Peter. "Joe Beef of Montreal: Working-Class Culture and the Tavern, 1869–1889." *Labour/Le Travailleur* 8/9 (Autumn-Spring 1981–82): 9–40.

Dowe, Dieter. "The Workers' Choral Movement before the First World War." *Journal of Contemporary History* 13 (April 1978): 269–96.

Dugaw, Diane M. "Anglo-American Folksong Reconsidered: The Interface of Oral and Written Forms." *Western Folklore* 43 (April 1984): 83–103.

Dunaway, David King. "A Selected Bibliography: Protest Songs in the United States." *Folklore Forum* 10 (Fall 1977): 8–25.

————. "Unsung Songs of Protest: The Composers Collective of NewYork." *New York Folklore* 5 (Summer 1979): 1–20.

Emrich, Duncan. "Songs of the Western Miners." *California Folklore Quarterly* 1 (July 1942): 213–32.

Evanson, Jacob A. "Folk Songs of an Industrial City." In *Pennsylvania Songs and Legend*, edited by George Korson, 423–66. Baltimore: Johns Hopkins University Press, 1949.

Faler, Paul G. "Working Class Historiography." *Radical America* 3 (March 1969): 58–68.

Fones-Wolf, Elizabeth, and Kenneth Fones-Wolf. "Trade-Union Evangelism and the A.F.L. in the Labor Forward Movement, 1912–1916." In *Working Class America*, edited by Michael Frisch and Daniel Walkowitz, 153–84. Urbana: University of Illinois Press, 1983.

Foster, John. "The Declassing of Language." *New Left Review* 150 (March-April 1985): 29–45.

Gilbert, Alan D. "Methodism, Dissent and Political Stability in Early Industrial England." *Journal of Religious History* 10 (December 1979): 381–99.

Green, Archie. "A Discography of American Coal Miners' Songs." *Labor History* 2 (December 1961): 101–15.

————. "A Discography of American Labor Union Songs." *New York Folklore Quarterly* 17 (Fall 1961): 186–93.

————. "American Labor Lore: Its Meanings and Uses." *Industrial Relations* 4 (February 1965): 51–69.

————. "Industrial Lore: A Bibliographic-Semantic Query." *Western Folklore* 37 (July 1978): 213–44.

————. "Recorded Labor Songs: An Overview." *Western Folklore* 27 (January 1968): 68–76.

Green, James R. "The 'Salesman-Soldiers' of the 'Appeal Army': A Profile of Rank and File Socialist Agitators." In *Socialism in the Cities*, edited by Bruce Stave, 13–40. Port Washington, N.Y.: Kennikat Press, 1975.

Greenway, John. "Folk Songs as Socio-Historical Documents." *Western Folklore* 19 (January 1960): 1–9.

Griffen, Clyde. "Christian Socialism Instructed by Gompers." *Labor History* 12 (Spring 1971): 196–213.

Griffiths, Carl Warren. "Some Protestant Attitudes on the Labor Question in 1886." *Church History* 11 (June 1942): 138–48.

Hand, Wayland. "The Folklore, Customs, and Traditions of the Butte Miner." *California Folklore Quarterly* 5 (January 1946): 1–25 and 5 (April 1946): 153–78.

Hand, Wayland, Charles Cutts, Robert Wylder, and Betty Wylder. "Songs of the Butte Miners." *Western Folklore* 9 (January 1950): 1–40.

Hobsbawm, Eric, "Religion and the Rise of Socialism." *Marxist Perspectives* 1 (Spring 1978): 14–33.

———. "Methodism and the Threat of Revolution in Britian." In *Labouring Men*, edited by Eric Hobsbawm, 23–33. London: Weidenfeld and Nicolson, 1968.

Holt, James. "Trade Unionism in the British and U.S. Steel Industries, 1888–1912: A Comparative Study." *Labor History* 18 (Winter 1977): 5–35.

Kealey, Gregory S. "Critiques: Labour and Working-Class History in Canada: Prospects in the 1980s." *Labour/Le Travailleur* 7 (Spring 1981): 67–94.

Kramer, Aaron. "The Crest of a Great Wave: Seven More Yiddish Proletarian Poets." *Jewish Currents*, January 1986, 26–32.

Krueger, Thomas. "American Labor Historiography, Old and New: A Review Essay." *Journal of Social History* 4 (Spring 1971): 277–85.

Loveland, Ann. "Evangelicalism and 'Immediate Emancipation' in American Anti-Slavery Thought." *Journal of Southern History* 32 (May 1966): 172–88.

McCutchan, Robert. "American Church Composers of the Early Nineteenth Century." *Church History* 2 (September 1933): 139–51.

McKay, Ian. "Historians, Anthropology, and the Concept of Culture." *Labour/Le Travailleur* 8/9 (Autumn-Spring 1981–82): 185–242.

Merrill, Michael. "Interview with Herbert Gutman." *Radical History* 27 (May 1983): 202–22.

Montgomery, David. "Labor and Republic in Industrial America, 1860–1920." *Le Mouvement Social* 111 (April 1980): 201–15.

———. "The Shuttle and the Cross: Weavers and Artisans in the Kensington Riots of 1844." *Journal of Southern History* 5 (Summer 1972): 411–46.

———. "To Study the People: The American Working Class." *Labor History* 21 (Fall 1980): 485–512.

———. "Trends in Working-Class History." *Labour/Le Trevailleur* 10 (Spring 1987): 12–22.

Nicholl, Grier. "The Image of the Protestant Minister in the Christian Social Novel." *Church History* 37 (September 1968): 319–34.

———. "The Christian Social Novel and Social Gospel Evangelism." *Religion in Life* 34 (Autumn 1964): 548–61.

Nickerson, Bruce. "Is There a Folk in the Factory?" *Journal of American Folklore* 87 (January-March 1974): 133–39.

Ozanne, Robert. "Trends in American Labor History." *Labor History* 21 (Fall 1980): 513–21.

Palmer, Bryan. "Classifying Culture." *Labour/Le Travailleur* 8/9 (Autumn-Spring 1981–82): 153–83.

———. "Discordant Music: Charivaris and Whitecapping in Nineteenth-Century North America." *Labour/Le Travailleur* 3 (1978): 5–62.

———. "Most Uncommon Common Men: Craft and Culture in Historical Perspective." *Labour/Le Travailleur* 1 (1976): 5–31.

———. "On Language, Gender, and Working-Class History: A Response."

*International Labor and Working Class History* 31 (Spring 1987): 14–23.

———. "Social Formation and Class Formation in North America, 1800–1900." In *Proletarianization and Family History,* edited by David A. Levine, 229–309. San Diego: Academic Press, 1984.

Quandt, Jean B. "Religion and Social Thought: The Secularization of Postmillennialism." *American Quarterly* 25 (October 1973): 390–409.

Rediker, Marcus. "Getting Out of the Graveyard: Perry Anderson, Edward Thompson, and the Arguments of English Marxism." *Radical History* 26 (1982): 120–31.

Reinders, Robert C. "T. Wharton Collens and the Christian Labor Union." *Labor History* 8 (Winter 1967): 53–70.

Reuss, Richard A. "Folk Music and Social Conscience: The Musical Odyssey of Charles Seeger." *Western Folklore* 38 (October 1979): 221–38.

———. "The Roots of American Left-Wing Interest in Folksong." *Labor History* 12 (Spring 1971): 259–79.

Ritter, Gerhard A. "Workers' Culture in Imperial Germany: Problems and Points of Departure for Research." *Journal of Contemporary History* 13 (April 1978): 165–89.

Rodgers, Daniel T. "Tradition, Modernity and the American Industrial Worker: Reflections and Critique." *Journal of Interdisciplinary History* 7 (Spring 1977): 655–81.

Rollison, David. "Property, Ideology, and Popular Culture in a Gloucestershire Village, 1660–1740." *Past and Present* 93 (November 1981): 70–97.

Saxton, Alexander. "Blackface Minstrelsy and Jacksonian Ideology." *American Quarterly* 27 (March 1975): 3–28.

Scott, Joan W. "On Language, Gender, and Working-Class History." *International Labor and Working-Class History* 31 (Spring 1987): 1–13.

Seeger, Charles. "Folk Music as a Source of Social History." In *The Cultural Approach to History,* edited by Caroline Ware, 316–23. New York: Columbia University Press, 1940.

Shalhope, Robert E. "Republicanism and Early American Historiography." *William and Mary Quarterly* 39 (April 1982): 334–56.

Snyder, Robert. "The Paterson Jewish Folk Chorus: Politics, Ethnicity, and Musical Culture." *American Jewish Quarterly* 74 (September 1984): 27–44.

Stansell, Christine. "On Language, Gender, and Working-Class History: A Response." *International Labor and Working-Class History* 31 (Spring 1987): 24–29.

Stegner, S. Page. "Protest Songs from the Butte Mines." *Western Folklore* 26 (July 1967): 157–67.

Suderman, Elmer F. "Criticisms of the Protestant Church in the American Novel: 1870–1900." *Midcontinent American Studies Journal* 5 (Spring 1964): 17–23.

Tenfelde, Klaus. "Mining Festivals in the Nineteenth Century." *Journal of Contemporary History* 13 (April 1978): 377–412.

Thorp, Willard. "Catholic Novelists in Defense of Their Faith, 1829–1865." *Proceedings: American Antiquarian Society* 78 (April 1968): 25–117.

Tucker, Bruce. "Class and Culture in Recent Anglo-American Religious Historiography: A Review Essay." *Labour/Le Travailleur* 6 (Autumn 1980): 159–69.

Wangler, Thomas E. "John Ireland and the Origins of Liberal Catholicism in the United States." *Catholic Historical Review* 56 (January 1971): 617–29.

Weber, William. "Artisans in Concert Life in Mid-Nineteenth Century London and Paris." *Journal of Contemporary History* 13 (April 1978): 253–67.

White, Dana F. "A Summons for the Kingdom of God on Earth: The Early Social-Gospel Novel." *South Atlantic Quarterly* 47 (Summer 1968): 469–85.

Wheeler, Robert. "Organized Sport and Organized Labor." *Journal of Contemporary History* 13 (April 1978): 191–210.

Zeiger, Robert. "Workers and Scholars: Recent Trends in American Labor Historiography." *Labor History* 13 (Spring 1972): 245–66.

## Dissertations

Arnquist, James D. "Images of Catholic Utopianism and Radicalism in Industrial America." Ph.D. diss., University of Minnesota, 1968.

Barkey, Frederick A. "The Socialist Party in West Virginia from 1898–1920." Ph.D. diss., University of Pittsburgh, 1971.

Bennett, John W. "Iron Workers in Woods Run and Johnstown: The Union Era, 1865–1895." Ph.D. diss., University of Pittsburgh, 1977.

Carey, Ralph Allison. "Best Selling Religion: A History of Popular Religious Thought in America as Reflected in Religious Best Sellers, 1850–1960." Ph.D. diss., Michigan State University, 1971.

Charles, Norman. "Social Values in American Popular Songs (1890–1950)." Ph.D. diss., University of Pennsylvania, 1958.

Cotkin, George Bernard. "Working-Class Intellectuals and Evolutionary Thought in America, 1870–1915." Ph.D. diss., Ohio State University, 1978.

Garlock, Jonathan Ezra. "A Structural Analysis of the Knights of Labor: A Prolegomenon to the History of the Producing Classes." Ph.D. diss., University of Rochester, 1974.

Hall, James William, Jr. "The Tune-Book in American Culture: 1800–1820." Ph.D. diss., University of Pennsylvania, 1967.

Jentz, John Barkley. "Artisans, Evangelicals and the City: A Social History of Abolition and Labor Reform in Jacksonian New York." Ph.D. diss., City University of New York, 1977.

Nicholl, Grier. "The Christian Social Novel in America, 1865–1918." Ph.D. diss., University of Minnesota, 1964.

Reuss, Richard A. "American Folklore and Left-Wing Politics 1927–1957."
    Ph.D. diss., University of Minnesota, 1971.
Rosell, Garth. "Charles Finney and the Rise of the Benevolence Empire."
    Ph.D. diss., University of Minnesota, 1971.
Scholl, Stephen Carl. "The Decline of Millennialism in American Protes-
    tant Theology." Ph.D. diss., Indiana University, 1974.
Waksmundski, John. "McKinley Politics and the Changing Attitudes to-
    ward American Labor, 1870–1900." Ph.D. diss., Ohio State University,
    1972.
Walsh, Joseph Howard. "Protestant Response to Materialism in American
    Life, 1865–1900." Ph.D. diss., Columbia University, 1974.
Whalen, Robert Kieran. "Millenarianism and Millennialism in America,
    1790–1860." Ph.D. diss., State University of New York, Stony Brook,
    1971.
Wilt, Paul C. "Pre-Millennialism in America, 1865–1918." Ph.D. diss.,
    American University, 1970.

# Index

*Books in the Series*
*The Working Class in American History*

Worker City, Company Town:
Iron- and Cotton-Worker Protest in Troy
and Cohoes, New York, 1855–84
*Daniel J. Walkowitz*

Life, Work, and Rebellion in the Coal Fields:
The Southern West Virginia Miners, 1880–1922
*David Alan Corbin*

Women and American Socialism, 1870–1920
*Mari Jo Buhle*

Lives of Their Own:
Blacks, Italians, and Poles in Pittsburgh, 1900–1960
*John Bodnar, Roger Simon, and Michael P. Weber*

Working-Class America:
Essays on Labor, Community, and American Society
*Edited by Michael H. Frisch and Daniel J. Walkowitz*

Eugene V. Debs: Citizen and Socialist
*Nick Salvatore*

American Labor and Immigration History, 1877–1920s:
Recent European Research
*Edited by Dirk Hoerder*

Workingmen's Democracy:
The Knights of Labor and American Politics
*Leon Fink*

The Electrical Workers:
A History of Labor at General Electric
and Westinghouse, 1923–60
*Ronald W. Schatz*

The Mechanics of Baltimore:
Workers and Politics in the Age of Revolution, 1763–1812
*Charles G. Steffen*

The Practice of Solidarity:
American Hat Finishers in the Nineteenth Century
*David Bensman*

The Labor History Reader
*Edited by Daniel J. Leab*

Solidarity and Fragmentation:
Working People and Class Consciousness in Detroit, 1875–1900
*Richard Oestreicher*

Another Civil War:
Labor, Capital, and the State
in the Anthracite Regions of Pennsylvania,
1840–68
*Grace Palladino*

Coal, Class, and Color:
Blacks in Southern West Virginia, 1915–32
*Joe William Trotter, Jr.*

For Democracy, Workers, and God
Labor Song-Poems and Labor Protest, 1865–95
*Clark D. Halker*